GENDER RELATIONS AND CULTURAL IDEOLOGY IN INDIAN CINEMA

A Study of Select Adaptations of Literary Texts

GENDER RELATIONS AND CULTURAL IDEOLOGY IN INDIAN CINEMA

A Study of Select Adaptations of Literary Texts

INDUBALA SINGH

Foreword by

P.K. NAIR

Film Archivist, Film Teacher and Film Festival Consultant
Founder-Director, National Film Archive of India (NFAI) Pune

DEEP & DEEP PUBLICATIONS PVT. LTD.
F-159, Rajouri Garden, New Delhi - 110 027

GENDER RELATIONS AND CULTURAL
IDEOLOGY IN INDIAN CINEMA
A Study of Select Adaptations of Literary Texts

ISBN 81-7629-989-8

© 2007 INDUBALA SINGH

Printed in India at MAYUR ENTERPRISES,
WZ Plot No. 3, Gujjar Market, Tihar Village, New Delhi - 110 018.

Published by DEEP & DEEP PUBLICATIONS PVT. LTD.,
F-159, Rajouri Garden, New Delhi - 110 027 • Phone : 25435369, 25440916
E-mail : deep98@del3.vsnl.net.in • ddpbooks@yahoo.co.in
Showroom :
2/13, Ansari Road, Daryaganj, New Delhi - 110 002 • Telefax : 23245122

for my parents,

RAGHU and KHEM
who induced the passion for good cinema in me

and

DR. PRITAM PAL and RAMINDER
who have been great motivators

Contents

Foreword

There was a time when Cinema related research was frowned upon and virtually discouraged by academicians in the University circuit in this country as they looked down upon cinema with utter contempt and ridicule, unworthy of any kind of academic space. But things have changed dramatically, of late. It's heartening to note more and more research students in all parts of the country are picking up film related topics for their M.Phil. and Doctoral thesis and the authorities concerned have started encouraging them. Better late than never.

Normally, those who come from the literary discipline would always like to look at Cinema as an extension of Literature. May be due to the fact, the latter came first and Cinema later. Well Cinema is not just putting images to the literary text. It's much more than that. In fact the literary text and the text in cinema are two different entities. Those who really understand the medium of cinema (and they are not many) will know that. In this context, one should appreciate the author for taking pains and making an honest effort to understand the intricacies of the film medium before venturing on a subject dealing with film and literature. This is amply reflected in the work. In view of this, the work is different and needs serious attention.

The selection of authors from R. Tagore to Khushwant Singh and the film adaptations are well chosen covering the span of a whole century, from the classical to the modern, within the framework of the study of gender relations in the backdrop of the country's changing socio-cultural political scenario. Though primarily confined to the North, a sincere attempt has been made to take regional and language specificities into account in the study. This is to be appreciated. The bifurcation of the six films into two chapters in terms of their gender equations arising out of strong cultural tradition and changing socio-political events, throws some light on the author's ideological position to the subject. This is commendable as I have been noticing in the past more often than not student researchers tend to fight shy of taking strong positions while drawing up conclusions of their studies. If you do not have an opinion on the outcome of the data collected, arranged and rationally analysed and find yourself constrained to express it in clear terms, to that extent the study will be wanting in contemporary relevance.

Happily, the present study not only breaks the jinx but also explores new grounds for others to follow. Let there be more such studies to prove the point that "Cinema is not just leisure time entertainment and not all that "disrespectable". Its importance in culture studies cannot be overlooked. High Time Cinema Studies get its due and legitimate space in the academic arena.

P.K. NAIR

(P.K. Nair (1933) Film Archivist, Film Teacher and Film Festival Consultant; Founder-Director, National Film Archive of India, (NFAI) Pune. Pioneered the film preservation, documentation and dissemination activities of NFAI and developed it to an institution of international reckoning. Served as chairman and member of several National and International Film Festival Juries. Actively involved in the spread of Archive movement and film literacy in the subcontinent, as well as promotion of Indian film studies within and outside the country. Continues to guide Indian and foreign scholars in their research projects on Indian Cinema).

Preface

The cinema is still the most powerful form and medium of communication and entertainment inspite of the continuing growth of television, satellite, multi-media and interactive forms of communication on discs or via the Internet. Cinema not only makes a crucial contribution to the content and grammar of popular culture, cinema was, is and will always remain a medium of messages and values. Cinema hence can be said to be a national, multinational and global institution though it has a language far more complex than words. However, cinema can best be understood with a grasp of common thread of expression and tradition. Real literature and fables make good stories. The art of the storytelling lies in the imageries created merely out of words. The study of literary adaptations for films is becoming more and more common in cinema all over the world. In a polyglot nation like India, cinema too has had popular literary texts in various languages adapted for the screen. Every part of India has its rich oral and cultural traditions. Yet cinema is a powerful cultural practice and institution which both reflects and inflects the discourse of nationhood.

Cinema is the most effective medium for putting across an idea. The challenge of cinema, or any art, is newness and to provoke thought. Only then will society move and expand. In fact that is a filmmaker's responsibility too. Issues such as women's rights, gender equality, India's economic structure and political conditions intrinsically reflect social consciousness if one really chooses to be aware of it. Understanding gender relations has become a subject of much discussion and debate. A century and a half ago there was no theory of gender in modern sense. Theories on gender emerged in modern shape with rationalist and skeptical culture. They came into existence by gradual transformation of the older discourses of gender which were religious, non-rational and moralistic. Gender relations is an issue, which affects the human relations and the very fabric of the society all over the world. Power is seen as a central characteristic of gender relations. Dynamic culture superimposed and articulated with contradictions poses a set of questions that meander around gender. Gender relations in Indian cinema are still operative in both modern and post-modern times according to Prakirti or nature and Purusha or the in dwelling principle in keeping with the Puranic traditions and the two epics Ramayana and Mahabharta. Film-makers still draw inspiration, passion and philosophies from them as part of the Indian cultural ideology though the ideas of human love are very powerful driving forces in Indian cinema.

This book picks up not only an interest in the process of adaptation from text to screen in Indian cinema but at the same time looks into the aspect of gender relations with reference to cultural ideology. Adapting from different languages or adapting to a relevant setting is the skill of the director. What happens to popular literary texts, novels, or a short story when they are transformed onto the celluloid and how the politics of gender relations operate is the basic concern of the book. Though there are numerous films in Indian cinema adapted from literary texts, however just a few films have been taken up which formed a part of my doctoral dissertation. Content is not an end itself. It is said, "the power of ideas" to work for larger concerns lends creativity a cause. Since gender is itself a cultural construct, it opens the way for the radical, complex perspective in deciphering the hidden edifice of ideology operating within the literary texts in the cultural context. When adapted on the celluloid they need to be examined and re-examined as to how the film-maker articulated gender relations on the celluloid. The Indian film industry produces a cinema which has a global reach and is as popular as Hollywood cinema if not more. Even for a Western intellectual critic, the nation in discourse of cinematic narrative will be intelligible only if he/she understands the Indian cultural context. Thus any responsible understanding of India's cinematic situation must be rooted in the understanding of the various socio-cultural dynamics that shaped it.

DR. INDUBALA SINGH

Acknowledgements

I extend a sincere note of thanks to Mr. P.K. Nair Ex-Director NFAI and Mr. Sasi Dharan, Director, National Film Archives of India, Pune (NFAI). I had the privilege of sharing intellectual discourses with them and my sincerest thanks to Mrs. Joshi, Aarti and Lakshmi, who enduringly assisted me in tracing the relevant material in the Archives. I register my heart-felt thanks to Prof. Suresh Chabria, Director Film Appreciation Course, Shri Hariharan, Film Consultant/South Indian Film Director, Ms. Gayatri Chatterjee, film critic/writer and Ms. Hemanti Bannerjee, Documentary film-maker. They all helped me in evolving and defining the critical perception of my book. The multi faceted and varied discussions with them and my course-mates in the month-long Film Appreciation Course, I attended at Film & TV Institute, Pune, sharpened and chiseled my sensors for analyzing the various aspects involved in the film making.

I am indebted to S. Khushwant Singh, eminent writer, Dr. Yogesh Parveen, Historian and Nawab Jafar Mir Abdullah of Lucknow for sparing their valuable long hours for me exclusively. They proved to be of immense help to me in acquiring an insight into my subject

I owe a whole-hearted gratitude towards Dr. Anu Celly, Associate Professor, Department of English, Panjab University, whose unflagging guidance, intensive intellect and personal dynamism has been a source of constant support to me.

I wish to thank Ms. Christine Singh of British Library and the staff members of Central and Panjab University Library, Chandigarh, who provided me all the reading material required.

My friends Rekha Dhingrani, Kanwaljeet Bawa, Dr. Tejinder, Ms. Swaran Garewal, Ms. Ranjana Sharma, Dr. Apar Sareen, Kiranjit, Inderjit, Dr. Amandeep and my brother Col. Balwan Singh, deserve a loadful of thanks from me for always standing by my side and goading me to finish the task successfully.

I thank Shri Vivek who unfortunately passed away recently, Arvind, Ganesh and Mr. Rishi, who all made available their endless hours for typing out my manuscript. My thanks are due towards Gopal, Ravinder, and

Gurmukh Singh, my "Men-Friday" without whose running the household tasks and chores, this book could not have seen light of the day.

I cannot help but express my gratitude to University Grants Commission for granting me Fellowship for pursuing and completing my book.

It would be extremely unfair to close my acknowledgements without mentioning the members of my family, who for 5 years, unflinchingly supported and encouraged me. They endured my mercurial changes of mood and passion for cinema with indulgence, My daughters Shireen, Pearl and my husband S.P. Singh, who was a personification of patience during these five years came through the litmus test with ceaseless perseverance, to emerge as a confidante and soul mate in the true sense.

DR. INDUBALA SINGH

1

Introduction

To make a film is to create a whole world and to make a film also means to take a position. The single most significant fact about the appeal of cinema at the turn of the millennium has been that almost everyone now is a film buff. "In an era of pandemic imagorrhea there truly does exist a literacy of the filmic image," according to Gilbert Adair, "cinephilia, or its crude facsimile, is currently an indispensable item in the thinking person's intellectual baggage. The cinema now comes to us or, at any event, meets us halfway, diffracted through such parasitical media as television, video and advertising" (Adair 3). All roads lead, or can be made to lead to the cinema. In fact, its contribution to the content and grammar of popular culture is undeniable. Not only has it been the major art of the twentieth century, but it also remains the cultural form of greatest significance at the beginning of the new millennium. Cinema has produced the canonical texts upon which so much today's visual culture is built and to which so much of contemporary culture is indebted.

The most popular form of aesthetic entertainment for the average Indian is the film. Indians are great cinema lovers. Cinema is very much a part of our culture and has been so, for almost a hundred years. Indian cinema has a long history, rich in character and anecdote and replete with the stuff of analysis ready for myriad interpretations. "Indian cinema is a modern cultural institution whose unique features can be related directly or indirectly to the specificity of the socio-political formation of the Indian nation state". (Prasad vii). It is not a coincidence that the film industry in India is the largest in the world. Whether it is the 'formula' of a Bollywood film or the films produced in different languages in the states of India or the so called 'art films,' all these provide a mirror in one way or another into the way in which our mind works. It is in a way a projection of the whole tapestry of Indian culture. It can be treated as an entry point for understanding the legitimization of social and political power through narrative forms, commanding the widest of social constituencies. The broader issues of social and political ideology are refracted in cinema through the characteristic concerns. With the help of categorization with genre and stylistic analysis, along with the wider perspective within changing cultural and social set up, it can lead to revelations of progression or regression.

Reflection on the film as a medium began with the medium itself. The etymological meanings of the original names given to the cinema pointed to diverse ways of 'envisioning' it. 'Biograph' and 'animatographe' emphasized the recording of life itself and 'vitascope' and 'bioscope' to the looking at life and thus shifted emphasis from, "recording of life to the spectator and scopophilia (the desire to look) a concern of 1970s psychoanalytic theorists" (Stam 22). Since the beginning of film as a medium, analysts have sought its 'essence' and its unique features.

> "Cinema was very quickly perceived to be an art and theorists and film makers proudly asserted cinema's links to other arts because films embody, communicate, enforce and suggest meanings. Film theorists often suggested that film constitutes a language or a 'visual esperanto'." (Braudy and Cohen 1)

Cinema may be considered to be an art form and theorists and filmmakers have proudly asserted cinema's links to other arts.[1] Film theory developed as an evolving body of concepts designed to account for cinema in all its dimensions, namely the aesthetic, social and psychological.

Film theory is rarely 'pure', as it is laced with an admixture of literary criticism, social commentary and philosophical speculation without being deterministic.[2] The genesis of the film theory occurred in France. The earliest reference to film as an art occurred when the filmmaker Louis Feuillade made an attempt to align cinema with other arts in his advance publicity sheet for his series Le film 'esthétique' (1910). He perceived cinema as a popular art and as economic art (a synergy between technology and the aesthetic). A year later Ricciotto Canudo published in France his manifesto *'The Birth of a Sixth Art'* in which he established the two main lines of debate that would preoccupy theorists well into the 1920s and in the 1930s regarding the debate around cinema's realism on one hand and the other around a pure non-representational cinema based on form and rhythm. After the First World War, there were debates, mainly among French critics and filmmakers which addressed the issue to high and popular art, realist versus naturalist film, the spectator screen relationship, editing styles (a debate much influenced by the Soviet cinema of the 1920s), unconscious and psychoanalytical potential of film. In the 1930s, following the advent of sound, the debate shifted to the very polemical issue of whether sound was a good or bad thing for the aesthetics of cinema. The two main theories developed after the Second World War viz. the *auteur* theory (1950s) and the second structuralism (1960s). Before that in 1948, Alexandre Astruc's concept of cinema preceded these theories, in which he propagated cinema as a language. (caméra-stylo as he defined it).

Cinema, however, "is primarily a visual experience sustained by the cameraman and the director. It is also an aural experience, a constantly changing mix of music, voice and noise. But most films also require the services of a writer. Though a few pictures may simply be found, most of them are thought up, plotted and written down". (Scott 167).

Films are thus, essentially the work of a 'writer director' yet film, like literature is essentially a 'story telling' art, dealt with as a literary genre. Cinema could be drama, which is classical, which in traditional Indian aesthetics has been called *dr'sya kavya*, i.e. visible poetry. Even in this traditional definition, the conception of literature as a verbal art is transcended by the inclusion of the visual. Obviously, speech in cinema aesthetics is only one out of several languages and as a rule, a subservient one. Most of what the film has to say, "is to be 'read' as precepts, preverbal and concrete observations and simple identifications rather than words." (Pfleiderer and Lutze 7).

Filmmakers talk about stories and scripts as most filmmaking actually begins with a story or script. Film theorists talk about cinema as a narrative. Essentially, they are talking about the same thing but using different words to do it. "The study of a film's narrative is both the study of its story and also the study of how the story is told by means of *mise en scene* (i.e. what is to be filmed traditionally) cinematography, editing, sound and its structure". (Roberts and Wallis 53). Cinema watchers are aware that one of the factors which attracts them to a film is its 'type' i.e. genre which simply means type. Genre analysis is popular, not the least because it relates directly to the way the industry works and how films are consumed.

In the study of literature, genre theory was already current when Aristotle wrote his *Poetics* in the fifth century BC. What is odd is, that it took serious film criticism until the 1950s to get a grip on this most obvious of analytical tools. Genre criticism brings the audience into the realm of film theory. It's understanding is predicated upon the understanding of conventions and characteristics and the sense of verisimilitude. Genre characteristics are based on the use of plot, visual imagery, character setting, narrative development, music, metaphor, space and symbol. When one takes up several films, one expects to see similarities in a number of these specific characteristics.

Serious genre criticism began with André Bazin, the key figure of the *Cahiers du Cinema*. In the 1950s the young writers of *Cahiers du Cinema* argued a new theory, i.e. *politics des auteurs*. This began the critical tradition of '*Auteur theory*' (stamp of the director as an author of the work created by him, with a desire to raise film to the status of a unique art form). They argued that film's generic ideas produced creative conventions in cinemal language, which can be developed by individual artists (*auters*) into a personal vision. The emphasis on artistic creation and the term *auteur* (author) placed the director, and not scriptwriter, centrally as the author of the film. However, if the film maker was to be seen as an author he would have to exhibit '*auteur*' characteristics e.g. visual style with reference to *mise en scene* and cinematography, narrative structures and features and the handling of situation and themes. These characteristics will be seen as a characteristic genre of an *auteur's* work. His spirit presides over the entire operation. Whatever the approach of the director, there is usually a place for creative inspiration of other members of the production team.

In the 1960s, structuralism and *auteur* structuralism replaced *auteur* theory. Structuralism was a theory, which was believed, could be applied to all aspects of society and culture but it ended up in rigid formalism that removed any discussion of pleasure in the viewing. The central theorist in the debate of auteur structuralism was the semiotician Christian Metz (1972). His theory purported to reveal all hidden structures behind filmmaking. Analyzing the film scientifically and objectively evaluating it, at the same time determining the filmmaker's style, is limited to formalism. In the period from 1970s to 90s it became evident that a single theory would never be sufficient to explain and analyze film and nor talk about the spectator-text relationship. The term post-structuralism then came up which defined the *auteur's* place within the textual process. The importance of intertextuality was established. There is no such thing as a 'pure' text, all texts have intertexual relations with others. In the final analysis, "post structuralism opened up textual analysis to a pluralism of approaches, which did not reduce the text to the status of object of investigation but as much subject as those reading, writing or producing it" (Hayward 389).

There exists a close relationship between literature and film art, since cinema depended for its narratives on the novel or short story. From Feuillade to Chaplin, from Griffith, down to Antonnioni and Kurosawa, the filmmakers have drawn from literary works. Indian cinema too has made abundance use of classics in Indian literature. The Indian film inherited two traditions. First, the subject matter of a large percentage of films was drawn from the Indian mythology. Secondly, a cinematic style became unique to India, in the sense, of being a combination of opera ballet and drama fused with a new technology. In addition to the films based on old Indian themes, there were several films made, which portrayed contemporary life. Cinema, however, as elsewhere, was in India, too, dismissed as a vulgar form of mass entertainment and was regarded with hostility by conservative opinion. However, its influence in shaping public opinion and human minds is tremendous. Not only does it engage the audience (viewers) for three hours but has far-reaching impact on the psyche too. The cinema is a very powerful medium for projecting ideas. Its potency, directness, reach and pliability, is unparallel. It holds up a mirror to life. Cinema is the only medium through which we can directly deal with the problems and paradoxes of a given society and bring about a change. The cultural patterns go on to form a large design in the film making process. It provides an insight in one way or another into the way in which the Indian mind works in its collective conscious/psyche. It is rather the kaleidoscope of the Indian culture.

Literary adaptation to films is a long established tradition in cinema starting, for example, with early cinema adaptations of the Bible. By the 1910s adaptation of the established literary canon had become a marketing ploy by which producers and exhibitors could legitimise cinema going as a venture of taste and thus attract the middle classes to the theatres. "Literary adaptations gave cinema the respectable cachet of entertainment-as-art. In a related way it is noteworthy that literary adaptations have consistently been seen to have pedagogical values, that is, teaching a notion (through cinema) about its classics, its literary heritage" (Hayward 4). Many-a-times a literary adaptation creates a new story. It may not be the same as the original yet it takes on a new life and so also the characters in it.

Whatever a film has to say is essentially somehow implicit in the story that it tells. The Anglo–American cinema has always leaned heavily towards adaptation, a skill that brought fame to both the directors and writers. However, studying both fictional and filmic sources can be fraught with problems particularly in making decisions about giving the 'appropriate' amount of attention to each medium and fostering the skills specific to each form. The chief problem lies in testing one's prejudices relating to this kind of hybrid 'study'. Many people are apprehensive that such adaptation of the novel on to the celluloid and the comparison of a novel and its film at times results in an almost unconsciously preferring the fictional origin over the resulting film. The pitfalls are created by demands of authenticity and fidelity of the screen version and whether core meaning and values of the ordinary text are realized in the film medium. Even when literary text is the subject of an adaptation, it may not be a text that many potential viewers are familiar with. Thus, it becomes widely known through the process of realization on screen. Moreover the attempt to inspire visual responses on the reading audiences can lead to an approach of a happy compromise for both the two media, "since literary criticism and film criticism can each benefit from the other." (Whelehan 4).

There have been apprehensions with regard to the adaptation of novels on the celluloid. Critics have felt that the characters of the novels undergo a simplification process when transferred to the screen; however, it is a myth that film is not very successful in dealing either with complex psychological states or with dream or memory, nor can it render thought in a palpable manner. Such fears can be dispensed with, as films with their narrative strategies also involve metaphors and symbolism in decoding and organizing the relationship between plot and story. The film 'triggers' the viewers to arrive at cognitive mental responses and formal patterning through various aesthetic aspects of films like lighting, tone of voice and so on. The whole realm of emotional effect would be encompassed along with the other formalities such as class, gender and sexuality as having an effect on viewing. The author says a person smiled, however, the celluloid would convey whether it is an embarrassed smile, confident smile, teasing smile or a smile of friendship or a hesitant smile.

'What is cinematic representation?' has been the concern of film theorists since the early days of cinema when intellectual enthusiasts of the medium at once celebrated the capacity of the mechanically reproduced image to capture reality in a way that seemed peculiarly modern, yet also viewed with suspicion the power of new medium upon the minds of the masses.[3] Films may have a non-verbal experience but it encompasses its narrative based on cultural experience of literature. People love to see films based on works of literature that they have read; yet, at times they are disappointed with its adaptation because they perceive the film in terms of a written narrative; while actually, "a film is primarily something to see, not to be read about. No description of a film can take the place of seeing it." (Das Gupta Chidananda Talking 118). The film is made of images and sounds, which evoke feelings, and a beautiful evocative image often becomes memorable. While encompassing narrative strategies, there are certain key shifts made in the process of transition from the classic to popular cinema. Film is decidedly a mechanical art, much more than painting or music or literature. The film director establishes a form of structural analysis, which is able to embrace fiction cinema, history, and painting and so forth as important narrative features. Thus it produces an atmosphere essential to the shaping of the text, which would include the portrayal of viewpoint and focalisation.

> "The fear that the film medium could 'steal' the constituency of a reader is always there. However a successful film can bolster the sales of the novel substantially and when a film becomes a financial or even a critical success the question of 'faithfulness' of adaptation of the novel is hardly given any thought. If the film succeeds on its own merits, it ceases to be problematic." (Bluestone 8).

For the study of the film as a work of art composed of converging systems of signs, verbal as well as non-verbal, perhaps the most satisfying approach is offered by cultural semiotics. Culture interpreted as 'collective memory' may be considered,

> "as a totalising main concept comprising the total of various secondary modellizing system, (like art, myth, religion, science, ideology and forms of social behavior etc.). These systems are 'secondary' in so far as they are based on the 'primary' system of natural language, which makes it possible to study culture as a hierarchically structured system of signs" (Pfleiderer and Lutze 10).

The related question of culture recognition and its assertion gets marked in fact, while trying to understand such an implication. One cannot help overlooking the complex outlook of aesthetic sensibility and the way viewers recognize and identify with particular codes. Aesthetic experience has often been said to be characterized by a peculiar detachment; it requires a disengaged and purely contemplative attitude or it can just consist in the simple consciousness of the material before us.

Cinema is an ideological apparatus by the very nature of its very seamlessness. Mainstream or dominant cinema in Hollywood or elsewhere puts ideology up on the screen. The workings of ideology can be examined in gender, race, class, age, and so on. According to Louis Althusser, ideology is produced, "by the subject for the subjects, ideology interpellates individuals as subjects, ideology constructs the subject and that the subject is an effect of ideology". (Althusser Essays 44). Ideology has had profound implications for the theororizing of spectator-text relations.[4] The recognition and identification process by which ideology functions is the one that the film readily re-enacts. Holiywood has been a prime example of mass entertainment industry operating in a nation-building context too. In fact the America constructed in the minds of people all over the world, is by virtue of Hollywood's cinematic products. According to Ashish Rajadhyaksha,

> "The India of its movies, like Hollywood's America, has spawned its own cinephilia. In their scale and pervasiveness, the Indian films have borne often unconsciously several large burdens, such as the paradigms for notions of influential Indianness collectivity and key terms of reference for the prevailing cultural hegemony". (Rajadhyaksha and Willemen 10).

In many crucial aspects, the Indian film industry modeled itself on the Hollywood Studio in adopting and adapting some of its cinematic techniques and plot devices. In fact Bombay production practices were originally based on imitation of Hollywood. The term 'Bollywood' for Bombay production came up during the early 1980s in English language, covering Hindi popular cinema. According to Govind Nihalani "even though it was found to be amusing in the early days of its coinage, the word obviously summed the popular perception of mainstream Hindi cinema as glamorous, melodramatic, loud and frivolous". (Nihalani Bollywood 24). It was felt as a derogatory connotation, firstly, because it seemed to point to the parasitic relationship that the Hindi mainstream cinema had come to establish with Hollywood. However, gradually, the word picked up a fair amount of enthusiasm by the Indian diaspora, particularly in Britain, as some television programmes were made on different aspects of 'Bollywood'. Soon it found its way into the writing of western critics, though the sense of 'wanna be' Hollywood continues to be implied. Lately, the word seems to have found wider acceptance. Nonetheless, it is a cinema of entertainment geared to promote and represent an imaginary mythical India. "Ideology is the discourse that invests a nation or society with meaning. And since it reflects the way in which a nation is signified, it is closely aligned to the myths" (Hayward 192).

In 1969, 'Third Cinema' was a term coined by the Argentinean film theorists and filmmakers Fernando Solanas and Octavio Getino in their manifesto 'Towards a Third Cinema' in which they called for a decolonization of culture, through a counter cinema. The concept of Third Cinema was used to distinguish it from First Cinema, Hollywood and Second European art cinema and the cinema of *auteurs*. The naming of Third Cinema was intentionally playful, a riposte to economists and to dominant western cinemas. Third Cinema refers to films made by countries of the so-called Third world countries i.e., which do not belong to the developed industrial countries. However, the two terms Third Cinema and Third World Cinema are not to be confused. Third Cinema, which sought to promote socialism, as it is ostensibly political in its conceptualization, and ideologically counters the filmmaking practices of two. At the same time, not all Third world cinemas, which sought to promote socialism, as it was ostensibly political in its conceptualization, does this. However, India has and still does produce another cinema that resists. One such cinema is the so-called New Indian cinema whose beginnings, in 1969 coincide with the publication of Third Cinema manifesto.

Film studies led to participation and re-definition of culture as an object of study and inevitably led a conceptual shift towards a radical contemporaneity. In fact, film theory was supposed to function with pre-supposition that there was some profound, ineluctable kinship between cinema and culture. As a result, many investigators of the cinematic institution felt that film technology had been invented to meet an already existing cultural need. 'Cultural studies' has been defined, "as a kind of disciplinary omnivore. 'Cultural studies' is committed to the study of the entire range of society's arts, beliefs, institutions and practices." (Grossberg, Treichler and Nelson 4). However, while film semiotics was concerned with specific cinematic codes such as sound imagery, metaphor and allusion, the movement came to be known as 'cultural studies' and was interested in embedding media like cinema within a larger cultural and historical context. Cultural studies, which gained ground in 1960s, draw on diverse intellectual sources like Marxism, semiotics and later feminism and critical race theory. The culture in any represented cultural ideology can be both anthropological and artistic in its contents.

The conceptualization of cultural ideology in Indian films is manifested through the narrative vision of the directors of the fiction on which they are based. An endeavour to study gender relations in the Indian films based on fiction with reference to cultural ideology can help in understanding the transition from the text to screen. Why does a film become a hit, an actor a superstar, an actress an icon? How do dreams get peddled and ideologies or attitudes and ethics get integrated in the story? Is there magic behind the magic of make-believe? These are some of the questions, which get raised in one's mind. This book proposes to examine the facets of woman's image vis-à-vis. the gender relations, the aesthetics finding portrayal'in Indian films based on fiction. Contradictions abound in Indian cinema, as much as they do in India. Some texts are film friendly and can be presented accordingly and directors do a better job in evolving the feelings in the visual medium strongly. The aesthetics of the cinema can be an instrument for enhancing the effects of the ideology and underpinnings of the protagonists per se in cinema.

At the phase of its inception, during the 'silent era', Indian cinema introduced the genre of the mythological film, which catered to the popular taste and plebeian filmgoer. It is just not an accident that the first Indian film happened to be a mythological. Dhundiraj Govind Phalke popularly known as Dada Sahib Phalke celebrated as the first filmmaker of India made 'Raja Harishchandra' in 1913. He chose the life of Raja Harishchandra as the subject of the first film for the simple reason, that a story from *Mahabharta* is well known throughout India and had been performed as a folk play several times. The path of Indian cinema thus started with the pre-cinema efforts of story telling from the *Puranas*. Thus, when technology made it possible to tell stories, he conceived filmmaking as a nationalist movement making it a specific 'Swadeshi' enterprise. Film technology had arrived in India during the colonial rule. It captivated the audiences, as it had done else where in Europe and America. Basically, it was the part of movement to promote indigenous enterprise, that the idea of Indian cinema was conceived. In fact the film theory in India occupied some of assumptions of the Hollywood film text with some particulars films in abstract general form, which however stood for all possible texts in the dominant mode. "It was at the stage of 'not-yet-cinema', a bastard institution in which the mere ghost of technology was employed for purposes inimical to its historic essence". (Prasad 6). A middle class social cinema of reform evolved in the 'sound period' in alliance with literary culture. It continued along with the heyday of nationalist ideology and the interplay with social aspirations, after independence too. A more specifically art enterprise attuned to cinematic language, emerged in the early 1970s with systematic state investment in art cinema. However,

> "the so called 'parallel cinema' emerged as the object of middle class spectatorship especially in the wake of the 'massification' of the commercial form into an encompassing and alienating package of spectacle, action and titillation". (Vasudevan Making 102).

The legacy of past however survives better in the popular films made by the big commercial film companies of Bombay and Madras. In fact a certain kind of cinema exists only because of a certain kind of state exists and film technology with cinematic institution arrived to meet the cultural need of the times. Cinema in India developed specifically with the socio-political foundation of the Indian nation state.

With international recognition of Satyajit Ray's 'Pather Panchali' in Venice (1956) Indian cinema entered an age of liberation and awareness. Till then Indian cinema nursed a feeling of inferiority of not being up to the standards of European and Hollywood cinema. It was not only hailed as a great Indian film but Indian cinema became aware of itself-its 'Indianness'. According to Govind Nihalani "this awareness evolved into a greater and wider awareness about cinema as an art form based on its power and potential as a communicator of ideas as experience and as a medium to provide debate on issues related to people and society. A general kind of feeling evolved that films could be made outside the traditional commercial structure." (Nihalani Talking xi). Within this ideological sphere there was a need to establish aesthetic conventions and meet new socio-political challenges. Three distinct aesthetic formations of cinema were made as a result of it-the new cinema, the middle class cinema and the popular cinema.

The study of popular cinema was taken seriously in its nascent stage in the 1960s as an alignment of cultural studies. This led to an opposing of the question of criteria to pronounce power culturally in the cinematic institution that was challenged by divisions such as gender, race or class. Film studies in the 70s were often in the grip of patriarchal or otherwise ideologically maligned texts. Critics explored the ways meanings are constructed through signs and chose semiotics to explore the value of different stories or images. Film theorists made huge claims for textual study, usually in terms of 'meaning' and of 'codes' embedded in the narrative of film "Questions were asked as to whose interests are being taken into considerations and to what assumptions?" (Branton 134). It was then that the Feminist film theory in the 70s developed. Feminists in United Kingdom have incorporated historical materialist approach of work done in cultural studies which "has examined popular culture within the sphere of class, gender and race and in relation to power and resistances to that power" (Hayward 123). In the United States, Feminists more specifically turned their attention to the, "notion of the social as a practical field in which technologies and discourses are deployed" (De Lauretis Alice 84). The cultural studies debate also had an impact and effect on the feminist-film theory.

Feminism has been dramatically one of most forceful social movements of the twentieth century. When the women set out to change the world and their position in it in the 1960s, it, seemed like an uphill task. It, however, rather altered the consciousness of the women themselves and women world over have mobilized themselves ever since and have come centre stage. In fact, the very social fabric of the western countries changed dramatically as a result. At the same time, many have derided feminism. It has been blamed for the break down of the family life in the west and its influence elsewhere. However, the polemics of militant feminism of the decades between 1960 and 1980 is being requisitioned and redefined. We have at this juncture the fiery feminist of the yore, Germaine Greer of 'The Female Eunuch' fame saying, "nothing has really changed." (Greer The Whole 2).

The feminism of the post world war two transformed the lives of women not only in the United States but throughout the world and brought about upheavals in law and customs of every day life. It rather altered the consciousness of women themselves. In 1920, the American women achieved the goal in the form of a constitutional amendment giving women the right to vote, making suffrage an outstanding victory. However, soon after women suffrage was won in the United States, the movement that had brought it about faltered and came to a standstill. Feminism entered a long period of dormancy. Several important feminist books were published during those dark ages, notably works by Virginia Woolf and Mary Beard. The disappearance of feminism from the stage of history for several decades meant that the emerging women of the sixties had to rediscover basic truths about the oppression of women for themselves.

The first indications of a feminist re-awakening in The United States affirmed, the equal rights of men and women in its 1945 charter and a few years later established the U.N. Commission on the status of women to advance this ideal and the pace quickened. Betty Friedan's 'The Feminine Mystique' was published in 1963. Finally in the late sixties, a vigorous feminist movement arose in the United State and rapidly spread to other countries developing a network of informal women's groups. Nearer home, we have had an Indian counterpart to Germaine Greer's 'The Female Eunuch', 'Caste as a woman' by feminist Vrinda Nabar and many more writings like those of by Kamla Bhasin, Rehana Ghadially, Indu Prakash Singh, Malladi Subbumma, Meenakshi Mukherjee, Malasree Lal etc. and various other journals and articles on the subject.

An acclaimed actress and activist Shabana Azmi feels that women have been duped into a spurious version of equality and says that, "far too long our voices have been silenced". (Singh 7). Sadly most women in the third world, even if they come from better classes, have little control over their lives. According to Vrinda Nabar, popular journals at times promote this ignorance by suggesting that Indian woman has never had it so good as she storms male citadels, rewrites the home equations and is on the threshold of a brave new sensual world. Vrinda Nabar feels that, "we are asked to believe that from testing waters, she has plunged into the deep water". (Nabar 5) It may be true to some extent. However, still quite a humbler segment of women are still deprived of basic education and the declining sex ratio is an ample proof to convey the status enjoyed by the girl child who will be a woman tomorrow. Even though a growing number of women are getting educated and well employed, there is still a large section of population that recoils from the feminist rhetoric. Suma Chitins feels that, "it is possible that they do so because they are too entrenched in tradition to recognize their oppression." (82). Sometimes, even women writers are clearly as imbricated in the ideology of their times as men are. Even, "middle class women, white women, upper caste Hindu women might find their claims to 'equality' or to full authority of liberal individualism at the expense of the working classes, non white races, dalits or Muslims". (Tharu and Lalita 38).

The assessment of the status of women in India can be made vis-à-vis her position in the social framework. During the pre-Vedic and Vedic period, women rather enjoyed an equal status in the discharge of their social duties. However, deterioration set in the status of the Indian women when Manu, the great Hindu law-giver, made a formidable list of do's and don'ts which came to be attributed to the women and for men, such as to be on guard in the company of females, as it was the very nature of the woman to seduce man in this world. "This not only deprived her of her social rights and deprived her of education which she enjoyed earlier but restricted her to the domestic chores which led to her economic slavery to man." (Gupta, A.R., 6). Thus, for the establishment of the definition of the ideal Hindu women, the two emblematised Hindu women who were chosen to personify the ideal Hindu woman were Sita, from the influential '*Ramayana*', and the legendary Savitri. In both cases, what the Hindu woman was expected to do and not to do was subject to the dictates and commands of her husband. To be servile to his demands was her '*dharma*'. The Indian culture, thus, in its powerful manifestation, became a male preserve. Yet, it is impossible to escape from the spirit of female power.

In fact, the struggle for the upliftment of women began in India in the nineteenth century. It was an offshoot of the fight against colonialism and the aspiration for national freedom. Political leaders, social reformers, missionary workers formulating virtually an all male hegemony, were interested in improving the status of the Indian women. At the same time, there were notable shifts in feminist theorizing from the early years of second-wave feminism in the west. "Theorists started insisting on broadening their scope beyond the exclusive focus on male dominance and assert their commitment to plural perspectives replacing it with the multi-faceted exploration of the contingencies of gendered identity." (Kemp and Squires 6). In fact, a look at much of the literature of mainstream feminism of west reveals that as a result of the common perception of feminism, the idea of woman as a monolithic construct was being obliterated.

A new expression over the evolutionary nature of feminism called post-feminism has now gained greater currency. As per the opinion of Ann Brooks, post-feminism claims, "feminism's 'coming of age' with its maturity into a confident body of theory and politics, in relation to other philosophical and political movements similarly involved in demanding change". (Brooks Ann 1). The concept 'post' implies a process of an ongoing change. Once seen, crudely in the *status quo* as anti-feminist, the term is now understood as a useful conceptual frame of reference, encompassing the inter-section of feminism with a number of other anti-foundationalist movements including post-modernism, post-structuralism and post-colonialism. At the same time, it does not assume that either patriarchal or modernist discourses or frames of reference have been replaced or suspended. It signifies, rather, a shift in the direction and emphasis within feminism and is seen as the culmination of a number of debates and fiercely fought arguments from both within and outside feminism. Annette Kuhn feels that,

> "to put forward the case for a feminist cultural politics, is to hold a notion that ideology has its own effectivity both in general and social formation and in particular with regard to sex/gender systems." She feels, if it is accepted, "the 'cultural' may be subsumed within ideology... then it becomes possible to argue that interventions within culture have some potential to transform sex/gender systems" (Kuhn 5).

If one poses a relationship between feminism and cinema to discuss gender relations, then there are connections that can be made on an analytical level between different sets of practices and when they are taken together they might provide a basis for certain types of intervention in culture.[5] However, the feminists many a times have conveyed that it is felt that there was no such methodology as a perspective through which they could look at films. There was felt a need to engage an intervention within feminist theory or culture, since film theory is something different from the general run of feminist film criticism.

In 1972, the first issue of the short lived American journal 'Women and Film' was published. The need for transformation of woman's stereotypical image, oppressive ideology and a need for the creation of a feminine critical aesthetics, was felt. There have been two types of feminist film criticism motivated by different geographical and ideological contexts, each though speaking in a different voice. The distinction between one's own voice and the voice of history is a handy one by which to distinguish two types of feminist film criticism. These two types could be characterized as either American or British. The American one is seen as sociological subjective, often speaking one's own voice and other British seen as methodological or more objective, often speaking the voice of history. The originally American approach is exemplified by early 'Women and Film' articles, and the British one is exemplified by articles in 'Screen' and 'Camera Obscura'. They were committed to using some of the most advanced tools of critical analysis like semiology and psychoanalysis and later on moved beyond regarding the image to analysing, the structures and codes. Two of the most important critics following this approach are Laura Mulvey and Claire Johnston.

Claire Johnston has critiqued the image of women in male cinema in her article 'Woman's Cinema as Counter-Cinema'. She finds the woman figure "to be a signifier not of woman but of the absent phallus, a signifier of an absence, rather than any presence, ... there is only the male and the non-male in order to be accepted into the male universe the woman must become a man" (33). Hollywood has been viewed as a dream factory producing an oppressive cultural product and same can be said about Indian cinema. Myths of women have operated in cinema, wittingly and unwittingly, of propagating primitive stereotype of woman with same modification. Panofsky locates the origins of iconography and stereotyping on account of the difficulties to decipher what appeared on the early screen "of identifiable standard appearance, behaviour and attributes of medieval personifications of vices and virtues. They were convincingly put as modern equivalents in the types of the family man and villain, the vamps and the straight girl". (Johnston 31).

Myths governing the cinema were in no way different from those governing other cultural contexts. Women in any fully human form had been left out of film as women were earlier left out of the literature with the deliberate intent of erasure. Most of the filmmakers were men and they did all the writing and film making from a male point of view, which was the starting point of a deterministic and normative point of view. The role of a woman in film after film revolved round her physical attraction and mating games she played with the male characters. Man on the other hand was not shown purely in relation to female characters–but in a variety of roles. Men in films were judged through courage in war, struggle against nature, intellectual activity and a thousand other things but with faith in themselves as a symbol of power and authority. Even when a woman is the central character, she is portrayed through the common myths of self sacrifice and martyrdom, as docile, submissive, self-effacing, and even when she gains eminence, she is portrayed as a victim of discriminatory circumstances who rises, through pain, obsession or defiance to become the mistress of her fate. But in the distinguished women's films, the combination of director and actor serve the same function as the complex perspective of the novelist. They tend to take the woman out of the plural into the singular, out of the collective identity into the radical adventurer, out of the solitary into the social, out of the contrivances of puritanical thinking into enlightened seeking self-interest. In the sociological analysis of woman in cinema, there still persist rejections in terms of realism. The reality of myth still operates and persists in the psyches. The directors in their findings and insights assume the image of woman and manipulate it with different manners within the different text of author's work as they adapt it on the screen desired from their *auteur* perspective. "Within such a sexist ideology and a male dominated cinema, the image of woman is portrayed on item subject to the law of verisimilitude, which is responsible for the repression". (Johnston 38).

Laura Mulvey, in her seminal article 'Visual Pleasure and Narrative Cinema' (1975), examines the classical narrative cinema. She sees psychoanalysis as a useful weapon for feminism. Mulvey feels that the mainstream film coded the erotic into the language of the dominant patriarchal order, which has women at its center by skillful manipulation for visual pleasure. "The cinema satisfies a primordial wish for pleasurable looking, but it also goes further, developing scopophilia in its narcissistic aspect. The conventions of mainstream film focus attention on the human form. Scale, space, stories are all anthropomorphic". (Mulvey 61). However, the concept of voyeurism around the way the cinema is structured, is linked to the scopophilic instinct of the male pleasure in his own narcissistic image, according to her.

'Scopophilia' or pleasure in looking, can be divided into, "fetishism and voyeurism. Through, the speculative structure of voyeurism and fetishism, women are simultaneously looked at and displayed with their appearance and code for looked-at-ness". (Mulvey 65). Theoretical approaches were and continue to be strongly male centred in popular as well as art cinema. Mulvey suggests that she is often fetishized or fixated upon, and constructed not only by the male characters but also by the female spectators. The females are theorized as being 'male' not literally but in the way of looking at women, considering that patriarchy is so well entrenched in their psyches. As a result feminist film theory has assumed a high status for psychoanalysis. Mulvey used the film theory taking Freud and Lacan as a basis and felt that the women viewers have two choices, either to look in a masochistic way with women constructed solely according to their narrative passivity or to take up the male viewing position. She goes on to consider the 'woman' as the object of the male gaze and man as the bearer of the look and woman displayed as sexual object is the leitmotif of erotic spectacle. She holds the look and plays to and signifies male desire. However, the position of the male figure is very differently located in terms of narrative structure by virtue of which he controls the film fantasy and the narrative dynamic.

> "Within the patriarchal culture, woman stands as a signifier for the male other bound by a symbolic order in which man can live out his fantasies and obsessions through linguistic command by imposing them on the silent image of woman still tied to her place as bearer and not maker of meaning." (Mulvey 59).

The patriarchal structuring of a mainstream film establishes looking as a male activity and being looked at as a female passivity. The only way in which male viewing pleasure can be rendered unproblematic is, if the castration threat that women pose, is removed. By turning her into a fetish object herself, exaggerating stylizing and fragmenting female beauty, cinema unconsciously fetishes the female for representing it in a phallus like way, thus undermining the threat posed by women. Men turn the represented figure itself into a fetish so that it becomes reassuring rather than dangerous. Mulvey uses the concept of fetishistic scopophilia to describe a process whereby the physical beauty of the object is built up, transforming it into something satisfying in itself. In viewing films, the question of 'male gaze' has been commented upon by Ann Kaplan. The gaze in dominant cinema is supposed to be built upon notions of male-female differences created by a culture. The three looks that derive from this gaze are supposed to be "the gaze within the film text – how men gaze at women, the spectator's gaze that identifies with the male gaze and objectifies the women on the screen and the camera's original gaze that goes into the very act of filming." (Kaplan Women 175). Kaplan makes a very interesting observation in an article "Can One Know the Other" about the cultural assumptions of the Indian diaspora about femininity, marriage and male/female relations. She comments on the system of Indian marriages as shown in the film '*Mississipi Masala*' by Mira Nair, which still functions within the Indian cultural context. Women are thought of as commodities and where gradations of skin colour still generate a prejudice against the darker looking. There is no doubt that the male gaze still dominates and determines the 'value' of woman in the 'market' of marriage.

One strongly feels that the feminist theories and criticism of the 70s and 80s have concerned themselves centrally with the authorship made by women, shuttering attention away from classic text to experimental cinema. Kaja Silverman felt at times, "the author often emerges within the context… placed definitively 'outside' the text and assumed to be the punctual source of its sounds and images." (394). She thus felt that there is no sense in which the feminist author, like her phallic counterpart might be constructed in and through discourse that might be inseparable from the desire that circulates within her text which is believed to formally articulate in recurring diegetic elements. She felt ironically that the male third person closed off avenues of enquiry that should be followed up. It is rather a key for understanding hierarchies of gender work in cinematic authorship. Cinema represents social and cultural realities of our lives. How cinema might be moving its audiences into perceiving equations or imbalances in gender relations, is a matter of grave concern which needs an inquiry. Even in India, it is strongly felt by gender sensitized women like Bina Agarwal that "men's emancipation is originally linked with that of women and achieving gender equality is therefore not just women's concern-it also deeply concerns men". (Agarwal 36).

No matter how much we would like to avoid the belief, but the initial effort to improve the status of Indian women and contemporary women's movement, is to a considerable extent, the product of an idea that had its birth in the west. However, our own historical and cultural experience has provided its own unique momentum and direction. "Unlike western women, Indian woman's identity is deeply embedded not in her individuality nor in the marital twosome, but in the entire family, caste, class and community". (Ghadially 16). It is, in fact, this rootedness, which is responsible for her inability to untangle herself from this intertwining network. However, a question that haunts every feminist is "What is the essential nature of woman? What are her immutable attributes, abilities and predilections? How are gender relatives perceived"? (Kemps and Squires 6). A fundamental goal of feminist theory is to analyse gender relations, how gender relations are constituted and experienced and how we think or equally important, do not think about them. Since all our laws and constitutions, our codes and customs of social life are of masculine origin; the equation of gender relations is inherently tilted. However, the study of gender relations includes, but is not limited to, what are often considered the distinctively feminist issues vis-à-vis the situation of women and the sphere of male domination. The strength of such a study lies in the critical distance gained in considering existing gender relations, a critical distance which provides an opportunity for renegotiating these relations afresh.[6] Feminist theory might then be best characterized as a critical analysis of the dynamics of gender and sexuality. If one is conscious of one's place in society and aware of one's right and duties as a member of the society, one should speak. To convey a message, one needs a medium.

Mass media is powerful in its potential to influence. The previous century has been a century of media revolutions. It has been employed as an instrument of social and technological changes. In a vast country, mass media is the best way to reach out to the majority of the population, in a quick and efficient way. Indians, as it is, have been more and more dependent on the Indian Cinema and theatre for their entertainment. Even with the advent of T.V., Internet, and Cable T.V. with its multifarious channels, Indian movies still form the biggest chunk of entertainment. From the day the first film was shown, in India in 1896, its popularity was established.

Popular Indian cinema has attracted a considerable amount of attraction as the site of alternate folk culture. It has woven its stories around popular folk stories, thus projecting the unbroken continuity of the Indian culture. However, the 'innocuous' story telling technique, which was employed, still prevailed. The impasse of this kind of cinema led to the compromise formation such as middle class cinema. This kind of cinema was distinguished by the narratives of upper caste, middle class life, with ordinary looking de-glamorised stars and it consolidated itself by elaborating a negative identity based on its difference from the mainstream popular cinema. Remaining within the norms of the structure of established industry, middle class cinema represents a first serious successful attempt at realistic cinema, for aesthetic purpose. The success of these films was based on the identification strongly felt by the ordinary middle class urban cinegoers with its middle class characters who were recognizable in identifying them with their own persona. "While the 'normal' audience was still there, and 'a new type' of audience was perceived as growing for cinema which could be drawn to an alternative cultural space". (Prasad 130).

The genius of a middle class cinema was rooted in the aesthetics based on dis-identifying with the so-called popular cinema. However, while it represented the urban working class, it excluded the rural Indian figure with its feudal social order. This was, then the phase when the new cinema arrived which was also called artistic cinema for its thematic content and aesthetic sensibility. A number of highly gifted directors have been associated with it such as Shyam Benegal, Govind Nihalani, Mrinal Sen, Ritwik Ghatak, Adoor Gopalakrishnan, Saeed Mirza, Kumar Sahani, Ketan Mehta, Aparna Sen and Vijay Mehta. When Shyam Benegal's first film *Ankur* was released in 1974, it seemed to many that 'New Cinema' had just arrived. However, for the filmmakers, *Ankur's* new modes of perception and technique were still hazy and barely formulated and *Ankur* was looked at in context of its theme. Aruna Vasudev felt it to be, "an evolutionary history culminating in the emergence of the good film and demonstrated that the triumph of the realist aesthetic was not a forgone conclusion". (Vasudev The New 40). Shyam Benegal's *Ankur* attracted even Satyajit Ray's attention for its camera work and the aesthetic of realism as a dissemination of socio-political ideology. Asish Rajadhyaksha affirms that "the neo-tradionalism of Indian popular film culture was a political and not a technological issue". (Rajadhyaksha Neo-Traditionalism 26).

Sadly, new cinema's shrinkage coincided with the technical freedom and films were being made with an eye on the overseas market for commercial gains. The commercial cinema resources are getting mobilized for better trade with financial budgets climbing in terms of not lakhs but crores. The higher the investment the more conformist the commercial cinema tends to become to reconstruct its investment in the process losing out on form and content. "Cinema has become a tool for instant gratification of the keeper-consumerist audience and as a consequence the lasting impact that film should have is missing." (Branton 147).

Popular cinema is tendentionally capable of being described as a melodrama and opium for the masses. The same phenomenon has been termed as a feminization of mass culture and has been shown to be a feature of cultural theory in the modern west "thus the gendered polarization of culture into a masculine sphere of heterogeneous and formally diffuse mass culture has led to an affirmation of melodrama as a feminine form." (Gledhill Home Is 6). Its pleasures are viewed as designated but real and valued pleasures of the female audience. However melodrama in its earliest manifestations was diffused and fragmentary to be called a form in its own right. It achieved its highest level of formal consistency later when it came to be specifically addressed to women in the Hollywood movies.

In the earlier phase of Indian Cinema, woman figure was portrayed basically as a chaste wife, an ideal submissive and virtuous daughter-in-law, and a nurturing mother or either a courtesan. Thus the basic two true archetypes of popular cinema have been, "firstly one *Mother India's*, matriarch, an upholder of *dharma* and the true emotional center of hero's life. The second is '*Pakeeza*' romanticized apostrophe to women, as the pathetic, impossibly innocent 'other' to be rescued from the penumbra of social opprobrium. Every *tawaif* and her cousin is descended from *Pakeeza* and is a reflection of pale, derived poetic pathos". (Rao Maithili To be 242). In the 70s and 80s, heroes pursued their own dreams and fought their own battles. The heroine took on several functions of the vamps of yesteryears dancing away with explicit gyrations portraying an aggressive sexuality.

The mid and late 80s did see another 'avtaar' of the heroine as the female avenger on account of rape and revenge formula. The heroine's uncompromising attitude and fight for justice came as a kind of assurance for her selfhood. In the 90s, family returned with force as a central theme of commercial cinema. If the declining of the parental authority was a reflection of the ontological social reality of the disintegrating joint family in the 70s and 80s, the family as the basic social unit made up for it by following the "back to roots" syndrome. Diaspora and Hindu nationalistic fervour in the 90s led to culture becoming a source of national identity, giving the crucial sense of belonging. Nationalism is very much on the agenda of commercial cinema now, in thematic terms.

In the films in preceding decades, the hero was on the search for the symbol of order. In the films of the decades of 90s the protagonist was seen as a liberator of community, which is largely passive. The new cinema came as a fresh breather showing a gentle respect for the marginalized individual, be it a man or a woman. However, the art movies of 70s presented the woman neither as a focused protagonist nor as the basic subject. Very often, the women were only presented as the marginalized and oppressed class in a more sensitive manner in the pre-emptive set of categories as that of caste and class. Most of the commercial cinema tends to represent the establishment and is no doubt basically regressive in character. Yet the so-called commercial mainstream cinema does project powerful women.

The study of the women's representation as such in Indian movies has long been neglected. Women characters have been marginalized in some way or the other, viewed rather as props to the male counterparts in the society. The few systematic studies that have been conducted on the topic of treatment of women in the Indian cinema unequivocally claim that the social roles portrayed in them are strictly dichotomous as well as stereotypical. The traditional role of the subservient female and dominant male repeatedly gets reinforced on the Indian screen. The roles, which women play in society and the images, one has of the Indian heroine, is developed by social situations, which are deeply rooted in the myths and legends of culture. In the Indian culture, inspiration of ideal womanhood comes from the mythical figure of Sita. She is presented as a model or an icon, as an archetype, which ought to be emulated. She came from the earth, like a line drawn with a sickle, (a phallic symbol), in the oral traditions of the many *Ram Kathas* scattered as memory, all over the country. The virtuous woman in the Indian films, too, has been resplendent with characteristics such as chastity, patience and selflessness. The symbolism in Indian cinema has varied in accordance with the portrayal of gender. "The men in the popular Indian cinema have mostly stood for power, while the woman has been a measure of that power, a subject on which the power is exercised either as a victim or an object." (Kazmi Nikhat The Dream 21).

Realism in the cinema is a combination of the referents of reality that endorses "the image as realistic, the conventions of rendering plausible whatever is shown and the entirely self sustaining diegetic nature".

(Vasudevan Making 272). Indian cinema has a great deal to say about all these categories. At first it demarcates the category of subject as constitutive of all ideology. At the same time, it specifies this action to its constituting concrete individuals as subjects. What seems to emerge in Indian cinema, is, an emphasis on emotion and spectacle rather than tight narrative, on how things happen rather than on what will happen next.

> "The spectator is addressed and moved through these films primarily by, the theory of *rasas* (flavors/moods) which is concerned with moving the spectator through the text in an ordered succession of modes of affect *(rasa)* by means of highly stylized devices. All Indian classical drama, dance and music draw on this aesthetic." (Thomas Rosie 118).

The oldest known available Indian work on the literary theory of theatre is Bharata's *Natyasastra*, most probably written in the third century A.D. Although the work refers specifically to Natya (drama), its influence on Indian literary criticism like that of its famous western counterpart, Aristotle's *Poetics*, was and still is considerable. The most important chapter in the *Natyasastra*[7] is the sixth, on rasa or the aesthetic and imaginative experiencing of the drama. "*Natyasastra* or *Natyveda* as it was called was created as a fifth '*Veda*' and was composed incorporating all the arts and sciences after meditating in solitude". (Rangacharya 1). In the western critical canon, Suzanne Langer immediately comes to mind as the foremost exponent of aesthetics, valorizing the importance of feeling in act. She refers most pointedly to *rasa* as 'vital feeling' when she states, "*rasa* is, indeed, that comprehension of the directly experienced or 'inward life' that all art conveys." (Langer 323).

The complicated doctrine of *rasas* centres predominantly on feelings experienced not only by the characters but also conveyed in a certain artistic way to the spectator. The duality of this kind of *rasa* imbrications was not lost on the directors like Satyajit Ray, Bimal Roy, Basu Bhattacharya, Guru Dutt, Gulzar who made films based on Indian fiction. The works of literary texts, which they chose to transform into cinema, taking their filmmaking in new directions, dealt with distinct ideological concerns. They made woman centered films, in which one can trace with a remarkable gender sensitivity and historical insight, the troublesome journey that the trapped Indian woman has had to make under the patriarchal gazes and the threat of a conspicuously deterministic Indian masculinity. Since any worthwhile examination of women and their struggle must include a parallel investigation of men and man-woman gender relations this would form the framework of my inquiry during the study. Post feminism is often used to signal a complete break in a previous range of usually 'oppressive' relations, which are to be overcome and replaced in the content of a new range of gender relations' vis-à-vis changing cultural relation. It however, does not assume that either patriarchal or modernist discourses or frames of reference have been replaced or suspended. It is interested in the shifting of boundaries, the undoing of binary oppositions and is investigated for its literariness, its slippages of meanings.

The social fabric of the western countries has changed dramatically as a result of feminism reaching out gradually in every nook and corner not as theory but as a way of life. The point is, whether the roles that women play in society and the images one has of the Indian heroine, are developed by social situations or deeply rooted myths. Are the roles she is expected to play dictated by the mythical view of femaleness and where does the contemporary woman stand today and how gender relations are perceived? How films reflect and cultivate interpretations of sexual difference, which control representations and erotic way of looking? Consistent with the cultural norms pertaining to the status of women in India is the honour of the family, which is closely linked to the female behaviour. The need to preserve honour is expressed through elaborate codified behaviour patterns that require the women to be dependent. Whether women are seen as protagonists only in women oriented movies or simply marginalized in formula ridden *masala* movies, it is in this backdrop that the present study is conceived. It is pertinent to examine texts, which are film friendly and deeply implicated in the propagation of existing beliefs and attitudes. The directors with their visionary wisdom transcend such invisible barriers, and simulate and implement projects aimed at improving women's status and show gender relations with a more balanced perspective. They deliver and deliberate, alongside, the growth of women's consciousness also and offer best chances for bringing about real changes and not cosmetic ones. They, thus, simulate and exhibit the development of gender relations and role of women as partners in building up a holistic better society.

In the Indian context, films have been used as a form of critical intervention on various myriad manifestations-like feudalism, casteism, myth, rituals and cultural conventions which go on to inform our cultural ethos. Certain movies, in the name of realistic cinema, equally exploit the women as a commodity. On the other hand, women in Indian cinema are expressing their sexuality but are unwittingly surrendering to the male gaze. The question of male gaze and voyeurism and the role of women as an 'object' as it has been explicated by feminist film theory in the west, is a very significant malaise. The film's media is more powerful in transcending the written words of the text and in going beyond the same, in establishing gender equations as a part of man-woman relations. The extent, to which the film media demonstrates the phase of cultural transition vis-à-vis the workings of human psyche and the behavioural pattern of interpersonal relations, is my study.

Gender relations mean going beyond feminism, in the sense that one may understand what are the cultural norms which denigrate woman and do not give woman an identity, a voice of her own and the rightful status of even being a human being with dignity. Gender relations are constituent elements in every aspect of human experience. Gender relation is a category

-meant to capture a complex set of social relations to refer to a changing set of historically variable, social processes. Gender, both as an analytic category and as a social process is relational. According to Jane Flax, "gender relations are complex and unstable processes constituted by and through interrelated parts. These parts are interdependent that is each part can have no meaning or existence without the others". (Flax 175).

Gender relations are identified as terms of dominance, difference, antagonism and solidarity that are constantly at work. The gender arrangements of a society involve social structure, for example, in religious, political, conversion practices, all of which place men in authority over women. The patriarchal structure of gender relations leads to socio-cultural structures, which ultimately, get established as an ideology. As a result such a structure of gender relations has no existence outside the practices through which people and groups conduct those relations.

> One, "often experiences disparities in gender relations as a part of our lives that are working on one gender logic and another part on a different logic. When this happens in public life, not just in personal affairs the complexity within the gender system becomes highly visible". (Connell 56).

While attempting to understand, gender relations there is a need to investigate both social and philosophical barriers in the comprehension of gender relations. Cinema has been a vital element of one's existence. Whether it is just a vehicle of escape from reality or has been influencing the attitudinal changes in society, is debatable.

Various directors like Satyajit Ray, Basu Bhattarcharya, Guru Dutt, Vijay Anand, Pamela Rooks, Hrishikesh Mukherjee, Muzaffar Ali and even female directors like Deepa Mehta and Kalpana Lajmi, have strived hard with their artistry to transform the fiction based on Indian literary writings on the celluloid. It is my contention that the aesthetic, which is used by filmmakers, may be examined as a critical variant or variable which may be so effective in enhancing the impact of cinema. Aesthetics can have an evocative and potent impact along with visual pleasure. It is my concern to examine how successfully, with their dramaturgy and deep insight, the filmmakers transcend the fiction and portray the problematic of the hegemonic overtones of gender relations. Do they really talk a language, which is discernible to a gender sensitive mind? The purpose of cinema has always been to entertain but whether it entertains intelligently or mindlessly, is a pertinent issue.

Hindi cinema may well appear like a tree rooted deeply in Indian tradition. A traditional feature of Indian drama is its mythological foundations and the myths of culture function as a set of basic images, which in their applicability share a collective conscious. The cultural explanation characterizes Indian cinema as a repository of a traditional aesthetic that composed different *rasa* or moods, in line with ancient canons of Hindu aesthetics. The techniques in Indian popular cinema are shaped by traditional narrative, whereas those of the artistic cinema are western in nature and are largely neo-realistic. However, in terms of experiences explored, they are much closer to Indian reality than the so-called popular cinema, which are mostly fantasies. They cater to ideas pre-shaped in the minds of the public and by meeting their expectations and anticipation, do utmost to impress for the commercial success of the film.

Aesthetically, Indian cinema is indebted not so much to high classical drama as to the so-called secondary varieties of traditional drama *uparupakas* with their predominance of non-verbal elements such as dance and music. "Bharata was conversant with ten kinds of *rupakas* i.e. major types of drama and his description remained authoritative for later theorists. In course of time, all kinds of novelties were introduced, leading, to further divisions and sub divisions". (Gupta, Chandra Bhan 164). The aesthetic experience is one and yet it assumes different forms at different levels. In the aesthetic experience one has a direct and immediate apprehension. Yet the aesthetic emotions cannot emanate either purely from the individuals resourceful mind or purely from the object. They result from the unity of the experience as such and this unit precludes the possibility of an illusion, whether deliberate or unmotivated. Aesthetic experience comprises,

> "the aesthetic objective, the stimulus and the immediate cause of feeling and on the one hand and on the other it includes the purely mental aspects of sensation feeling emotion, imagination and the resultant meaning embodied. In ordinary perception we take the object as a means to an end. But in aesthetic perception we are concerned with objects in terms of existence or reality, which excludes all practical interest". (Pandit 26).

The individual who approaches the aesthetic state is one whose heart is genuinely moved to look into the inner life of things. In a folkloristic rendering, the popular film is rooted in the persistent morality of Indian culture in which music has an expressive equivalence to speech. In contrast to a literary disposition whose reading practices interiorise the reader/ viewer's relationship to the text, such morality is said to sustain an externalised declamatory and musical form in Indian cinema. The aesthetic experience is a state of harmony and it is free from all contradictions.

Cinema has often been dismissed as a vulgar form of mass entertainment and was even considered therefore, non-literary and unworthy of serious consideration. However, its influence in shaping public opinion and human mind is tremendous. Cinema is a cultural institution and various literary and artistic intelligentsia of filmmakers have been interested in shaping and nurturing their desire for a traditional and authentic India. The imperatives of a modern national identity has accrued from a broad engagement in the popular cinema by the left wing intelligentsia and those more loosely associated with the Progressive Writers' Association and the Indian People's Theatre Association such as Rajinder Singh Bedi, Sadat Hasan Manto, Ismat Chugtai, K.A. Abbas, Kaifi Azmi, Zia Sarhady, Shaheed Latif, Chetan Anand, Krishen Chander, Sahir Ludhianvi, Mrinal Sen, Bimal Roy etc. There have been a series of writers in different various Indian languages who have contributed immensely to the edifice of India literature and inadvertently to the kaleidoscope of Indian cinema. There have been enough unities underlying the differences in Indian languages yet bringing nearer to the idea of Indianness as there has been an "unbroken continuity of themes, genres, symbols, canon and traditions." (Das 24). Each of the Indian language is not merely the language of a part of India, but essentially represents thought and culture in its manifold forms.

Film, as an art form embraces both elitist and popular concepts of art and work closely with literary aesthetics. The two art forms-verbal and visual are not merely parallel but interactive, reciprocative and independent. The visual medium offers choices, which the written narrative may not, in choice of perspectives through *mise en scene*. *Mise en scene* is what cinema has in common with theatre. However, cinema goes beyond placing things. Films through different elements using aesthetics, setting, costume, expression, make up, movement, lighting etc., aid the construction of meaning. To look at mainstream popular cinema, is to critique an art form in which the functioning of reality and fantasy acquire altogether different dimensions, which aim at mass audience and pure entertainment. However, it is an entertainment medium enjoyed by millions, yet it also helps to develop an understanding of the institutions and social context within which it is situated. Through such a set up and strategy, cinema also reveals the society's unconscious positioning of men and women along with their prejudices, stereotypical mind sets, even while assuming a language of their own, with a set of messages to be decoded. The viewer's sense of identification with what occurs on the screen is central to the film going experience.

This book is based on issues whether cinema facilitates the subversion of ideology and whether cinematic representation overrides the cultural content and ambience set in fiction. Films are a medium of presentation of certain facets of a culture as well as of character with its entire attendant trapping of ideology, representing visual features and pleasure through aesthetic vibrancy. Acting process, directive genius, cinematic codes and technical approbation always provide physical and psychical place for individual spectators and even impress on the collective psyche. Visual culture implies "the existence of particular structures for the gaze for seeing and for the enactment of desire, voyeurism or fear in looking." (Evans and Hall 176). Certain themes, imbued with visual metaphors and technologies of looking and seeing, have become the staple diet. The politics of representation is important for the cinegoers. The male gaze and the possibility of a female gaze, the mirror stage fetishism and voyeurism in the reproduction of image so strongly propounded by the feminist film theories in the west can enhance the critical study of cinema in juxtaposition with the representation of women in it. Aesthetic aspects of representations like the use of imagery, symbols, motif, space, setting and lighting of camera as well as the conventional theatrical devices like costume, spectacle, music etc. all of which go on to highlight the story, are also to be taken into account. Aesthetics and ideology get inter-linked leading it to acquire a pivotal role in the dissemination of critical response regarding the forms of influence that cinema has on individual and collective human conduct and interpersonal gender relations.

The need of the hour is to view Indian cinema as a modern cultural institution whose unique features can be related directly or indirectly to the specificity of our socio-political formulations. Meaningful Indian cinema is committed to the progressive social goals and has not just been conceived for disengaging the spectator from his pre-designated location. The manner, in which the cultural ethos of the Indian society with its myriad manifestations influence the making and presentation of Indian cinema and to the extent to which Indian filmmakers have been able to evoke man-woman relationship based on fiction by Indian writers, is the subject of my study. This book proposes to study the rich and varied film *oeuvres* which are based on the works/texts of Phanishwar Nath 'Renu', Mirza Ruswa , Mahashweta Devi, Rabindra Nath Tagore, Prem Chand and Khushwant Singh. The films taken up for the study would be *Teesri Kasam, Umrao Jaan, Rudali, Ghaire Bhaire, Gaban* and *Train to Pakistan*.

"The opening chapter is an introduction or rather a gateway to the edifice I have built up my work on in consequent chapters. It has defined the aims and objectives of the book by bringing forth a discussion on feminism and film theory and as to how these two complement each other and their points of convergence and divergence. An attempt has also been made to trace the history and evolution of Indian cinema and view the film as an art form and a genre, which depends on a variable use of aesthetic. The second chapter focuses on the cultural context in the Indian set-up and Indian cinema viewed as a cultural institution, whose unique features can be related directly or indirectly to the specificity of the socio-political formation of the Indian society."

The third and fourth chapter involve a critical study of films based on fiction with regard to the use of aesthetics by the filmmaker and how it has an evocative and potent impact on the dynamics of visual pleasure. The third chapter includes films like *Teesri Kasam, Umrao Jaan and Rudali*. The shift in man-woman relationship will be perceived in them vis-à-vis conventional societal norms related to class, traditional myths and rituals, casteism and religious diversities, which form the Indian cultural scenario. The fourth chapter includes films like *Ghaire-Bhaire, Gaban and Train to Pakistan*. Gender relations have been perceived in the backdrop of freedom movement and how they disturbed and affected the equations in man-woman relationship.

The last chapter is a sum up of the main arguments of all the preceding chapters in order to explore the relation between films and literary texts. It views the manner in which the writers' referential sophistry gets transformed on the cinema of make-believe through the art and craft of filmmaking, which lends to it something more meaningful, thus, converting it into a more palpable and expansive discourse. The visual media has the potent aesthetic tools of set designing and spectacle, music and sound effects, expression and metaphor, action and performance and space and costume which help the filmmakers to make a more powerful intervention on the theme of the text.

The book summons up the cinematic interpretations of the literary texts on which all these six films are adapted. The interpretations been highlighted by a combination of methods, at times by an analysis of shot-by-shot frame, narrative construction, motif and image. The study is an attempt and a sincere endeavour to have a felicitous research to convey the vision of the literary works taken up respectively. It relates to an attempt to understand how these films enable one to understand the visuality of literary texts on which they are based and the aesthetics employed in the method of interpretation from text to the screen image by the filmmakers respectively along with the issue of gender relations and implicit ideologies of culture. A film version of a literary work refers to the original text but then there are versions employed by filmmakers, marked with challenges as to how to show cinematically what they read in the text. "The juxtaposition of transportation strategies from the literary to the filmic, offers object lessons in the field of text-into-film adaptation which would take a life time of work to vet each adaptation." (Bignell 122).

This book attempts to trace the theme of gender relations against the background of cultural ideology, as and how it reflects in Indian cinema drawn from its rich repertoire. An attempt has also been made to correlate it with the contemporary situation both in terms of the ideas at work as well as the broader contextual reality of our everyday lives. The focus here is on the Hindi cinema; the closest one can come to a 'national' cinema with the works in other languages also taken into account. To be able to grasp the significance of Indian cinema, an awareness of the deeply entrenched values, traditions, and contemporary events in this complex and multi-faceted society is essential. This would include issues of gender, class, conventions, stature etc. India's cinema encompasses them all. Indian cinema like other cinema industries both reflects and is reflected through the country's political, economic, social and cultural aspects.

Notes and Referneces

1. Cinema has been defined in terms of other arts, like "sculpture in motion" (Vachel Lindsay); "music of light" (Abel Gance); "painting in movement" (Leopold Survage); "architecture in movement" (Elie Faure). It simultaneously established links with previous arts while positing crucial differences : "cinema was painting, but this time in movement, or it was music, but this time of light rather than notes. The common point of agreement was that cinema was an art." (Stam 33).

2. It can be carved into, "epochs of theory pluralism and theory monism three epochs: 1910-30s, a period pluralism, 1940s-60s a period of serially monistic theories, 1970s-90s pluralism once more". (Hayward 386).

3. The question was taken up with renewed insistence by post-'68 film theorists who developed a semiotic theory of 'filmic illusion' to explain the power of movies. The cinematic image was conceived as a sign that produces in the spectator the impression that what it represents is real. (Allen and Smith 39).

4. For Althusser, 'ideology' described the process by which social institutions cultivated individuals compliant to the social system by appealing to their need to be recognised, or acquired a social identity.

5. The form of commercial cinematic representation, as both model and vehicle of ideology, was not gender neutral but structured gender relations at the expense of women. "Feminists were quick to embrace the concept of ideology as a way of performing that representations generally, and gender representations in particular, are socially constructed and thus subject to change." (Hammett 245).

6. Feminist film theorists have suggested two possible mechanisms for evading patrarchical ideology. The first appeals to the potential of critical self-awareness or critical distance; the second invokes the authenticity of every day reality and lived experience.

7. According to Bharta, *rasa* consists in the active creation of one of eight defined *emotional* states that figure as the theme or subject of an artistic work. The four positive emotional states that Bharata singles out are *sringara/rati* (love), *hasa* (mirth/ laughter), *utsaha* (dynamic energy), and *vismaya* (wonder/astonishment). The four negative emotions, in their turn, are *birha rasa/soka* (sorrow/grief), *bhaya* (fear/terror), *krodah* (anger) and *jugupsa* (disgust). Later speculation includes in this pantheon the ninth positive emotion of *sama* (serenity/calmness).

2

The Cultural Context

Films, whether they are works of art or depict the realistic milieu, are definitely not larger than life. Yet they have something to convey to the cinegoers-certain ideas, some mature or vulnerable at times and some impressions. They definitely convey a message, right or wrong and leave an impression, sometimes indelible, sometimes passing and fleeting for a moment. To understand and grasp the Indian cinema in a lucid manner, there is a need to be perceptive to India's values and its tradition, its mythology, its contemporary history, which go on to form its cultural context. Indian cinema has been a receptacle of such cultural norms. It is, "ineluctably rooted in its tradition, moving with seeming ease between present and past. It requires an intrepid spirit to decipher its codes to comprehend the variations as much as the unifying principles in the films." (Thorval vii). Inspite of the erosion of the traditional forms, these values have established themselves, as an integral part in the aesthetics of filmmaking, be it through the aesthetics of dance, melodrama, costume, music, spectacle etc. In fact,

> "the cultural industries are institutions in our society which employ the characteristic modes of production and organization of industrial corporations to produce and disseminate symbols in the form of cultural goods and services, though not exclusively, as commodities. In fact, the control of cultural production (capitalist-political-economic) has led to a highly commodified modern mass culture working on the individual spectator at levels which integrate psychoanalytical with the ideological lures." (Branton 67).

For the study of cinema to be taken seriously, one of the first moves of the nascent cultural studies in the west had been to question the power relations in cultural institutions. It is necessary to decode deployment of meaning in its relation to ideology.[1] A medium as powerful as cinema needs to be interrogated, as to the message it conveys and the values, which are carried in it. It is difficult to repudiate the view that cinema has tremendous power to influence.

It is basically hard to define and pinpoint as to what culture means. However, "culture can be referred to as configurations of behaviour manifested and carried by individual, but also as characteristic of a group on the whole." (Subramanyam 15). In order to examine the nature of culture, a possible starting point is the way in which O'Sullivan and Hartley have described culture as, "the institutionally or informally organized social production and reproduction of sense, meaning and consciousness." (44). It can be perceived as a kind of training of minds, tastes and manners. Rather, culture can be studied and psychologically interpreted in the behaviour of individuals embedded in the structure of society. It is possible to claim that culture is an ideological construct made up of collective products such as myths, rituals, art, music, dance etc. However, culture cannot be guaranteed by any single factor but can be seen as the articulation of a large set of elements. Raymond Williams attributed culture to the working class as well as the élite and stated: "There are no masses but there are only ways of seeing (other) people as masses." (32). Culture of any place or region is, however, closely tied to its history, geographic location and the moment in time when culture is being studied. O'Sullivan and Hartley felt that the notion of culture has gone through several conceptual changes at various points in time. They feel that the term is multi-discursive and can be mobilized in different ways in different discourses. In India, too, culture has been formulated in a manner specific to India, its history and its specific practices.

India, with its range and density of diverse cultures opens up the space to the traditional moorings of its culture. There has always been strong link between tradition and culture in India, rather, only those cultural expressions forms and artefacts that have been in existence for long, are considered a part of authentic culture as they have withstood the test of time. In fact, Rustom Bharucha feels that Indians do not necessarily think about culture, still less think through it, "What matters is that we live it and uphold its value at all costs. Culture, it could be argued is a visceral matter rather than an intellectual problem." (68). The heart of a culture involves language, religion, traditions, values and customs. Different societies follow different trajectories even when they are subjected to the same forces of economic development, in part because of situation specific factors. However, society's cultural heritage also shows how a particular society is shaped, "Whenever the culture discourse is considered seriously it gets reduced to tokenistic issues, thus, eluding real genuine issues which affect India today." (Thapar India 68). It rather leads to condescension of culture. However, it is undeniable that there is so much to cultural heritage of India that it is impossible to gauge and fathom its depth. In fact, one wonders as to what should be the starting point to comprehend its multivalence.

India's culture blossomed more than 3000 years ago. It has given successive generations of Indians, "a mind-set, a value system and a way of life which has been retained with remarkable continuity like enduring imprints on Indian consciousness." (Singh, B.P., 1). The mainstream theory of Indian culture lies in its historical heritage and its close relationship with religion. Culture in India needs to be considered in connection with the diversity of languages, religions and regions that India represents. India's culture provides a mirror in which one sees India as a land of myths and legends. This has been possible on account of the idea and the reality of India playing a central role in her creative manifestations, be it in literature, painting, music or drama. These creative manifestations of the past legends and myths have imparted to creative men and women, experiences of modern cultural forms along with forms for experimentation and expression.

The entire corpus of literature in India, right from the *Vedas* of antiquity, the *Upanishads,* the *Ramayana* and the *Mahabharta*, the works of Bharata Muni, Kalidasa, Bhavabuti and Bhasa right upto Panditraja Jagannatha of the 17th century, are replete with observations, suggestions, descriptions and exhortations that bespeak of a dynamic culture. Indian culture has been, however, conceptualised around specific stages in Indian history. First, there is the ancient culture of the Aryans, followed by the culture related with Islamic insurgence and then later the culture of the west represented by the British colonials. What one needs to do is "to explore the hybridity of culture instead of legitimising indifference to other cultures and explore dialogic interactivity across cultures in India. This can be practiced by implementing the notion of culture as an aesthetic discipline, an artefact." (Bharucha 45). A particular image of amalgamation helps one to imagine the intricacies of metabolism in the interaction of culture. At the same time, it can conceal the violent and divisive sources of segregation and discrimination in a dialectal relationship with factors pertaining to gender, caste, class and the creed and the extent to which this can help in steering clear of seemingly cultured attitude through negotiable rules of behaviour. Culture is contradictorily also the *raison d'etre* of countless humiliations and cruelties relating to difference in languages, myths, rituals and social interaction. The apparent flexibility gets totally centralized as a cultural ideological stand and rather than being a *panache* boon of civilized society, it becomes a trapping impediment of normal human relationships and gender relations, leading to power clashes between the two sexes.

Anthropologists, who make comparative, study of human cultural experience and social interactions realize that,

> "there is no culturally innocent or culture free reality and any claims to have a privileged handle on reality to be able to perceive an extra-cultural reality–are in themselves cultural. Rather accounts of cultural

patterns and practices differ quite often, radically from one's experiences. In fact, anthropological studies attempt to forge close relations with other cultures or the cultural 'other'." (Bharucha 23).

Since gender is so omnipresent in human life and shaping the decisions, choices and life styles of individuals, it plays a crucial role in the lives of human beings. Rather, gender in varied perspectives across the boundaries of time and space, plays a more crucial role in the life of women vis-à-vis their position in comparisons to males.

In the Indian scenario, the Indian thought originates in remote antiquity. Considering India's long past, it has sustained a highly individual ethos and stratified society. According to B.P. Singh, "Its survival values, over a long stretch of time are still organized on a relatively primitive basis and yet regarded by progressive Indians." (63). Indian society has always been rooted in modes of hierarchy in principle and practice. Such strictures are archaic but we have come to respect them as the products of an impressively penetrating insight. The cultural ideology-field around gender is centered on Hindu ideology and bound with its practices. This is then articulated within the social and cultural practices and the complex chains particularly are grouped around religion. Such articulated elements produce popular culture in India, which in turn is a reproduction of the set of conventions that are imbibed. The traditional baggage determines the inferior status of women and the female child enters the world in a devalued form. It is the birth of a baby boy, which is considered a blessing. It is a mindset that is as formidable as fortress. The seeds of gender inequality so prevalent in our society are sown as such at her birth.

Dynamic culture superimposed and articulated with contradictions, poses a set of questions that meander around gender. The position of women has always been secondary to that of men and the construct of womanhood has been produced and dominated by the male hegemony. This has been possible by the articulation of a variety of social and cultural practices that place men in a position of dominance. The literary tradition of *Ramayana* which depicted Sita as the quintessence and epitome of womanhood, went on to have a stronghold on the mind-set, not only of men but women too, leading to a stereotypical stance for the women of India. The structure upon which the contemporary Indian society rests has its roots in ancient India. Patriarchy is maintained and reinforced as a cultural pattern intersecting with the structure of power. Gender relations and powers are expressed, reinforced and simultaneously reproduced through culture. It is through culture and heritage, through which patriarchy operates subtly in day-to-day life. The cultural reinforcement and reproduction of patriarchy takes place through the embodiment of such a cultural construct. Through the cultural construct of femininity, woman is expected to accept her femininity as natural and to fall into the trap of stereotypes.

Cinema like other forms of art functions is a source of communication in conveying messages. While the role of media in early liberal thought was defined mainly in terms of a watchdog, the expectations from this medium widened with the development of mass society within this spectrum. One may legitimately question the role of cinema in representing women's concerns and their presentation and participation in this public space. In commercial Indian cinema, there is an urge to cater to ideas pre-shaped in the minds of audiences and by meeting their expectations and anticipations, this not only endeavours to impress a vast number of audiences but leads to a "feeling of Indian collectiveness." (Bathla 15). The foundation of Indian cinema was undoubtedly defined for this purpose and its major aim was to provide an insight to a culture process of society. Indian cinema defined for this purpose, the myths of a culture as a set of basic images that used the myths in genres of sociological films. In keeping with the cultural pluralism that India represents, our cinema reveals tremendous cultural diversity too. Indian cinema is to be viewed in its spatial perspective as multi-hued as life itself. However, through cinema, an ideology to keep women away from the power system has been attempted through the construction of private and public realms for women and men respectively. Although, commercial Indian cinema caters to the public and helps them to escape into the illusions of fantastic dreams and opiates the masses, yet, the strangehold of patriarchal mores and near total suppressions of women's autonomy in society is brought about in an arresting manner in the Indian cinema.

Cinema is a powerful cultural practice and institution which both reflects and inflects the discourse of nationhood. As a result, the concept of national cinema is at the base of any discussion of popular culture of any country. Indian cinema's style is unique and recognizably Indian.

"Nationhood as with all forms of identity revolves around the question of difference with how the uniqueness of one nation differs from the uniqueness of other comparable nations". (Dissanayake 145).

Nation may be understood as an imagined community and nationhood is a cultural artefact of a particular kind. Any investigation into the ways in which cinema constructs nationhood must consider issues of ethnic loyalties, its political character, history, religious affinities and its local patriotism. The concept of national cinema, hence serves to privilege notions of coherence and unity and to stabilize cultural meanings. Cinema narrates story in images and whatever is perceived and imagined in literary texts gets transformed on celluloid as images and sound. A film tells the story of a literary piece to be adapted for celluloid through its myths, legends history of a country, its music, spectacle which all get invigorated as the ethos of the culture of a nation.

Both the sociological status of a family and the gender relations, become a part of the nation's myth-making and ideological productions, which get reflected in literature, paintings, and cinema too. Even if the scriptwriter respects the original story, he/she tries to "preserve the richness and density of the novel while simultaneously cutting it down to a fraction of its original length", says Sooni Taraporewalla, an internationally acclaimed scriptwriter. (quoted in Kanga Fareeda 3). However the way cinema works, "to capture the complex and dynamic relationships between temporality and spatiality, is not available to any other media." (Harvey 145).

The film theorists like Professor Kwame and Anthony Appiah argue against the pseudo universalism of Euro-centric theorizations. Ukadike, another non-western critic asserts that, "Eurocentric paradigms cannot take on the mantle of universal templates or they will hamper a deep understanding and appreciation of cinemas in the non-western world". (quoted in Dissanayake 148). Interestingly since the last fifteen years there has been a rhetorization about issues as to the nature of cinematic representation vis-à-vis the role of ideology in cultural production and also regarding the importance of female sexuality in cinema, in the genre like that of melodramas. However critics like Paul Willemen have cautioned that the melodramas in the west cannot be judged in terms of western conceptualisations of melodrama. He says, "Melodrama functions differently in different cultural contexts and the melodramatic traditions evolved differently in Asia, Latin America and Africa." (Willemen 40). In India, film melodramas bear the cultural inscriptions of folk theatres as well as the Parsee theatre of the nineteenth century. This bond had magnificently served the silent film. However, the ethos of such a cultural construct found its way during the sound period and the same reflects in the latter phase of Indian cinema and even in the contemporary. Rather, analytical tools developed by western film school, such as those relating to point of view, the gaze and textual subjectivity also have limited application in Indian cinema. Indian cinema did and does emulate Hollywood mode but the role of its own aesthetic intertexts and cultural contexts are crucial to the understanding of Indian films.

Since cinema came as a part of technology from the west and is related with different life styles and beliefs that define human society, it is inevitable to understand its patterning of meanings only in the context of a socio historical consciousness which seems to permeate its forms. According to Dr. Kishore Valicha, an avid film scholar, "the key to cinema lies in culture". (Valicha vii). The meanings in cinema and in cinematic articulations are inseparable from various social, intellectual and cultural developments. Hence, it is necessary while dealing with the cinema of a particular society, region, country to relate its cinema to certain thematic concerns (or myths) that are a part of the cultural context of that society region and country.[2] These often go back in time to an ancient part for intelligibility of certain cultural constructs of that society in cinema. Certain cultural and artistic forms in cinematic representation make sense only in the light of these cultural contexts.

Even though cinema is mainly a technological art and its development is related to the emergence of modernity on the account of growth of science and technology which transcends boundaries and languages; however, many cinematic forms cannot be understood without significant semiotical meanings such as codes, conventions and even a technology that is a part of the knowledge of cultural phenomena. In order to understand and decode various signs that are used in it and to perceive its cultural meanings, be it in Indian popular cinema or serious art cinema, such a work, according to Kishore Valicha, can be described as an axio-aesthetics of the Indian cinema. According to him,

> "it is not a pure kind of aesthetics concerned with enunciating only formal cinematic principles. It is an aesthetics with the total hermeneutic functioning of Indian cinema with relation of cinema to society, culture and the *weltanschauung* what makes for cinematic meaning in a cultural sense." (Valicha x).

In fact, film codes pertain to the world and society we live in and narration in cinema is culturally determined discourse and hence is a kind of meta reading. The semantics of the Indian film cannot be separated from the sociological or even the philosophical thought nor the cultural current that distinguish any historical age.

Film is not an isolated art form as it inhabits a common expressive culture fed by tradition, cultural memory and indigenous modes of symbolic representation. Hence, films and other arts are mutually implicated in the productions of meaning and pleasure, which definitely need to be examined. The complex way in which traditional arts, be it in the setting, costume, characterization, music, locations as well as the way cinematography, take place in the film, are all vitally connected in the orchestration of meaning.

Indian cinema has its own unique and recognizable style. Even what is projected beyond the screens and cinema halls through the film's advertising and promotional material, all forms part of the visual culture of the Indian film. This all-pervasive visual culture as it reflects the harmonious whole of everyday Indian life,

> "is an integral part of the complexity that comprises Indian cinema. Indian commercial cinema is often considered vulgar and kitsch by some and glamorous and trend setting by others; however, it permeates every aspect of India and Indian diasporic culture." (Dwyer and Patel 8).

"In fact Indian cinema has its own narrative structure, in the lack of realism and multiplicity of emotional context". (Thomas Rosie 117). These are some of the aspects, which inform us of the cultural specificity as certain defining features of Indian cinema. "It reflects its own powerful personal levels of association that the public have with male/female roles, and the familiar subject matter of family social order and morality." (Dissanayake and Sahai 82).

In the myths of India, one tends to bring the intuitive collective wisdom of an ageless, anonymous and many-sided civilization. Hence, there is every reason to feel diffident while commenting on any Indian myth. However, the cultural values stabilized by Indian society in its early phase had a sound idealism, which promised a sustained evolution along healthy lines. The pursuit of legitimate economic motivations was endorsed without reservations by the cultural mentality even while aggressive competitiveness was restrained by the emphasis on humanity and compassion for others. Gender relations were perceived within the paradigm of pristine purity in the age of the mythological beginnings.

"The God and Goddess are the first self-revelation of the Absolute, the male being the personification of the passive aspects which is known as eternity, the female of the activating energy (*Shakti*), the dynamism of Time. Though apparently opposite, they are in essence one. There are many representations of sacred union of the Two-in-One *Shiva-Devi Parvati* as the primeval pair in close embrace and has set the model for countless couples". (Zimmer 128).

There is much to be said of such symbols, ornate and ambiguous though they may appear to be, developed in sterner tradition. *Shiva* symbolism delves deeper into the mystery of the two-in-one other than any other Hindu tradition of *Shakti* worship. That is what makes it particularly interesting and illuminating.

History of Indian scriptures is represented as a ceaseless conflict between the *Dharma* and *Adharma*, between the moral, idealistic, spiritual forces and the unregenerate forces of darkness, lust and evil in which *Dharma* always wins. To understand the central evaluative and moral concepts of the Hindu Great Tradition and culture is to recognize that there are certain criteria. Hindu ethics has its public face *Dharma* or normative rules and its private wisdom or pragmatic rules to distinguish between the principles men espouse and the tactics they adopt. The oldest major Indian sources of ethical ideas are the two Epics, which continue to be the inspiration of all teaching on morality. The *Ramayana* and the *Mahabharta* are the two immortal epics of India that have loomed large since time immortal, over the aspirations and ambitions, hopes and frustrations, emotions and thoughts of generations throughout the length and breadth of this country. These two epics from the pens of Valmiki and Ved Vyasa respectively encompass within them engrossing tales, and graphic narration and description. An Indian sense of community has been especially,

"fostered by common cultural legacies among the most remarkable of which have been the great Indian epics the *Ramayana* and the *Mahabharta* like the Iliad and the Odyssey. They are oversized tales of adventure involving gods, heroes and mortal men, as well as mythical animals. Each has a unifying plot, holding together a vast panorama of people and incidents like the Bible. Each is also a compendium of folk history, poetry and wisdom. Told, sung and acted along before Christian era, these tales have conquered the waves of invaders that have swept over and fragmented India. The stories found their way eventually in verifying versions into all languages of India". (Barnouw and Krishnaswamy 64).

Their numerous characters and situations, inform the trend of our national ethos and ideals and films too. They have embalmed in their immortal pages, for posterity, the essentials of Hindu *Dharma* that continues to guide and lead, entertain and inspire their followers as no other books or scriptures have done. The influence of *Ramayana* has been much potent and pervasive on the mass mind in India. It not only excludes both serenity and wisdom but also helps to harmonize all discords in our culture of diverse strands.

However, the concept of Sita in *Ramayana* as *pativrata*, self-effacing, obedient to a fault is prevalent in traditional Indian society. Sita immortalized in the *Ramayana* is the ideal woman, the ideal wife who is steadfastly loyal to her husband and obeys his wishes unquestionably. The *Ramayana* says that a wife's god is her husband and he is her mentor, friend and teacher too. In traditional Indian society, the lives of women were severely circumscribed and role models from the scriptures essentially determined women's roles. They were similarly constructed and filmed as that of a daughter, wife and mother. Women had a subservient role to play with no independent thought or action of their own. The enormous success of the televised *Ramayana and Mahabharta*, which indicates the orthodox view of the *Bhartiya nari* as an impossibly ideal, lifeless, colourless oppressed prototype, is a part of our popularly accepted syndrome. Interwoven with all these are the symbols of womanhood, *purdah, haveli, chudiyan, mangalsutra, kumkum sindoor* and the colour red, which constitute a rigid code of bondage and solely female circumscribed. "These are grim pointers to our blinkered perception of culture's strangehold". (Nabar 44). The Indian women see them without exception as heavy with suggestions of romance, lyricism, beauty and enchantment, fulfillment etc. Women who seek to live by traditional norms find happiness while those who dare to transgress them are punished and victimized in the mythologies.

Symbols of forms of oppression for a significant number of Indian women are part of our cultural heritage. Sita, wife of Rama, the protagonist of *Ramayana* and Savitri, married to Satyavana who refused to give him up to *Yama*, god of Death and ultimately prevails with him and gets her husband back from him, are both ideal wives who seek fulfillment through selfless service of their husband. Draupadi, wife of the five Pandav brothers in the *Mahabharta* is rather more independent and is shown as having very forceful views. All three women are regarded as valid symbols of Indian womanhood and have an enormous hold on the Indian psyche as the level of popular and creative consciousness. The code of conduct called *stree dharma* for a woman in the orthodox Hindu worldview, to a kind of faith and this cultural construct of dutifulness is relevant in the contemporary Indian society.

> "*Purush and Stree* which signify male and female respectively encompass the two genders imposing a casteist hierarchy as it were on the sexual one. Rather called as *purush jati* and *stri jati*, it means and imbibes class, nature and caste as well". (Nabar 201).

The concept of equality as a correlate of the concept of individual freedom is alien to Indian society. Women have been conditioned to revere the father and the husband, as a devotee serves God. Rules of proper conduct for the Hindu wife and husband are clearly laid down even in our *Dharma Shastras* and these works have had a great influence in shaping the mind set and behaviour of women. Indian women's identity is one that is usually connected to and defined by societal and cultural norms and is defined in terms of gender relations within the parameters of patriarchal familial structure. Sita, Savitri, Gandhari and other characters in these stories exemplify the ideal behaviours for the women. "The term '*pativrata*' connotes to a wife who has accepted service and devotion to her husband and his family as her ultimate religion and duty". (Chitnis 90). The ideal of *pativrata* is romanticized through legend, folklore and folk song and reaffirmed through ceremonies of different kinds e.g. *karva chauth* a ceremony in which wife fasts the whole day for the long life of the husband etc.

The discrimination between the sexes in India begins even when the child is in the mother's womb. None of the conventional blessings showered upon a pregnant woman mention daughters. A woman in India is made to feel morally obliged to give birth to a son and female infanticide and foeticide is a form of such discrimination and its manifestation. The girl child, in India even before she is born, has long been an object of fear, disappointment and revulsion. The female foeticide is privately sanctioned act and declining male-female ratio on account of it is an eye opener of the modern 21st century India. There have been claims of infanticide prevalent even in *vedic* times when women were accorded equality with men in the pre-Manu India. In the west too gender infanticide, is practised in several cultures. As Simone de Beauvoir points out that orthodox patriarchal regimes gave the father absolute control over the lives of children but "every new born male is allowed to live, whereas the custom of exposing girl infants is widespread". (Beauvoir The Second 83).

Pre-Manu India accorded women equality with men in the performance of ritualistic *vedic* sacrifices and women even could become priests. The *vedic* age was more liberal in its attitude towards women than the long period following the composition of the laws of Manu which became the canon law of Hinduism. According to Manu, "though destitute of virtue or seeking pleasure elsewhere or devoid of good qualities, yet a husband must be constantly worshipped as God by a faithful wife. Let her continue till her death forgiving all injuries, performing harsh duties, avoiding every sensual pleasure and cheerful practicing the incomparable rules of virtue, which have been followed by such women as were devoted to only one husband." (quoted in Krishnaswamy 9). Manu also draws a distinction between the image of woman as a sexual partner and the woman as mother. Thus the dual status of the women figures very early in the Indian history and although her position in society has varied to some extent at different periods and in different regions, the ambivalence and duality of her role has continued to be an important feature of Indian society. She is deified in the *Vedas* as bearing *Shakti*, centrifugal source of energy for the creation of the world and at the same time spurned and rejected as being a sinner and a destroyer. Malpractices like sati, child marriage, female infanticide, the low status of widows and *purdah* have had serious consequences for Indian society.

Culture certainly impinges upon media and as a result of it, Indian cinema has become a party to the production of social consciousness. Such an approach looks at the cinematic media as an institution which operates within a given culture in relation to ideology which is not imposed but appears to exist by virtue of an arrived at consensus. The cultural map of the social world is fragmented into different spheres by the media and in the process it constructs 'meaningful' and 'meaningless' elements, making them a part of culture and accentual value system. In other words, women's subordination cannot be understood as a part of class relations, without looking into the component of male domination and the marginalization of their issues. The complexity underlying the process of domination of women can be understood from the institutionalised and systematized phenomena of gender relations. The exercise of power over women is dispensed and anonymous and it operates in a manner, that the concept of subjectivity can be understood subtly with all the complexities underlying its subjugation. It is rather constituted through a process in which a subject forms or recognizes an idea in which he/she believes in and acts in conformity with these ideas. The process becomes determined by dominant ideological value patterns. This can be perceived as the end product of the process of cultural reproduction and the individual is constituted and constructed as a subject not only accepting those very dominant views but also by duplicating and reproducing the same. Thus, stereotypes can be perceived in gender relations, "as the result of various social structures unconsciously reproduced by both men and women independent of their personalities or choices." (Grosz 17).

The filmmakers over the years have allowed their imagination a free rein, even though it is underscored with the constraints of the commercial viability of the final product. They have used, misused and abused the stereotypical images of women in Hindu mythology, modernized and contemporarised it for mass consumption. Sita has been an eternal favourite because of her tenacity to endure and tolerate all forms of humiliation at the hands of her husband. Indian cinema filmmakers have used her appeal for mass audience as she offers the ideal popular image of a woman, who is willing to sacrifice everything inspite of the injustice perpetrated on her in order to sustain the honour of her husband and of his family. As an icon, *Durga or Shakti* is the militant manifestation of Parvati, Lord Shiva's consort. Some of the traits of Durga's persona as such may be perceived in the context of certain Hindu philosophical ideas. As *Shakti* she epitomises divine power and surpasses the gods in what is considered to be a male preserve. Interestingly, though gods because of their failure to meet the cosmic crisis precipitated by the rampaging demons create Durga, she fights for the divine cause by creating female helpers from herself such as Kali and other deities known as *Matrikas* or Mothers. As the repository of Supreme power, she reverses the traditional role of passivity for women.

However, the fact that Draupadi of *Mahabharta* had five husbands has rarely been used or misused by a filmmaker in the form of a myth onto any transposed contemporary Indian situation. The reason is that she being a polyandrous woman, is hard to digest for the Indian male psyche who prefer the Sita/Savitri, Durga, Kali, Shakti, Kunti image, as it suits their sense and sensibility. Spivak underscores the manner "in which Draupadi's legitimate pluralization becomes the means to demonstrate the male glory". (quoted in Chatterji Shoma The Distorted 51). There is a fundamental parity between perpetuating of mythical stereotypes like Sita and Draupadi and our present day reluctance to admit any change that threatens the androcentric patriarchal set up. Since the inception of Indian cinema, the movies of such-like identification steadily came to acquire the ability of offering a temporary palliative to crores of Indians who are overstressed by endemic pressures of poverty, unemployment and disturbing family relationships. Many of these films relocate ancient Indian myths and mythology in modern situations which people find easy to identify with or admire.

Identification is a key term, which is often used to suggest an utter absorption into the narrative forms which film usually, takes. This "is often, then used to suggest that the identification of a spectator into a film, or character or scene produces a particular, often a single, social identity often assumed to be negative or oppressive". (Branton 143). Identity and identity construction can become central to the investigation of cultural consumption. Judith Butler in her book *Gender Trouble* argued against regulation of gender relations and reinforces a binary-view of gender relations in which human beings are divided into two clear-cut groups, women and men. She believed that gender should be seen as "a relation among socially constituted subjects in specifiable contexts". (Butler Gender 72). In other words, rather than being a fixed attribute in a person, gender is a flux variable that shifts and changes in different contexts and at different times.

However, the misuse and abuse of mythology in Indian cinema cannot be absolved from its inherent dangers, as these images form a mindset, leading to a vicious circle that offers no escape. Taking elements and cues from myths in scriptures, the filmmakers have been perpetuating certain pre-ponderous elements of myths through the films. The business of the film is to create images through pictures. The mythical aspect would be more potentially tapped if the image were a populist one. Popular Indian cinema has been creating instant mythology and not authentic characters of credible people and this is truer of the heroine than the hero. One the other hand, Indian Cinema is

"so driven by its phallocentricism that its heroes inevitably acquire longer than life dimension with archetypal overtones. The heroine is strait jacketed into a chaste wife, like the mythical Sita-Savitri. Her suffering makes her only more virtuous. She is a nurturing mother either self-effacing or an avenging demon, Durga/Kali or a titillating seductress oozing oomph as a vampish character". (Rao Maithili To be 241).

On the other hand, there has been a dichotomy of good or bad son; either he is the dispossessed son or a lone warrior claiming his patriarchal inheritance. He is either an avenger or the dutiful Ram like monogamous husband. Again there is a stereotypic syndrome, but it is more potent when two or three aspects get combined to give newness to the hero's role. However, the beautiful educated heroine always finds her ultimate *'nirvana'* from wallowing in servitude and subservience not only to her husband but also to other members of the family of the house too. The heroines are supposed to have those mythical classic virtues that define themselves by a set of relationships and modes of conduct created by a social cultural construct. There cannot be a deviation at different stages of their lives as girls, wives and widows. As Manu, the famous lawgiver, codifier of sixth century BC says "In childhood, a woman must be subject to her father, in youth to her husband and when her lord is dead, to her sons". (quoted in Krishnaswamy 9).

The fact Manu gets updated in this process all over again, is corroborated with the fact that the so-called emancipated Indian girl with an outgoing outlook turns into the docile *'pativrata'* chaste wife after marriage. The female stereotype has been reinforced in movies after movies perpetuating the archetypal myth of the chaste Indian woman. Another character is that of a *bhabhi*, brother's wife, which is a strong flashback to the archetype of the ideal Indian family woman. Her only *raison d'etre* is to please others and relentlessly work for their welfare, be self-effacing to a cloying degree, always ready to hold up the sky when it threatens to fall, always 'in place' to be the sacrificial lamb who is innocent. Yet beleaguered by all and sundry, still smiling and loving, despite a life of compromise, she tries to emulate the ideal Indian woman defined in every mythological or religious story. In movie after movie, the daughter-in-law in Indian cinema has been venerated as *pativrata* or *adarsh mata*—the ideal, which all women should idolize. The women viewers often cry in empathy and men bask in the desire for an ideal screen wife. Elderly women look at their modern *'bahus'* within the same perspective. They give them meaningful glances to suggest that they should be more like the ideal screen idol. When a woman in the family rebels and questions archetypal situation or tries to defy her family or society at large, she stands to be ostracised and accused of destroying social traditions. However, according to Rita Felski "Even the most stereotypical and conventional of texts may articulate moments of protest and express utopian longings, while the most fragmented and aesthetically self-conscious of texts cannot escape". (Felski : The Dialectics 18).

The universal 'Mother' was often identified with '*Kali*', the goddess of destruction as enacted by Nargis in '*Mother India*'. The film fully exploited the emotional possibilities and painted a mystical picture of the suffering mother figure. However, in the patriarchal Indian society, the mother is an archetype of stability and continuity in her role as a pro-creator, *Prakirti*. As *Prakirti*, she is inseparably connected with the physical world. According to the scriptures, she personifies earth itself and stands for cosmic stability and sustains the creatures of this earth and provides for all from her own body. In fact, '*Mother India*' is one of the numerous Indian films, which propagate the almost divine prototype on motherhood. It idealises the woman and the mother, as an almost sacred concept, a central theme of Indian cinema even today. In fact, the mother or the mother-in-law is placed at the centre of the female power. This rather re-establishes male hegemony as she does not betray tradition and social mores. In fact, in the *Mahabharata*, Draupadi as a wife is 'won' after a tournament of archery where various men participate. However, she, as a wife of all the five *Pandavas* is constructed as a person who is inserted within the patriarchal hegemony at the behest of the mother of *Pandavas*. The Kaurvas later on, not only use her as a power in a gambling game but she is also disrobed publicly. This only shows that both the *Pandavas* and *Kauravas* did not really care too much about the dignity of women, including their own wives.

There has been an attempt on the part of parallel art cinema to break the tradition of a stereotype syndrome. In such a milieu too as, the paramount importance is one's survival, the Indian woman strives and seeks to be emancipated even though poor, tries to be independent even though she is bound by tradition. There have been path-breaking filmmakers in the days of yore who have gone against the current of a set of cultural construct of masculinity and femininity. There had been men behind women much before feminism made its dent in pre-Independence and post talkies Indian cinema, which has proved to be strongly supportive of women protagonists. Filmmakers have periodically attempted to explore a woman's psyche. However some did it with admiration towards women and some with the typical male chauvinistic gaze. The heroine in the Indian cinema had often been shown as the idolized Indian womanhood or repressed as the sex symbol, though at times she regained self-esteem from time to time. Her image as a person of substance has its own ups and downs with the changing trends and milieu.

Yet, popular culture drew on a melodramatic framework to provide archetypal symbolic enactments. Gender representation was at the heart of such cultural negotiations. Central to such negotiations was always the figure of woman which served as a powerful and ambivalent patriarchal symbol, heavily over determined as an expression of the male psyche. The image of woman "has been a site of gendered discourse drawn from specific, socio, cultural experiences of women and shared by women, which negotiates a space within and sometimes resists patriarchal domination." (Chatterji : Shoma, The Distorted 45).

There have also been various sensitive male filmmakers not indifferent to equations in gender relations. Satyajit Ray being the frontrunner in this respect and Basu Bhattacharaya, Bimal Roy, Shyam Benegal, Mahesh•Bhatt, Raj Kumar Santoshi, Sanjay Manjrekar, Ketan Mehta, Madhur Bhandarkar to name a few. Satyajit Ray's films like *Ghaire Bhaire, Charulata* etc., Basu Battcharya's *Anubhav, Aavishkar, Teesri Kasam*, Shyam Benegal's *Ankur, Nishant, Bhumika* etc., Mahesh Bhatt's *Arth*, Raj Kumar Santoshi's *Damini, Lajja* etc., Mahesh Manjrekar's *Astiva*, Madhur Bhandarkar's *Chandni Bar*, Ketan Mehta's *Maya Memsahib, Mirch Masala* and Prakash Jha's *Mrityudand* to name a few, stand out as exemplary movies in which the visual and symbolic space is organized in a manner which addresses its spectators as a woman regardless of the gender of the viewers. The women filmmakers have also successfully attempted to portray women as subjects of such discourses, which negate or objectify them through their representations. Inspite of Silvia Bovenschen's belief that, "we are in a blind. How do we speak, in what categories do we think, ... Are our traditions and notions of happiness so far removed from cultural traditions and models."(quoted in De Lauretis Aesthetics 28). The women filmmakers have managed to perceive gender relations afresh by 'Re-vision', the act of looking back, for survival. Adrienne Rich feels that, "there are women who masquerade and women who wear the veil; women invisible to men in their society but also women who are invisible to other women in our society." (quoted in De Lauretis Aesthetics 8). There is not only the gender divide but also the class, caste divide in India on the same lines as the invisibility of Black women in the West. However, the gender, sensitised filmmakers irrespective of their gender, analysed the social and cultural constraints. They not only successfully try to articulate and reformulate them but, artistically and critically portray their ways of thinking as reflected in their *oeuvres*, some of which will be taken up for analysis of cinematic representation in the consequent third and fourth chapter. At the same time, they offer ideas and insights because of the breakdown of the beliefs under the cumulative pressure with the passage of time. The equations in gender relations were felt to be changing gradually and the female protagonists had to blend the old world with the new. Even if cultural conventions framed as unwritten code of an ideology were being defied; yet, respect for them and adhering to them was considered of prime value.

As pointed out by Sudhir Kakar, "in addition to the 'virtues' of self effacement and self-sacrifice, the feminine role in India, also crystallizes a woman's connection to others, her embeddedness in a multitude of familial relationship". (Kakar Feminine 51). However, if women have to gain understanding, they must get out of these self-trapped ruts and discard the vague notions of superiority, inferiority and inequality, which have hitherto corrupted every discussion of the subject afresh. There has been a near silence over the existence of women's movement in the Indian scenario since feminism is not rooted in the cultural reality of India or is rooted in the socio-economic reality of India. Within such a cultural reality, equality of gender relations is antithetical to the patriarchal values, which are basically family values of the Indian society. Hindu 'dharma' not having attributed the status of individuality to a woman, combined with the image of Sita, still persists as an ideal in the Indian society. The role of a woman is not based on her own interests; whereas feminism questions the power relations within the family structure. Moreover, a poor country grappling with the problems of poverty and basic needs like illiteracy, health, population, finds it difficult to confront the question of gender equality in relation and does not consider it a priority. The cultural atmosphere/climate in the country provokes a different kind of insight into the relationship between media and social movements and what can be a better source of communication than the cinematic media, which can bring out significant changes and equality in gender relation, is certainly a question to be examined.

Film is a mass cultural product undoubtedly and Indian cinema is framed with narrative references to Hindu mythology and replete with filmic gestures, suggesting crossovers with mythology from the great epics *Ramayana/Mahabharata*. Yet, the cultural context raises questions, which by and large remain as unresolved problems of power relation in gender relations around feminism. There are certain questions which get raised while viewing the cinema of any region as those of socio political and cultural values which get constituted in filmmaking and how are the cultural ethos constituted in films. Yet, there is a need to understand the cinema of any particular region or a country to have a fair knowledge of culture content of that region or country for a better intelligibility. It is on the basis of such knowledge of the culture content and it's nuances that the spectator can fully comprehend a film, to arrive at a better understanding of the film. The knowledge of cultural content may not be however misread as film theory but the cultural content can be seen rather as the outlines of a theory of cinema that can account for Indian cinema. Tejaswini Niranjana, a feminist film critic feels that, "the category Indian may no longer be limited to national boundaries... the categories of the Indian spectator may be seen as a category deployed to a range of spectators formations in parts of both the 'west' and the 'Third World' wherever people, whether ancestrally of Indian origin or not, see Indian films". (Niranjana Interrogating 8).

The cinema all over the world ought to address women across cultures, as individuals in their own rights, yet bound by shared experiences and shared emotions, similar constraints and a common desire to enhance the quality of life around them. Culture is a dynamic process, not stable and it constantly changes, evolves and regulates the lives of women through myriad manifestations in the form of convention, which looks at femininity as a construct. "Two facets of femaleness relate to the duality in the characteristic of the female as both the benevolent fertile bestower and the malevolent aggressive destroyer". (Wadley 25). The Hindu notion of divinity however rests upon the premise that *Shakti* (power underlies both creativity and divinity) is a female. Hence, the idea of all creativity in all the power is rooted in the femaleness and there would be no existence without that energy and power. *Prakriti* is the all-embracing material substratum of things. *Purusha* is sentience personified. *Prakriti*, which has always existed, remains in a state of dissolution. Nature is active and the woman is the field or earth in which man or the counterpart male aspect puts his seed. The concept of unity of *Purusa* and *Prakirti* underlies the beliefs regarding biological conceptions. There is a popular myth of Kali, one of the wives of Shiva who went on a rampage of killing and danced so furiously that the earth trembled. The gods were thus frightened, as they were unable to stop her and sent her husband Shiva to induce her to desist from further destruction. Kali, however, continued dancing and killing. Shiva lay down at her feet and when she realised it was her husband she was to step upon, an inexcusable act for the Hindu wife, she stopped the rampage and the earth was saved. This myth presented the idea that males have to control the dangerous female power and good females, goddesses or humans are to be controlled by males. However, only a culture without hope cannot forgive a culture that doesn't believe in progress or redemption. The woman in India has to overcome the legacy of age-old humiliation, dependence, resignation and silence.

The novel in India constitutes a rare religion of enlightened lucidity wherein the figure of the Indian woman picks up enough courage to raise her head and asks a few awkward but pertinent questions. Indian cinema will also have to reflect the same sensitivity in the balance of gender relations and not just make classification of woman into an idealized stereotype. The portrayal of a woman even in subtle ways, usually presents her as the guardian of culture and religion or an embodiment of purity and spiritual power, yet constantly requiring the protection of man as her lord and master. Indian couples were earlier reduced to the impersonal pattern of a joint family life with its emphasis on the subordination of emotional ties to the solidarity of the group. Nuclear family now-a-days, leads to an equation in the marital relationship, which is evidently visible among the Indian professional classes. At the same time, the pattern of liberalization in sexual mores which the west is so familiar with, has already reached India. It has not only led to a freer association between young men and women but even a new kind of emotional reciprocity is bound to be developed and is also perceivable.

Mythology becomes a tool to correct aspect in life as the Hindu view of life was always informed by two parallel themes, one that emphasized the legitimacy of desire and the other that stressed the joys of transcending such desires. The dialectics of mainstream Hindu culture did not mean that one path was right, and the other wrong. Both were valid, for the essential premise was that there was more than one avenue to experience the bliss of the infinite. In myths and legends, some well known, others obscure relating to goddesses and various incarnations of *Devi*, right from the ferocious *Durga* to the compassionate *Lakshmi*, the wise *Saraswati*, the blood thirsty *Kalika*, the faithful wife *Sita* kind a culmination in the sensual *Radha*, the Indian women find a symbol for the vicarious release of their repressed personalities. *Radha's* intense yearning for *Krishna* echoed their subconscious frustrations. Her uninhibited pursuit of physical fulfilment with *Krishna* and the secretive, illicit and adulterous nature of her affair with *Krishna* provide a particularly apt framework for women by and large to identify with *Radha*. The furtive rebel, determined to clandestinely break the stranglehold of social norms and customs, became an image that they could readily internalise. If *Radha* was the inspiration, Krishna was the object of the Indian woman's fantasy. Unlike other gods in the Hindu pantheon, Krishna's personality had a softness to it that made it conspicuously responsive to the longing and desires of women. Above all, he was human, treating women not just as sex subjects, but found them a source of inspiration and longing. In his company, they could relax the code of conduct imposed by an overwhelmingly male dominated society. They would assume a stance of familiarity, calling him a liar, cheat and so on. *Krishna* allowed women to play out the fantasy of being in control, of being able to bend the will of men to their commands. Traditional art forms, figures, rituals, myths, symbols and motifs are predominantly ingrained not in the religious sense but also as a cultural ingredient. Many of the practices which one sees as religious symbols, are cultural and have become almost national constructs.

Woman's right to be "human" is continually determined by ideological construction and social, economic and political forces which determine women's worth differently. One needs to expose gender as a symmetrical distribution of human rights in a man's world, which is fashioned by gender biases and it is the need of the hour to bring out not only its pervasiveness across religious, cultural and political boundaries but also the various ways in which it circumscribes the choices and roles available to women. These gender biases are additional impediments in the realization of women's human right manifested in gender discrimination which unravels in various institutionalised forms like unjust laws relating to marriage and inheritance, as well as cultural and social practices like genital mutilation, female foeticide etc.

Some stark realities have effectively been listed. The reality is that the substantive part of a common civil code relates essentially to gender justice. However, the record of the injustice perpetuated as cultural ideologues in this regard, is far from satisfactory. The agitation against the shooting of Deepa Mehta's '*Water*' depicting the sorry plight of Hindu widows in need of social reform in Varanasi is a sad reflection of it. The power equations between men and women are titled right at the onset. The Indian tradition in defining gender as a sociological and cultural construct has rather encouraged subservience of women and applauded their self-effacement yet there is much in the tradition and culture, which can help establishing gender equality in men and women.

Since cinema clearly opens a most useful window onto a culture of a society, a region and a country; hence, there is not a better way of studying Indian culture than through its culture specific cinema. To an extent it is true that most films create or try to create myth of some kind. Meaningful cinema, in which filmmakers show a greater awareness indicates that cinema is not only a vehicle of ideas, it can also have deep imprints on the psyche of masses. In today's chaotic media world with minds mediated by images of multifarious T.V. channels, which are culture resistant, cinema has assumed greater significance. Cinema is the only medium through which we can directly deal with society and bring about a change. Cinema generates new ideas in the same way that it sustains old ones.

A film structures what it has to say by using the language of cinema and codifying its artistic purposes and establishes what it has to convey carefully through consciously designed narrative manifestation. However, inspite of being consciously structured, the message in a film is inseparable from the objective socio-cultural constraints that both promote and hamper its development. To understand and decipher the message in Indian films, there is a need to relate to its fundamental socio cultural semantic structures with narrative in the film. According to Peter Wollen,

> "The cinematic sign, the language or semiotic of cinema like the verbal language, comprises not only the indexical and the iconic, but also the symbolic that cinema did not only develop technically out of magic lantern but also out of strip cartoons, wild west, shows automata, pulp novels... there is no pure cinema grounded on a single essence hermeneutically sealed from contamination." (Wollen 153).

Films however cannot help but carry information that is ideological in its content. However, an approach, which relates film to culture as a part of the process of understanding, is more appropriate in the study of Indian films. Indian films have a tendency to retain narration because non-narrative cinema is not a success in India. Human values and subjectivity interpenetrate cinematic structures and as a result in gender relations too. Films assume an epistemology ontology that links it with the ideology of the society within which it functions. Ideology arises from prevailing social conditions and also helps to perpetuate these conditions. Film can play a significant social and critical role. It can either reinforce the existing ideology or question it. It is on account of this cinema becomes an extremely compelling and decisive cultural medium.

The Indian films according to Chidananda Das Gupta "primarily catered to a spectator who had not severed his or her ties from the countryside and so had a traditional or pre-modern relationship to the image one which incapacitated him or her from distinguishing between image and reality" (Talking 24). However as India gained independence and the development of modern nation state, the middle classes were regarded as the bearers of a rationalist discourse. The dominant spectator of popular cinema, still according to Ashis Nandy a social psychologist, holds onto a notion of traditional community quite remote from the outlook of modern middle class. As such this spectator is attracted on to a narrative "which ritually neutralizes the discomfiting features of social change, those atomising modern thought patterns practices which have to be adopted for reasons of survival" (Nandy, The Secret 76). Popular cinema in India embraces the cultural indices of subjectivity and works in a psychic and sociological matrix. Even while attempting to transcend the oppositions between tradition and modernity, many dimensions of tradition as cultural constructs under the aegis of an ideology of modernity, get re-constructed in neo-traditional forms. Cinematic situations can best be understood when they are rooted in the understanding of the varied and various socio-cultural and economic dynamics that shaped them. It is the need of the hour to arrive at a perceptive analysis on how the cultural projection, subjected to hybridification, is a process invariably present in the encounter between technology, commerce and traditional power. In order to cater to the need to understand Indian cinema as precisely Indian, it is necessary to be aware of the cultural context, which leads to the cultural practices that get articulated in Indian cinema. According to Ashish Rajyadhyaksha, cultural processes are,

> "conceptualized as intricate, dynamic processes implicated in strategies of containment, subjugation, accommodation, collusion or resistance, not to mention emancipation than as emanations of fixed homogeneous social categories or groups such as sociological notions of class, gender or race". (Neo-Traditionalism 25).

The mythological film, India's oldest and unique genre, achieved for Phalke the first Indian fiction filmmaker, his dream for showing India's gods and goddesses. There is a domestic space, which has space for femininity and love while projecting gender relations. However "the role of melodrama rather than realism in its orthodox sense has played a pivotal role in the cinematic writing of the biography of the nation state". (Chakravarty 12). Both realism and melodrama have been acclaimed as aesthetic terms bearing an intimate relation to the democratic revolution accordingly. After Peter Brook's publication of book, *'The Melodramatic Imagination'* (1976) the tide has turned in favour of melodrama. "The feminization of mass culture has been shown to be a feature of cultural theory in the modern west". (Hussyen 76). Melodrama, however, functions differently in different cultural contexts and the melodramatic traditions evolved differently in different countries. The gender polarization of culture into a masculine sphere of autonomous modernist work of art and a feminine sphere of heteronymous formally diffuse mass culture which has led to an affirmation of a melodrama as a feminine form and its pleasures as the denigrated but real and value pleasure of female audiences. "However melodrama which in its early manifestation was to diffuse and fragmentary to be called a form in its own right, achieved at its highest level of formal consistency precisely at the moment when it came to be specifically addressed to women in Hollywood women's melodrama." (Gledhill Home Is 6). The relation between melodrama and realism can be best understood by reference to the fiction of social contract and the field in which the contract is held to be effective.

When a literary text is transformed from a novel, story or a play for a film, the work has to have certain appeal for its viewers. There is a need for them in the adaptation of literary text to the celluloid to recognize the adaptation as a shared expertise. According to Umberto Eco, "naturally all the elements, characters and episode must have some archetypal appeal". (Eco 395). According to him the term,

> "archetype need not have any particular psychoanalytic or mythic connotation. However it should serve to indicate a pre-established and frequently reappearing narrative situation cited or in some way recycled by innumerable other texts. It should be able to provoke a sort of intense emotion accompanied by the vague feeling of déjà vu that everybody yearns to see again". (396).

He calls this as "inter-textual archetypes" which may not be necessarily 'universal'. It may be of any recent tradition or standard situation that manages to be particularly appealing to a given cultural area or a historical period. Many a times when the filmmakers can't deal with the story, they put in stereotyped situations, which have already worked in some films. Surprisingly, as literature comes from literature, cinema comes from cinema.

While looking at gender relations and their representation in the adaptation of literary texts on celluloid, there is a need to look at what a feministic perspective does to literature. Jasondhara Bagchi, an Indian feminist suggests that, "feminism is emancipatory in its premises and offers the opportunity to look at the literary texts. It helps to release them from the prison of form and genre, making them more accountable to history and society, to emotional life as well as a silenced reason, and to the intimate politics which organizes and thus 'naturalizes' human experience". (quoted in Chaudhuri and Mukherji 1). Since gender is itself a cultural construct, it opens the way for the radical, complex perspective in deciphering the hidden edifice of ideology operating within literary texts in the cultural context. When adapted on the celluloid they need to be examined and re-examined as to how the filmmaker articulated them on the celluloid. The consciousness of gender runs through the literary texts, which encode our cultural existence in the binary constitution of our social being.

Literary texts require us to interrogate the texts through multifarious interpretations, irrespective of the gender of the writer, as reading gender through and across literary texts cannot be a theoretically predetermined exercise. The narrative of events portraying the knowledge, which the film provides of how things really are "is the meta language providing the truth against which we can measure the discourses". (MacCabe 75). In cinema, the meta language moves closer to the traces of the narration. This meta language is not present in the novel but is precisely significant because of its ambition to become a transparent medium for making visible the meanings immanent in the narrative.

Every story involves certain archetypes in its narrative, as cultural intervention, which get absorbed in the plot structure and may at times exceed or at times run counter to the plot structure, which absorbs them both. Anybody who views Indian cinema with a genuine interest, be it some one from the ordinary so-called masses or the intellectuals, understands how the array of the Indian cinema especially the commercial Indian cinema, produces its own specific pleasures. According to Rajyadaksha, "In order to understand how this array of possible pleasures is organized by and for particular cultural practices, it is necessary to look at the institutionalised histories of the practices concerned." (Neo-Traditionalism 22).

Even for a western intellectual critic, the notions in the discourse of cinematic narrative will be intelligible only if he/she understands the Indian cultural context. Any responsible analysis of India's cinematic situation must be rooted in the understanding of the various socio-cultural dynamics that shaped it. In fact while adapting literary text for the celluloid, both the filmmaker and the novelist meet in a common intention as to have an effective relationship between the creative artist and the receptive audience. "Because novel and film are both organic, in the sense that aesthetic judgments are based on total ensembles which include both formal and thematic conventions, we may expect to find that differences in form and theme are inseparable from differences in media." (Bluestone 2). There are apprehensions at times that the structures, symbols, myths, values which might be comprehensible to the writers and readers may be incomprehensible to the mass public audience of cinema.

However, the moment film goes from the animation of stills to telling a story, it is inevitable that the text becomes the ore to be minted. However, many a critic feels that, "language cannot convey non-verbal experience: being successive and linear, it cannot express simultaneous experiences; being composed of separate and divisible units, it cannot reveal the unbroken flow of the process of living. Reality cannot be expressed or conveyed, only the illusion of it." (Mendilow 18).

But if the history of aesthetics proves anything, it is that a given set of myths, symbols, conventions is unable to satisfy all spectators of films at all times in all places. Sartre, while speaking of literature said, "one cannot write without a public and without a myth, without a certain public which historical circumstances have made, without a certain myth of literature which depends to a very great extent upon the demand of this public." (51). In filmmaking also, modern folk myths perpetuate symbolic heroes, heroines, villains, vamps and comedians found in literature.

Myths, which are supposed to be at their simplest, provided fable, like narratives with didactic morals and repeated from mouth to mouth. The oral narratives provide the symbolic figures around which folk beliefs are organized. The epic traditions use the same thesis as an important ingredient in the enjoyment of the narratives with the presumption that the audience knows the theme in audience. According to Northrop Frye, "myth is a conception which runs through many areas of contemporary thoughts: anthropology psychology, comparative religion sociology and several others". (Frye 156). According to him, "myth is and has always been an integral element of literature". (Frye 156). While Indian cinema has made use of literature in literary adaptations on celluloid, it makes use of popular myths, which depend for their success on simple and recognizable meaning, which get reinforced and constructed in the films. While the formal structure of myths is assumed to be universal and encountered everywhere, it is embodied in any country in a symbolic content that is a society specific. Countless Indian films have used myths and fantasies in order to conform to social images and earned audience identification in return. Scared beings, semi–divine heroes, heroines, historical figures have all been absorbed into archetypal forms of myths. Carl Jung called archetypes as "collective unconscious" and feels that the "term archetype applies only indirectly to the representatives collectives." (207). According to him, just as all men and women inherit some bodily parts from the human and pre-human past, they have a common mental inheritance in the depths of the unconscious. These primordial images or archetypes are perceived anywhere. Hélène Cixous writes,

"we are caught up in a network of millennial cultural determinations of a complexity that is almost unanalyzable. We can no more talk about 'woman' than about man without getting caught up in an ideological theatre where the multiplicity of representations, images, reflections, myths, identifications, constantly transforms, deforms alters each persons imaginary order and in advance renders all conceptualizations null and void." (268).

In Indian archetypes also, among the emotive and persistent figures, it is possible to name male and female archetypes, which get represented in Indian films. Gender relations are evoked and also subverted accordingly through various myths and archetypes, which get intercepted as cultural ideology for Indian films. Myth and reality over lap continuously in Indian cinema as the protagonists reflect mythical characters. "Often, they are aimed at 'naturalizing' and even 'divinising' a particular world view". (Singh and Jaidev 3). Like history, they are not easy to disown even when they form archetypal patterns difficult to shed off from a culture collective psyche. On account of the conditioning as a mind set for many, they are not easy to disown as they would feel culturally impoverished and strangely weightless even though they are oppressing, since myths can subjugate both women as much as men.[3]

Indian cinema's undying obsession with Indian mythology since the time of D.G. Phalke's film 'Raja Harish Chandra' invites certain deliberations. The screen adaptation of the Indian mythologies was meant as a box office safeguard, as no other works clicked nor broke through the immense class/caste barriers than the two dearly loved epics, The *Mahabharta* and the *Ramayana*. Throughout the long trajectory of the Indian cinema, be it in the popular or art parallel cinema or the experimental cinema, one gets to see new myths churned out of the old. Exemplary epic figures keep returning reinforced under different deceptive garbs. At the incept of Indian cinema, even the question of mode of address on the screen as to how objects and figures were to be located with respect to the look of the spectators within the spatial and temporal co-coordination of the scenic construction, was based on the aesthetics peculiar to Indian films. The aesthetics of frontality and iconic as the *darsana*, was incorporated by early filmmakers starting with D.G. Phalke.

"Darsana is the power exercised by the authoritative image in Hindu religious culture in which the devotee is permitted to behold the image of deity, and is privileged and benefited by this permission, in contrast to accept looking of that assigns power to the beholder by reducing the image to an object of the look". (Vasudevan The Politics 139).

Cinema of any region, be it Indian or Latin American, African or third world cinema, usually suggests that the art practices of a region are being constructed as culturally symbolic of that region. The dominant effort of the Indian cinema has been to recast expressions of the traditional codes in an urban social context, which is in turn reformed by the mass communication that perpetuates it. Most of these are close to religious fervour, myth legends that get focused still as the pattern of ideals in Indian literature too. The functioning of reality and fantasy acquire altogether different dimensions in the films, which aim at mass audiences and pure entertainment. But, "at times, even through these they reveal the society's unconscious positioning on issues like gender, positioning of women and prejudices." (Jain and Rai Films 10). Stereotypes of gender relations become a language of their own and need to be decoded as they evoke memories of myths and traditions around them, of imaging men and women in their relationship. The cultural contents are sometimes reinforced and at times subverted with both progressive and regressive consequences as visible symbols. The role of culture and ideology in determining the outcome of women helps not only to establish the historicity of culture as well as their mutability. "What is interesting is that not only do culture and ideology shape the contours of subordination but they also mould the conceptualization of liberation". (Krishnaraj 2).

The Indian cinema is a uniquely appropriate site for the exploration of melodrama as a cultural form. The Indian cinema's women's melodramas have been male centred but at the same time they raised,

> "the question of women's desire and albeit with patriarchal scaffolding broached questions connected with the emancipation of women from the oppression of feudal orthodoxy". (Prasad 86).

In their narratives, one sees an attempt to represent the woman's point of view, or centred the narrative of a woman caught between desire and an oppressive tradition. Sparkling images of the mythology are all reserved for specific occasions. If celluloid is drawn to the deities of the religious mythologies, it is not so much for religious but creative reasons. Since, "art is selfish and righteousness unfortunately offers little scope of display of variety". (Somaya Cinema 65). The films take cinematic liberties and present synthetic reality and at times protagonists look too dynamic to the helpless and vulnerable.

Part of the history of modern Indian has been the enormously influential presence of what is now famous as the world's largest film industry. This however came as one of the legacies of the colonial state that Independence bestowed upon free India. Indian cinema, whether it was commercial or art cinema, has the expression of the aspirations of a people long bound by the traditions of a divisive society and colonial role. "India's film history has been largely written up from the standpoint of state policy on Indian cinema after 1947, with its efforts to install a respectably realist cinema" (Rajyadhyaksha Indian 151). Indian cinema was an expression of the freedom struggle itself, which was more than just a political movement. Indian cinema, in the pre-independence days, was actively involved in articulating the issues of freedom struggle. "Although the themes that directly dealt with the struggle were not always portrayed and much of this was due to censorship by the colonial government". (Dasgupta Susmita 368).

The issues of pre independence cinema did not only concern socio-historical issues along with mythology, but also addressed aspirations of the socially excluded individuals and these included the rights of women as free agents too. The individual was looked upon as a judge between contending particulars and values of tradition and universal values of modernity. Indian cinema addresses to a nation wide audience and there is an extension of the 'all India' aesthetic of fantasies that often came to be called 'masala' ingredient for Pan-Nationalism films. After independence, new cultural and ideological priorities laid down by the Indian constitution dreamt of self-rule and as a democratic state, also got articulated. They all go to form the cultural context of Indian cinema. However, there are many a gap between promises upheld and practised. The institutions of state, which were expected to protect the individual from the repression of the community, almost invariably did not succeed.

The fight for social order upholding established moral structures is an ongoing process in Indian cinema. Indian cinema and particularly Hindi cinema, though, has been a genre of the mass entertainer that has played the political function of culturally integrating the country, a role performed by default. It has used the cultural aspects of the Indian visual art, music; theatre and literature that systematically went onto formulate the cultural ideology complex. There are various phases through which Indian culture and Indian film theory has gone through, be it Nehruvian times, political crisis during the period of Emergency or during the resurgence of the new economic policy. Indian cinema, in its own way, reflected upon it all.

The themes of Indian cinema have been varied and keeping pace with the levels of social development, though it is difficult to pinpoint functional relationship between politics, economy or civic life and cinema. Indian cinema reflects on social issues and has even pre-dated certain issues, too, like the left students' movements, peasant rebellion and industrial unrest. However, 'the-girl-meets-boy' issue has been the centre of the stories with a heroine and hero and other related characters that get separated and unite again. At times one sees variations of the same 'done-to-death' plot replicated in every other film. Still, by and large, Indian cinema has been sensitive to the constraints that individuals have felt in realizing their aspirations in the various social categories to which they belong. The success of this medium lies in the fact that it is able to raise class specific constraints into matters of general concern. Indian culture has been pluralistic and aspects of pluralism have been reflected upon in Indian cinema. Even Indian literature is rich with well-conceived ideas and plots that are elaborately thought out. Therefore adapting literary texts for celluloid ensures strong content.

NOTES AND REFERENCES

1. Louis Althusser influenced the film theory during the 1960s and 1970s. He believed that in ideology the subjects also represent to themselves, "their relationships to those conditions of existence, which is represented to them there." In other words he believed

that, "they make ideology have meaning by colluding with it and by acting according to it because of the reassuring nature of national identity or cultural membership." For example, "Hollywood is about reproducing the institution, culture or ideology of the white middle class United States to which all should aspire, or, if they do not, they will perish. Almost a Taylorization of national identity (a compartmentalized assembly-line approach)"! (quoted in Hayward 323) Semiotics in film theory opened up filmic texts in the way thus illustrated above, showing how they produce meaning, have served among other things to uncover, make explicit the naturalization process of realist, mainstream cinema all over the world.

2. Myths shade into folk tales, which may be secular, literal, narratatively more predictable or coherent enough in not asking to be believed yet they become the cultural aspect of a society. Myths persist though often in a diluted form and "do not always travel without at least changing some part of their character." (Chatterji Shoma Subject 226).

3. Myth and morality conspire to bring about gender injustice. Myths oppress by denying their victims voice, visibility and dignity as they fabricate such foolproof constructs and allow no decent escape routes to those they target. "Seldom, ideologically neutral myths are constructed, sacrilized and disseminated for legitimising certain power filled practices attitudes and ways of seeing. Though myths can subjugate women as much as men can. Yet, the situation is asymmetrical, because while men have myths on their side women have myths against them". (Singh and Jaidev 3).

3

The Beleaguered Survivor

Filmmaking actually begins with a story and when one makes a movie, the story or the script provides the foundation that is integral to the production of a movie. Although the study of literary adaptations of films based on fiction is becoming more common and acceptable too, yet it is viewed with some apprehension as regards its impact on the value and place of the literary 'original'. "Studying both fictional and filmic sources can be fraught with problems". (Whelehan 3). According to Whelehan, there is a need to pay 'appropriate' amount of attention to each medium and fostering the skills specific to each form[1]. It, in fact, encompasses the positioning of literary work in the vistas of celluloid. Looking at the film and viewing it in its cinematic presentation involves not only the analytical work on narratological perspectives but there could be various impediments in uniting the study of visual and written narratives.

Interest in the process of adaptation from the text to the screen undoubtedly has increased over the years not only in the Hollywood film industry but also even in the Indian film-industry, immensely. However there are prejudices about this kind of hybrid study. There is always a fear of pitfalls created by the demands of authenticity and fidelity in successfully extracting the essence of the fictional text. It is the director's job to look as a viewfinder through the intense focus of his camera lens at the body of work, which is to be adapted and brought about on celluloid of the work of fiction at hand. The excitement, passion, surprise and beauty inherent to the director's vision can be released only when it is wedded to a firm grasp of the directorial craft. The conceptual aspect of this craft is fraught with a methodology that the director works out, while transforming the text to the screen or celluloid. The film is first conceptualised in the director's head. However the emphasis during the filmmaking, throughout, is on the craft of narrative or story telling. The goal or objective of the director is to be fully equipped with an essential tool that he/she can best utilize to craft the piece of fiction at hand. Film is our liveliest but not our likeliest art as it defies our expectations of what art should be. "It is mechanical in its mode and collectivist in its inspiration. It is the writer director duo coupled with others such as actors, cameraman, music director, art director, costume designer, editor etc, who together, assist in the cinematic representation, making it an art". (Scott 1). Aesthetic finesse, besides technological interventions, is undoubtedly an undeniable aspect in filmmaking. Each member of the production team is an achiever in the cinematic representation of the piece of fiction at hand, including the cameraman who sets out the visuals, the editor who sorts them out after they are shot.

The filmmakers state their viewpoints; assert their aesthetic perspectives to explain their philosophy and ideology during the process of filmmaking. Every filmmaker tries to project his/her cinematic language, his/her own grammar and articulates his/her passion that seizes and engages him/her during the process. Every individual filmmaker tries to articulate his/her sensibility in the cinematic form of the piece of fiction at hand and adapts an approach by which he/she tries to justify one's genuine commitment. A well-made film evokes a response of great fervour while viewing that a reader has while reading the piece of fiction. The motivation, the passion of the director is a very vital factor in the making of the film. It not only helps in understanding the piece of fiction through the craft and technique of the film that the director employs, but also helps in understanding the sensibility informing the film. Moreover, the director's involvement not only is conducive to understand the philosophy, ideology and sensibility of the writer but also in transforming the work of art to a higher level, aesthetically. An attempt to inspire the visual responses of the reading audience is highly challenging. Filmmakers are concerned and talk about both stories and scripts, whereas, film theorists talk about the narrative in a film. The study of a film's narrative is rather; "both the study of its story and how the story is to be told by means such as *mise en scene*, cinematography, editing, sound and in what order (structure) it should be". (Roberts and Wallis 52).

Adaptations from novels and plays have been there in the Hollywood cinema but the situation has not been too common in India. However there have been Indian films that have been adapted from novels, short stories for the screen with relative success, enough to inspire remakes of the same novels a couple of times. Many a great writer's works have been visualized on the screen, thus immortalizing his works. As far as 1908, Leo Tolstoy suggested a genuine respect for the opportunities that the film technology offers. He saw the advantage of the film medium lying in the more enhanced representation of reality. "This swift change of scene, this blending of emotion and experience is much better than the heavy long drawn out kind of writing." (quoted in Spiegel 162). Many a critic finds a kind of congruence between the two narrative forms, by the authors and *auteurs*. In fact, in the 1950s, the young writers of *Cahiers du Cinema* argued a new theory *'politique des auteurs'*. Auteur theory, as it was called, was supposed to actualize a prevalent need to raise the film to the status of a unique art form. The real implications of the term *'auteur'* (author) placed the director (and not the script-writer) as the author of the film. It was believed that the director 'wrote' in pictures. The *cahier's* position about the creative conventions in cinema and language was exploited and developed by many a director into a personal vision. In fact Luc Godard and Truffant felt that, "the filmmaker was to be seen as an author or auteur who exhibit through his/her films 'auteur' characteristic i.e. personal individuality in their visual style, narrative, structures and features, particular character traits/situations and sets of themes". (quoted in Roberts and Wallis 127).

Dramatic elements in the story help to enhance the aesthetic visual expression and a good screenplay narrates a story visually. Undoubtedly, an integrated story or script helps the director to achieve cinematic excellence. The first and the most important element of the shooting script is a screenplay, which is a more broadly visualized rendering of the film that emphasizes the emotional and logical flow of the story over the breakdown of shots. Rather, a good screenplay is "a form of language that allows the writer to imply a pattern of shots while still concentrating on the dramatic progression of the scene. (Grove Elliot 215).

Writing a screenplay is a complex job and a successful screenplay incorporates all the elements of characterization, plot, action, dialogue and setting in a bold, fresh and original way in order to enhance the story of literary text. According to Mahesh Bhatt one, "does not just believe in the message of writing, but induces it into filmmaking also. Script is not based on friction and conflict only, but in it voices have to be felt like the feeling of an exhilaration which one feels, that not only he/she can think of but anybody can feel". (Bhatt Mahesh in an interview with Star News). Aparana Sen an actress and a filmmaker believes that script writing is the backbone of the film, which one writes in the form of pictures. She says, "I see films as appealing directly to heart and nothing overtly intellectual about them. I basically see human drama in the core of films". (Sen Aparana in an interview with Star News). It's also necessary that the thematic motifs of the literary text should correlate the aesthetics of filmmaking and see how it can highlight and accentuate the theme of the story by the craft of filmmaking, perception, attitude and sensibility, all part of the journey as one employs the imagery of words on celluloid. Film scripting is a form by itself, unlike play writing or novel writing. According to Vijay Tendulkar, "the script is in words, but these words are supposed to have a graphic quality, a moving chain of visuals with minimal use of well worded crisp dialogues". (Tendulkar 319).

My basic concern in this book is as to how Indian films based on the literary texts in their adaptation get transformed on the celluloid. The films selected by me examine human predicaments in man-woman i.e. gender relations within the cultural ideological framework that informs the same.

The urge to probe and comprehend gender relations is the essence and concern of any civilized society where equipoise in relations is necessary. Such a study may help in understanding certain inherent problems integral to an ideology, which has been rooted in the so-called cultural trap. Women's image in film can no longer be seen as a simple matter of misrepresentation. Hence, one of the basic connections between what women experience in any culture and how gender relationship is perceived between spectators and the spectacle is very vital. The way a text unfolds on the celluloid in its cinematic representation cannot be passively imbibed. The way a piece of fiction is transformed on the celluloid becomes the site of a struggle between the way gender relations are perceived in society and represented in cinema. Each film is going to be read as a text and it will be seen as to whether films transcend the written piece of fiction or stir one's sensibilities with a transparent reflection of the cultural ideology.

When one decides to look at the Indian films from the point of view of gender, one cannot help but interpret and intercept it through the cultural ideology. It is difficult to read and critically evaluate Indian movies without an understanding of the social, historical and cultural tradition of India that I have tried to examine.. The films I have chosen for analysis in this chapter are *'Teesri Kasam'*, *'Umrao Jaan'* and *'Rudali'*. The shift in man-woman relationship will be perceived in these films vis-à-vis the conventional societal norms rooted to class, tradition, myth, ritual, casteism and religious diversity, which form the Indian cultural scenario. The central women figures in all these movies are survivor figures who strive to transcend a deterministic socio-cultural order that is inimical to the growth and happiness of women.

TEESRI KASAM

'Teesri Kasam' which means the 'Third Vow', when translated in English, was released in 1966 and directed by Basu Bhattacharya. The film was adapted from the short story i.e. 'Lok Katha' called *'Teesri Kasam, Mare Gaye Gulfam'*. Shailendar, the Hindi-Urdu lyric writer, had produced it. The *auteur* producer Shailendar was a quiet, shy, reticent person and deeply rooted in culture. He was an idealist and believed that his poems were not for sale and even when he was offered a wad of notes to write lyrics for films, he was ideologically hostile to the idea. He worked in IPTA plays. Raj Kapoor, the great filmmaker called him 'comrade' and his other friends also thought him to be a 'leftist' or 'socialist'.

The story of *'Teesri Kasam, Mare Gaye Gulfam'* written in 1952 by Phanishwer Nath 'Renu' in Hindi, was close to his heart and being a socio-realist, Shailendar ventured into his first film production with it. He wanted to reach to the people by actualizing a thought-provoking theme related to gender relations. The cinema is an essential part of popular culture as Jean Luc Godard had said, "we must put everything into cinema and by the unifying force of the filmmaker's mind turning narrative objective cinema into a direct personal communication between the filmmaker and his audience". (Das Gupta Chidananda Talking 4). This can be done if the filmmaker is aware of past forms of cinema and of the other arts. In India, films have "largely been a receptacle for the mixing together of other media, rather than a medium in itself". (Das Gupta Chidananda Talking 7).

The traditional Indian theatre form of *'Nautanki'*[2] of Uttar Pradesh has been beautifully incorporated into the film. There have been various traditions of the performing arts in India and *'Nautanki'* is one such tradition. They are all characterized by a multiplicity of genres, forms, style and techniques. Nevertheless, inspite of their complexities there is an eternal timelessness about them in terms of the evolution of artistic form and style in time and its socio cultural milieu. They establish a characteristic, "of the cultural pattern in the aesthetic in purely anthropological terms and are sometimes called 'folk' which imply community and means expressions that are participative and spontaneous-sometimes 'classical', indicating highly contextual forms" (Vatsyana 2). Often, local and indigenous myths and legends of the oral traditions got woven in them, leading to an adaptation of the local forms of dances and dance-dramas developed from the recitative words and its consequential interpretations. Such local and regional forms, in turn shaped many literary versions of the epics. They have also been the vehicles of the protest, dissent and reform as articulators of satire and social comment and thus played a vital role in being instruments of socio-cultural change.

The contemporary forms such as *Bhavai* in Gujarat, *Nautanki* in U.P., *Tamasa* in Maharashtra etc. belong to this group. The essence of these forms becomes transformed into a form of ballad recitation, folk drama, folk dance etc. A different order of relationship of word/sound movement and gestures emerges in the pageant forms such as these. "Here the literary word is set to melodic line in a given metrical cycle, and is then interpreted either descriptively or symbolically by the dancer. The styles commonly termed as 'classical' in the context of dance, all use this principle" (Vatsyana 8). Such forms are deeply rooted in village and folk culture and evolve a methodology of communication. The theoretical enunciation of these thought processes were made by the early Indian aestheticians in the formulation of *rasa* theory, which has guided the destiny of Indian art forms since centuries. In the Indian context, when one speaks of drama, dance or music one alludes to the fundamental principle of the 'word' movement or sound and does not refer to art in isolation or in mutual exclusiveness. The principles of eternity and of flux, of an ever-old and ever-new or renaming phenomenon were integrated into the Indian thought at its metaphysical as well as mundane levels.

'Teesri Kasam' based on *'Teesri Kasam, Mare Gaye Gulfam'* is one such story by Phanishwernath 'Renu' which Basu Bhattacharya transformed on the celluloid in search of native strengths both cultural and moral. Basu Bhattacharya was an eminent filmmaker noted for making films that explored the intricacies of human relationships. Bimal Roy's influence was

discernible in the film. Basu Bhattacharya claimed to be inspired by Satyajit Ray. The cinematographer Subrota Mitra who shot Satyajit Ray's early films beautifully filmed the film.

He later directed 'Anubhav' and 'Avishkar' and 'Grihapravesh', a trilogy with the common theme of marital disharmony which were stereotypical Hindi New Cinema products of the 70s, with a realistist's emphasis being reduced to a concern with the marital problems of upper class couples.

The film 'Teesri Kasam' discussed the problem of gender relations, though not in the marital sense but from a more wholesome humanistic angle. The emotional story of 'Teesri Kasam' exposes the gross exploitation of women especially in the area of performing arts. Phanishvernath 'Renu' in his introduction of the story says that he is aware that he has been called an incorrigible romanticist, sailing through life rudderless. However, he feels that none of his critics realized that he had been trying to seek himself in his stories in turn that dealt with human relationships, human conditions and a contestation of the Indian values.

'Teesri Kasam 'Mare Gaye Gulfam' is set against the backdrop of rural India depicting the story of a 'nautanki' dancer and of a country bumpkin who is a bullock cart driver. A simpleton, Hiraman has been transporting goods on his bullock cart over 20 years. Unwittingly, he keeps getting caught into situations which are not his own doings but for which he inadvertently has to pay a price from time to time. Hiraman, with his simplicity of heart and purpose, touches the inner chord of the human element in all of us. The writer evokes that simplicity in his characterization in a rural setting. It is, "the simplicity of popular culture although not as subtle or profound as superior culture. It is genuine in the sense of being spontaneous and earnest". (Kazmi Fareed 29). However, Basu Bhattachraya evokes the cultural climate coupled with the human element in a subtle manner, though overtly at times, through Hiraman's characterization of in his journey from innocence to experience. Hiraman is earnest and sincere in his job. When he gets to transport a courtesan who is a 'nautanki' dancer to the mela i.e. the fair, where her performing troupe is waiting for her, he gets apprehensive and rather awe struck. The very minute she boards his bullock cart he starts wondering whether she is a woman or a champa flower, and the poetic sensibility within him feels that she exudes such a fragrance.

When the cart gets onto the kutcha (rough road), the right wheel almost gets stuck into one of the pot holes, he hears a little sigh of hers which upsets him. Hiraman couldn't bear that and starts whipping the bullocks and cursing them for not being able to distinguish between the load of stuffed sack on the cart and that of a delicate woman's. She however pleads him not to whip the bullock in a soft gentle voice. He then feels that he had never heard such a beautiful child like voice. It sounded to him as if it was a voice just out of the gramophone. However, since he had not even cast a glance upon her, it added to the mystique of her persona. She was Hirabai, an actress of Mathur Mohan Nautanki company. Hirabai acted out the part of Laila of the famous Laila Majnu love legend in it. Hiraman, however was a simple straightforward man. He was not given to any vices nor any pleasures, hence had never been to a Nautanki nor heard of any Laila or Hirabai. At the onset of journey in the mid of night, Hirabai wrapped in a black veil alights his cart. He just gets curious and cautiously asks her accompanist who had come to see her off whether there was any material of theft in the boxes perhaps tobacco, being loaded alongwith her. He recalls an old woman in the black shawl i.e. wrapper who used to sell tobacco in the mela. The metaphor which the writer hints in the story is, that Hiraman is aware that there's something intoxicating enrapturing about Hirabai. Basu Bhattacharya uses it as a motif for celluloid. The metaphorical motif, the mystery of being wrapped in the shawl hints at the camouflage element in the characterization of Hirabai and Hiraman's perception of her subconsciously. While adapting the story he shows Hiraman getting more and more engrossed in thoughts about her. After hearing her lyrical voice he is so enchanted that he repeatedly turns back to have a glance of her. The camera rests on Hirabai's feet symbolically conveying reverence that Hiraman perceives her as a Devi (goddess). When the cart moves towards the eastern direction he feels that a light has entered into his cart. When Hirabai's nose pin shines he perceives it, as the twinkling of jugnu (glow worm) on her nose. He feels that there was deep mystique in the atmosphere which the director beautifully evokes through the scintillating photography of Subroto Mitra in the way he shows the journey from Champanagar to Sindhiya village. Even the name Champanagar invokes an ambience of land of fragrant flowers. Hiraman starts wondering en route whether she was an enchantress. However, when he turns back again to have a glance of her, he gasps. The moonlight falling on her face gives her an ethereal fairy like look. Enthralled and captivated by the incredibly beautiful actress of nautanki, he almost exclaims with excitement and when she opens her eyes he is almost dumbstruck.

Hirabai the female protagonist is however oblivious of the effect she is having on him and inquires his name. She tells him that they share the common *Hira* (diamond) in their name. However she tells him that on account of common '*Hira*' in their name they were both supposed to be namesake friends (*meeta*). He, however, does not realize that there was a difference between connotonising man and woman's name. "To believe that one's a woman is almost as absurd and obscurant as to believe that one is a man". (Brooks Ann 125). Gender equation in that sense gets established between them because of the commonality of the name. They also develop a rapport during the journey and Hiraman starts mulling over ways of addressing her. He feels the need to have a heart to heart, open talk with her and hence he resorts to speak in his village's dialect. As Raymond Williams points out, "verbal language is instinctively human, indeed constitutively human. It is a distinctively human opening of and opening to the world." (74). The director conveys this on the celluloid through his use of variable tones reaching a high or low pitch as required.

Hiraman's bearing projects a total submission of his self in the company of Hirabai, signifying a reverence towards a goddess enshrined in a temple. His instantaneous response to the sight of her feet, too, is symbolic of his attitude of respect towards her as to a *'devi'* (goddess). He is so overwhelmed by her company that he feels as if a new lyrical form of *raga* is ringing in his mind and his very being is shaken up. He is sensitised to the fact by now that she does not like his whipping the bullocks. Hirabai, on the other hand, gains cognisance of the fact that Hira's name deciphers the fact that he was a pure soul like an uncut genuine diamond. She realizes that he has a level of detachment from the affairs of the world. His bullocks are almost an obsession for him and his brother, who is a farmer and a sister-in-law back home, are the people that he is devoted to. He respects his sister-in-law more than his own brother. He had got married in childhood, but before the marriage could be consummated, his bride had passed away and he did not marry again. His sister-in-law had wanted him to remarry but only to a young unmarried girl. This speaks of the cultural mindset even of the simple rural folks. It also speaks of the custom of child marriage and a man's right to re-marry unlike the widow and that too a young girl half his age. Moreover, such customs are perpetuated not by men only but also by women who are trapped by the mind set of the patriarchal ideology, which adds to the complexity of the problematic of Indian womanhood.

Hirabai has seen lust in the eyes of men who hovered around her, but she has never seen such innocence and devotion of any man. He is oblivious to the idea that a woman who danced in the *Nautanki* was referred in a derogatory way as *"Baiji"*. (Nabar 46). Throughout the journey, he keeps her amused and narrates anecdotes and wins her affection by rendering old songs and above all treats her as a respectable woman. These lilting, touching songs are like a communion of the two souls wherein the commonness of their feelings merge together. They develop a pristine 'in-love' stage in their platonic relationship and a kind of emotional bonding takes place between the two. They are both caught up in, "the state of ignorance and wisdom which comes into being when man and woman encounter each other the first time". (Gandhy 145). To the audience, she represents all the preconscious qualities of a female, attractive yet captivatingly dangerous, mischievous yet unsure, not knowing what to do with her. Her spell is cast on him, forcing him to explore his intuitive wisdom. He sings songs of wisdom like *'Duniya bananewale kya tere man me samayi Kahe Ko Duniya banayi ..... Kaheko preet jaga yee"* translated as "Oh God! Maker of the world, why did you create this world. Why did you create love between man and woman?" They both get merged into a state of oneness during their journey. It is like a journey of each seeking the completeness in the other, like the *Shiv-Shakti* bondage inherent to the concept of *Ardhinareshwar*[3]. It is pertinent to take into account the fact that, "Indian mythology may seem licentious and full of contradictions to the Western mind, but it has a specific purpose. It expresses the full range of human existence. The individual has the liberty to act his or her instinctive nature". (Gandhy 149). While following their respective instinctive nature, they both elevate each other onto higher planes of self-realization.

While following their respective instinctive nature, they both elevate each other on to higher planes. He feels that she is an *Apsara* from heaven who had descended in her form. She is fascinated by his singing and appreciates him, leading to a kind of abashedness on the part of the simpleton Hiraman. There's a kind of verisimilitude in the affairs of his life *"Sajnava beri Hogayee hamar chithiya ho to sab koi bante Bhag na bante koi"*, translated "My companion has abandoned me and now abandoned I can't even share my suffering with anybody. Had it been a letter I could have shared it with some one but who can share stroke of ill luck of separation from one's beloved". Hira Bai feels his singing is so heart rendering and soul stirring that it seems as if mother Saraswati, goddess of learning, music and dance had blessed him, herself.

However, in the process of their journey together; unwittingly, he gets caringly protective towards Hirabai. He wants to protect her and obliterate her from piercing eyes of the world of patriarchy. Enchanted as he is with her looks, her poise, her bewitching smile, her carriage which he felt was like that of any respectable daughter-in-law or daughter of the village and not that of a *nautanki* dancer of the company. So much so that he feels that he is falling blindly in love with her. Even Hirabai regales herself in his company and is at ease with herself as a person. She's touched with his caring attitude and feels elated as he treats her like as a respectable woman unlike the other men she has known in the *nautanki* company. It is not desire (*kama*), or any such passion that holds them or binds them. It seems that Hiraman like Shiva has burnt *kama*, as in the myth reduced it to the ashes and conquered it.

Hiraman rather elevates Hirabai to the status of a deity. Their laughter rings with innocence over silly meaningless innuendoes of Hiraman's talk. However, when they pass though a village called Teg Chaiya, innocent children on seeing the curtained bullock cart, start singing a wedding song. Both of them fall into a trance and see a dream like vision of a newly wedded bride who is brought home in the form of Hirabai and Hiraman contemplating such an event quietly smiles with wistful hope in their eyes. The children innocently thus lend meaning to their relationship. The mise en scene is gradual, presented in motion with the bullock cart plying by. There seems to be no haste to move ahead which is symbolic of their relationship. Evolved by the singing of the innocent children, their togetherness as man and wife, Basu Bhattacharya beautifully evokes the nuances of the song. They could communicate with each other with great ease and when they traverse together on the lonely road Hirabai feels no fear of any kind in his company. He could now understand the language of Hirabai's eyes. Without any verbal communication he was sensitive towards her every action. They were unified in an equilibrium of a relationship of unsaid understanding.

According to the psychology of love, when there is total love between individuals, there is a manifestation of their best qualities, which come to the fore. It is a relationship, which is built on the enjoyment of togetherness like a communion between two souls yearning for love. They both feel in touch with each other's souls, connecting them and weaving them into a kind of instinctive consanguity. It is the highest kind of man-woman relationship, which transcends love to a spiritual level as "there is freedom from any desire and this state embodies ecstasy, creativity, vitality." (Gandhy 229). The film has a subtle evocation of the dimensions of platonic love and harmony. Hirabai's relationship with Hiraman signifies the female construction of self in relation to others, leads to a new life, which changes the consciousness of woman and her perception of the world. However, this construction of the self is in opposition to another which "threatens one's very being and reverberates throughout the construction of both class society and the masculinist world view that results in a deep going and hierarchical dualism." (Hartstock 156).

Hiraman realizes that Hirabai enjoys listening to anecdotal stories and music. He narrates a very symbolic legendary tale of Mshus Ghatvarin (washerwoman) to please her to her heart's content. Mahua, a young beautiful maiden was from the region of Panwar river as the legend goes. Her father was a drunkard, her step-mother was a way ward woman who indulged in relationships with evil kind of people who sold intoxicants of sorts. She maltreated Mahua and made her slog day and night. One day she sold her off to a merchant (saudagar) for a price against her wishes. Mahua felt trapped and stifled and hence tried to escape as she was being taken across the river. However, one of the merchant's servant fell in love with her when he had a glance of Mahua. On hearing about Mahua's escape, the merchant tried to get her back. Since Mahua could swim like a fish, she tried to make good her escape by swimming against the current of the stream. The servant who had fallen in love with her, beseeched her to stop lest she would get drowned. Mahua agreed to go with the servant who protected her from the merchant and accepted her as his wife. As a result, all her weariness got over and her mind was at rest after the long suffering of loveless life which she had lead. While narrating the tale, Hiraman visualised himself as the merchant's servant who wanted to help Hirabai whom he identified with Mahua. The story was a similitude for his love and concern for Hirabai and both feel overwhelmed. As the tale gets over they are in unison in their feelings for each other which is beautifully conveyed on the celluloid by the subtle expressions of both Hiraman and Hirabai. The lyrical quality in his voice mesmerizes her and she calls him her guru, her teacher, her mentor as he had taught her a new song with a new bhava (feeling).

The journey of Hirabai and Hiraman together correlates with the use of the bullock cart as the symbol of domestic sphere, a kind of a cocoon that offers shelter from worldly interventions. In fact, for Hirabai it is a cocoon, which detaches her from the external world leading to the discovery of her inner self. As Sue Thornham states that, "our identities are formed and constantly renegotiated in the interaction between unconscious processes (our 'inner' world) and the 'outer' world of society". (Thornham Feminist Media 225). She could relax, here, oblivious of the world, away from being the sumptuous feast for titillation from the prying eyes of the male gaze, of the 'voyeur', a term which came into the feminist film theory through Laura Mulvey's usage of the same term in her influential essay, 'Visual Pleasure and Narrative Cinema'. For a *nautanki* dancer where the audience comprises of male viewers, "the determining male gaze projects its phantasy onto the female figure which is styled accordingly". (Mulvey 59).

In the meanwhile Hiraman gets caught up at a halt with old associates from his village. Lalmohan, Dhuniram, Palatdas and others are excited in coming across the alluring *nautanki* dancer who provides in them, "their own anxieties which are intermixed with desire." (Kaplan Looking xviii). Meanwhile, Hirabai is extended a hearty welcome by the representative of the *nautanki* company as they reach the venue of the fair where her performance is to be held. Hirabai parts ways with Hiraman at this point, pays him the fare and he tries to smile at her but a realization dawns on him that she was going back to where she actually belonged. Hirabai addresses his bullocks as 'sisters' and moves on. Her bonding with the bullocks as sisters is symbolic, as she herself was being treated as dumb driven cattle, trapped as a dancer to perform as a source of pleasure. Her position is analogical with the victimization syndrome, as she is conditioned to be constructed in an image as, "a reductionist aesthetic," thus reinforcing the repressive cultural ideological concerns in juxtaposition with the essentialist images of women. (Felski The Dialectics 435).

Hiraman feels extremely depressed and upset at the parting but is also touched by her concern to extend passes to him and all his friends for the *nautanki* show. However, there was a hierarchy in the seating system for the *nautanki* show. There were people sitting at the back, on the floor, and in the front and some on the chairs respectively according to their class distinction. All types of men, from all walks of life, came to see the *nautanki* show including ones who pay 50 *paisas* or 25 *paisas* and are termed as (*athani chavani chaap*), *zamindars* and even policemen. They all are unified in their gaze rendering Hirabai's position to be fetished as that of an art d'object for the male '*voyeur*'. Hirabai, in such an audience stood, "in patriarchal culture as a signifier for the male other bound by a symbolic order in which a man can live out his fantasies and obsession". (Mulvey 62). Such a gaze according to E. Kaplan,

"is also not a relation nor a process, like the consumption of pornography, it is a one way gaze that seeks to alleviate the one gazing through sexual fantasies, and produces a sexual arousal in that subject which is enjoyed alone, not with an other." (Kaplan Looking xviii).

Such a gaze connotes a normative order that prevails the relationship between an active subject versus a passive object. According to Fredric Jameson who responds to Mulvey with the argument that

"reduces the woman to a mere body from a male position, the struggle is really about what he calls "the right to look" which men have and woman do not." (Jameson 7).

The extent to which the protagonist's sensibility is informed by the scriptures is indicated by the fact that Hiraman feels that he is her protector like the mythological husband figure Ram was of Sita in *Ramayana*. As a result, he is duty bound to ward off the advances of the other male voyeurs as they were like 'Ravana' the evil mythological character. He also sees himself as the male protagonist in consideration of all the female roles enacted by her. When she cries and sings *"Mare gaye gulfam"* translated "oh, I have been taken in." He starts wondering innocently who that poor *gulfam* is and does not realize what she wants to convey. Watching the *nautanki* show in the evenings has become a regular feature with him after a hard day's work of transporting goods like his friends. Hiraman realizes that she is the cynosure of common male gaze of all the male viewers watching the *nautanki* show. Hiraman, however gets possessive about her gradually and wants to hide her away from every prying eye. Both Hiraman and Hirabai feel repulsion against the wily ways of the *zamindar* who is infatuated by her and introduced to her by Birju, the agent of the company. Hopelessly, Hiraman wonders how far he would be able to protect her from the representative of the class caste conflict and ideology of hegemonic hierarchical relationships. The local *zamindar* seeks her out for sexual favours and is turned out by Hirabai. Inspired by the love and respect of Hiraman she herself wants to redeem herself for the sake of the purity of that unadulterated love that she wants to share. She thus portrays her vulnerability to deterministic moral codes by showing, "her continued identification with purity, despite contrary appearances". (Brooks Ann 37). However, she is made to realize callously by the local *zamindar* with a threat that she will have to pay a heavy price for refusal by being instrumental in causing the loss of Hiraman's life too. She realizes that sexual liberation which she is trying to seek for herself, as an ideology is simply not ordained for her. She is a woman shackled not only by her gender but also by her class and caste too. The sentimental contours of the story touch upon the gross sexual oppression of woman as represented by her sensitive portrayal through her gestures and demeanour. It is time yet again for Hirabai to regret being a female, to grovel at the feet of an unforgiving social system and to be smothered by its trappings. She has to part ways with Hiraman.

Indian culture ideology has for the major part encouraged the subservience of women and applauded their self-effacement. It has thus promoted women's subjugation, which hinders her from developing and moving towards establishing equality in gender relations. Hirabai's plan to move away from Hiraman is one such entrapping of cultural ideology. She does not want to seek her happiness in her togetherness with him any more as she fears for his life. She returns his money, which he had handed over to her care. It is symbolic of her constrained determination to wriggle out of a situation of becoming his partner in life.

Hiraman goes to see Hirabai off at the railway station to bid her the final *adieu* and both feel uneasy. Hirabai is touchingly patronizing in her behaviour and gifts him her *shawl* (wrapper). The pathos of their separation is negotiated when she reminds him the story of Mahua Ghatwaran that he had narrated to her and tells him that like Mahua she has been sold off too. She calls him *meeta* (dear friend) and tells him not to lose heart. After parting from her, he moves towards the bullock cart waiting on the road and looks into the empty cocoon of his love nest wherein Hirabai had spent some precious time with him. He feels that she has been playing the role of a fairy, a goddess and a friend to him. She portrays to him the image of woman, an archetype of love, the eternal image of a woman, who made him feel whole and complete. There was a special sense of connectedness to life that he felt with her, as she has lent a new meaning to his life.

What Jung describes, "as the classical anima" (Jung Development 198) can be applied to her as she actualizes the unconscious longing, which draws man into seeking himself. But as long as he is not conscious of this fact, he keeps seeking himself through the projected image of the woman of the mythological figure of *Ardhinareshwar* the figure which signifies missing half in him. He now understands the meaning of the significance of the word *Gulfam* which means a dejected soul like himself, which is so connotatingly elucidated and used in the title and the lyrics of the film. It thus gets conveyed through *Gulfam* that cultural ideology traps both the sexes. According to *Shiv Shakti* myth, male and female must separate, since, "the ultimate goal is to attain the inner balance of the male and female qualities within ourselves. We should be in touch with our souls". (Gandhy 273). The commonality in their name connotes both Hiraman and Hirabai as counterparts and counterfoils of each other. They live a life of relatedness during their journey where their own selves get connected with the other, neither in a state of independence nor co-dependence but interdependence. The man-woman relationship gets elevated on the spiritual plane as a sort of the communion of two souls.

According to Ashish Rajadhyakshha, "in the end the audience places its sympathy with the disillusioned Hiraman, rather than with the woman." (Rajadhyakshha and Willemen 362). Both Hiraman and Hirabai are from the lower strata of class and have borne enough oppression on account of the same; however, Hirabai suffers extra on account of her gender too. Hirabai understood the reality of life and tells to a friend that it's easy to act out *Laila*

Majnu's love legends but not so easy to act in real life, the role of the exalted mythical Goddess on a pedestal, which he bestows upon her. His innocence and affection persuaded her to fight off unwanted advances and leave the place. Yet she has to move on and face the reality of living in a way that she may realize that,

> "the cycle from Unmanifest to Manifest is incomplete. It is about the evolution of consciousness through a lifetime, the different energies that transform as an individual personality matures". (Gandhy 234).

She realizes that to awaken her other half is the nature of her dance and that she is the link so that *Shakti* can flow.

Basu Bhattacharya releases such a passion in the film while transforming the beautiful poignant short story of "Renu" on celluloid, through his vision. With such a vision he tries to realize in his first film the nuances of gender relations with a firm grasp of his craft in the 'classical' sense. He engages the audience in a cinematic story through a visual/aural narrative that is so enchanting. According to Nicholas T. Proferes,

> "Human beings are in need of a narrative and always have been and it has played a significant part in all the diverse cultures of the world and perhaps in the development of the species itself." (Proferes 6).

The film portrays aesthetically the visual elements of body language, appearance and facial expressions as great care seems to have been taken to show such nuances of language, expressions, feeling and nuances of folk theatre. The folk theatre culture, which has got lost with a callous attitude of indifference towards it has been cultivated and woven into the story in an appealing manner. This was perhaps the cause of film's undoing at the box-office.

The film is notable for its musical element, too, which has lent to it the ambience and cultural climate of the theatrical medium style songs. The picturisation of the songs evokes the traces of such a culture, which seems to have got lost in the rut of the commercial film. Shankar Jaikishan duo, the melody makers have successfully contributed to the repertoire of music in Indian films, within a dimensional canvas, that has an orchestral harmony. In fact, Hindi film music has played a significant role in the integration of folk music in India. Cinema has brought folk music from different rigors into the mainstream, culturally and musically and every region now has a style of its own. Visual images and dialogues aided by songs and dance react verbally in a way such as *'Pan Khaiye Saiyan Hamaro'* (My love can single out for the one who chews betel leaves) and *'Duniya Banane Wale'* (O, Creator of the world) bring alive the magic of rural existence. Those songs also connote an inward journey for both Hiraman and Hirabai, a movement towards self-assessment and redefinition.

Nautanki style stage setting is truthfully depicted in the film, lending a feel of the old charm of theatre without any heavy arc light glares. The scene, which strongly sets out is the one when Hiraman and Hirabai have parted. Hiraman is watching the train on which Hirabai leaves from the road. Far away, from the bullock cart, he can view the train leaving and he hears her voice as if in a hallucination, urging him not to whip the bullocks. Basu Bhattacharya uses sound as, "'design by inference,' which is known as the 'sound picture counter point' in common parlance" (Chatterji Shoma Sound 176). The sound of the train suggests the drifting apart and parting of Hiraman and Hirabai. The train is passing and it is viewed from the wheel side of the bullock cart. It conveys much as a metaphor of life passing by; yet, life has to go on. It is also symbolic of the lost world of innocence and simplicity and that leads to philosophic realism.

The innocence of Hiraman is soul stirring and effectively portrayed by the actor Raj Kapoor. "It is perhaps his best performance as an archetypal persona". (Rajadhayaksha and Willemen 362). The film sees Raj Kapoor returning to his role as an innocent country bumpkin. The film offered Raj Kapoor a chance to turn out one of his most sensitive performance. Waheeda Rehman, a trained classical dancer in *Bharatnatyam,* portrays the role of *nautanki* dancer with élan. She reveals her extraordinary facial mobility and dancer's grace. Her physical presence infuses an intense sense of impassioned liveliness into the simple folk story. The hero is realistically shown not singing but playing the *dafli*. A song sung by the group of villagers who are all bullock cart drivers and other workers at the *mela* '*Chalat Musafir Barfi ke sab ras pi liya re pinjarewali chidiya*' is heart rendering of the Hirabai's helpless state of being trapped in the collective male gaze. Waheeda Rehman in an interview to Shekhar Gupta, Editor-in-Chief of the Indian Express, on NDTV 24x7's Walk the Talk programme on Aug 26, 2006 was told that '*Teesri Kasam*' a classic was ahead of its times by Shekhar Gupta. She agreed to that saying that she always had a knack of choosing stories which were true to life like another adaptation of literary text '*Guide*' by R. K. Narayan. *Teesri Kasam* was a story where both the characters lose out. She told that Raj Kapoorji wanted to change the ending and the producer asked her the same. However she was against the idea as she thought that it would not justify the title of the film. Moreover the writer was feeling very upset as he felt his work was being compromised which eventually did not happen.

One may feel cynicism, certain ignorance towards the cultural underdevelopment in the commercial films; hence, when good 'art' movies are made, Hindi cinema appears to be dreadfully self-conscious, didactic and pretentious. But no-where does one feel that air of gross exhibitionism in '*Teesri Kasam*'. It rather smells of the very earthiness with its roots firmly on the moorings a cultural identity and a sense of identity and nostalgia about a lost world of theatre[4].

'*Teesri Kasam*' is an unusually sensitive film and subconsciously sensuous too. It uses the bullock cart journey as a metaphor to emphasise the emotional journey of protagonists, Hiraman and Hirabai. Deep-rooted prejudices against the lower class artistic women are questioned and the director shows a human side to the *nautanki* dancer, though he fails to provide fulfilment of her dreams to get re-integrated into the social fabric of Indian womanhood in the cultural ideology. Moments of reconciliation and transformation fall like a pattern even while essential conflicts about Hirabai's position amongst Hiraman's friends and their attitude and feelings towards her, are biased and coloured by set cultural constructs. "Fears about mass culture are often linked to a series of anxieties about femininity". (Huyssen 281).

A literary craftsman, Renu underscores the decidedly masculine nature of Hiraman's absolute independence from a subjection to all norms. Litterateur and scriptwriter Nabhendu Ghosh influenced the substance and concerns of Shailendar's cinematic universe in 'Teesri Kasam' and the beautiful sensitive lyrics of *auteur* producer Shailendar, add boldness in the content. The film attempts to analyse the social order of the given society based on class and gender. It combines cinematic craft with human story telling. His lyrics often worked in portraying and in raising the films above the normal standard and quality. His knack lay in the witty dialogues and realistic characterisation and a playful, intelligent genre revision, which enhances the strong literary flavour in the narrative of the film.

UMRAO JAAN

The film 'Umrao Jaan' released in 1981 may be considered not as one of those popular films, which are just romantic musicals that offer escapism and fantasy to the cinegoers, but as a classic in its own right. It is based on the first major Urdu novel of Mirza Mohammad Hadi Ruswa (1857-1931) which is biography in Urdu of the legendary mid – 19th century courtesan called *Umrao Jaan Ada*, who lived during the times of the zenith of Avadh culture and the moment of its disintegration. It is supposedly an account of the real life reminiscences of Umrao, a *tawaif* (courtesan) living in Lucknow's *chowk* (prostitutes quarters) who was personally known to the author. Woven into the tapestry of the light and shade of the period's refined decadence, is the life of a woman who, inspite of being the victim of the most adverse circumstances, matures into a highly cultured human being, an accomplished poetess in her own right. This writing of Mirza Hadi Rusva's novel had scandalized an earlier generation as it celebrates the figure of the low class courtesan as a cultured woman, who writes poetry and sings and dances for the pleasure of Lucknow's fabled connoisseurs of art and music With Rusva's novel 'Umrao Jaan Ada', the Urdu novel came alive to the realistic world of the courtesan giving a touch of social realism to fiction. This was a time, as the Urdu writer Joginder Paul points out in his article 'Urdu ka Aaga Peeche' (The Context of Urdu Fiction), when people generally liked the magical and innocent tales prevalent even in the nineteenth and twentieth century. "The earlier tradition of story telling, '*distaangoi and kissagoi*' was that of long intricate tales, told with a strong sense of drama and imagination". (Panja 145). However, this art acquired a variety of versions with the changing imagination of the people.

Khushwant Singh and M.A. Hussaini did the English translation of the immortal Urdu novel *Umrao Jaan Ada* for the Indian series of the UNESCO collection of representative works. They recount in it how Mirza Ruswa came to write the story of the courtesan of Lucknow. He happened to meet Umrao Jaan years before they actually had known each other at a poetic symposium. Umrao Jaan bemoaned and recited a verse whose last lines were "who will listen to the tale of my woeful heart. Far and wide I have wandered on the face of this earth. And I have much to impart"[5]. (words of Ruswa translated by Khushwant Singh and M.A. Hussan (1)). According to the translators, Mirza Mohammad Rusva accepted the challenge and what came out of the series of joint sittings with the famous courtesan and sensitive writer, is an Urdu classic par excellence.

Umrao Jaan was like a woman who had slaked her thirst at many a stream and wanted her experience to be told to the world. She goes through a series of emotional experiences. Her life was like a 'text' wanting to be authored. Rusva Mirza speaks of Umrao's patriotic idea of nationhood and dislike of the British too, in snatches of her conversation. At the same time, the exquisite civilization of the dream town of Lucknow during the time of Wajid Ali Shah comes to life. The atmosphere of Lucknow centered around inculcation of the art of poetry and music, which was imperative for any one who feels the need to be culturally refined. The aristocrats were given to sloth and pleasure, frolic and a leisurely life style. The writer sees and portrays decadence integral to the times of Wajid Ali Shah, set in a story in 1840 through the perspective of female protagonist, Umrao Jaan. All her life, she is forced to drift through life inspite of strong cultural moorings, like a homeless vagrant. Umrao, as a young girl is abducted from her simple and happy home in Faizabad by Dilawar Khan, an enemy of her father and bartered for money in Lucknow chowk to a *kotha* as a *tawaif*, (a nautch girl) in the house of infame. Known as Ameeran in childhood, she grows up and emerges from the trauma of kidnapping and concubinage to be Umrao Jaan, the famous courtesan of Lucknow and takes the city by storm with her creation of sensitive poetry and rendition of music. *Umrao Jaan Ada* is steeped in the ethos and ambience of 19th century Lucknow, the capital of Avadh, just before the annexation by Lord Dalhousie. The term 'courtesan' and 'prostitute' have been interchangely used within the context of the practice of mercenary exchanged, enforced on women. "Hence a complex picture emerges of an institution that was prevalent in all parts of India and towards which moral opprobrium existed side by side with wide spread social acceptance to become immensely popular with the elite of city." (Chakravarty 127).

In fact the term *tawaif* was used for the courtesans who were considered "professional women performing artists who functioned between the eighteenth and the early twentieth century in North India. The word 'tawaif' is believed to have come from the Persian 'tawaif' of circumambulation of *Kaaba* and refers to her movement around the 'mehfil' space, the circle of her patrons." (Subramanyam 63). They were intensively trained from an early age to dance, sing, converse, amuse, and excel in the "exaggerated politeness for which Lucknow had acquired a special reputation during the nawabi." (Chandra Moti 23). Moti Chandra traces the existence of courtesans all the way to the Rig Vedic age, thousands of years ago, cataloguing the available references to them in the major treatises and literary works of both ancient and medieval times. As artists, they were supposed to be respected for their talent and skill and were rewarded with payment and gifts. Association with a courtesan conferred status, which signified sophistication, wealth and cultural finesse in the life style of the patron. The courtesans were considered unique among women of their times and were even educated, charming, wealthy and politically powerful too.

> "The equation of sexuality with tradition is epitomized in the persona of courtesan. They represented a tradition and a form of cultural institution and their existence is traced back to ancient India. As late as the early 19th century, it was the *tawaifs* who knew the intricacies of culture and delicacies of language and poetry. Usually they were more than well versed in Hindi, Urdu, Persian, Oudhi and Brij poetry" (Reported in Booklet at National Film Archives of India Pune, 1953, quoted in Dwyer and Patel 206).

Till as late as the 1940s, they also performed in temples at various festivals and at *urs* festivals of *sufi* saints. Courtesans also took pride in claming a long ancestry and called themselves 'khandani tawaifs' (a traditional family of courtesans) implying a family of high status. They were sponsored, witnessed and patronized by the highest nobility in the exclusive (simultaneously public) space of the court or the *mehfil*.

In the Southern India the women dancers were dedicated to the temples and were called "devdasis" or "Maharis". (Shovana Narayan : 29). The institution of devadasis went through many vicissitudes of weather. The devadasis were dedicated to the service of the temple as a girl child by their parents for a variety of reason ranging from fulfilment of a wish of the parents, poverty or rescue of prostitutes from brothels. Since they were married to 'God' they could never be widowed and therefore their presence was considered acceptable on auspicious occasions. Outstanding performers enjoyed the friendship of kings and sages. These women usually followed the matriarchal system. They could also retire from their professions in old age. Daughters of these women usually followed their mother's footsteps.

However, the position of the courtesans was highly ambiguous. Since they are women placed blatantly in a patriarchal society, they are required to appear unveiled before men as object d'art. They perform and speak of private matters and even the secrets of love in the public space of the *mehfil*.

The courtesans did not marry, although they entered into relationships with their patrons. Such liaisons were not considered immoral. Nor were these relationships entered into or terminated arbitrarily. In a way, there was also a tendency to claim the courtesan as a kind of proto-feminist figure regardless of the fact that the courtesans, as much as wives, were circumscribed by the norms of feudal patriarchal society and hence were not totally free of essentialist determinism. They were respected though not respectable in the sense in which wives were considered. A wife is called *Begum Sahiba* but a courtesan is called *Jaan* like Umrao Jaan, Bismillah Jaan in the film. Marriage with a courtesan was frowned upon, though visiting her *kotha* was not considered reprehensible. Strangely in a patriarchal society, wives and courtesans are kind of mirror images of each other. Wives were the means by which patrilineage-established links with other families and thereby affirmed its social status. The courtesan, on the other hand, addressed the aesthetic and erotic needs of their patrons. The courtesans, thus, are not different from their respectable sisters. They are not different because they share the same ambiguity of status as well as the ideological circumscribing of their persons and roles. Each one lives up to the role socially defined and constructed for her with regards to both being as a representation of the patriarchal order.

The establishment of the image of courtesan and Madame or *Chaudhrian* in charge of the establishment is symbolically a representative figure of patriarchy that perpetuates it by her authoritative position, inspite of her entrapment in a mutually exploitative universal order. In fact, she herself is trapped in it. Yet the performance space gives them the possibility to transcend the same by subverting though not changing radically, the given condition of their lives. The courtesan is outside the proscriptive periphery of stereotypical role models of mother, wife and daughter on account of her alleged promiscuity. By virtue of her illegitimacy, she is contrasted with the unscrupulous purity as one of the argued pre-determined feature of womanhood in the patriarchal cultural ideology. She is an alien to the conventional societal set up of a family. In the *Natyashastra* the courtesans were called 'ganika.' "Ganikas or courtesans were dancing girls. They were also eloquent and clever and able to argue, at the same time amiable, poetic and well versed in arts" (Gupta Chandra Bhan 93).

Muzaffar Ali, the director of the film who adapted the novel for the celluloid, himself, is from Lucknow. Being the son of Raja Sajjid Hussain of Kotwara, he grew up amidst the remnants of Lucknow's grandeur and he is aware of the nuances of Lucknow culture. A case of obsession with the past marks Muzaffar Ali's films. Muzaffar Ali is himself a poet, an artist, a dress designer in his own right. Having studied at Aligarh Muslim University he learnt a great deal about the Urdu culture and poetry. Even when he studied science, he pursued a career in advertising at Clarion McCann where Satyajit Ray was the Vice Chairman. He, however, remained the quintessential artist at heart, all throughout. From his paintings he drew inspiration to make movies and from his movies he was inspired to design clothes. He attributes his diversification by saying "I think whatever I do is all related". (Walia 2). As a result when he made 'Umarao Jaan' he always sketched on canvas whether it was the scene of his film or design of an outfit. His earlier film "Gaman" (1979) is a story of a taxi driver who sets out for Bombay from his village in U.P. leaving his loving mother and wife, for livelihood. In 'Umrao Jaan' he laments the absence of courtly ways of life in Lucknow. Ali who traces his ancestry to one of the more important nobles in Wajid Ali Shah's courts, brings strong sense of nostalgia to this film. There has been a genre of the courtesan films in India cinema and the film 'Pakeeza' (the pure one) illustrated some of the significant aspects of the courtesan film. It is considered a classic in its own right and is considered "poetry and fantasy and nostalgia all orchestrated together in a grand scale". (Chakravarty 291).

The biography of Umrao Jaan Ada which Mirza Rusva penned, startles the reader with the intensity of emotions that it portrays human character. The pathos of Umrao Jaan's dilemma and suffering as she wanders into the wilderness with her wings clipped, unfolds the tragic but affirmative saga of her life. Rusva, with his mastery of Urdu prose, evokes the decadent culture of Lucknow, which stands out picturesquely through this novel. It is possible to see the image of woman assuming very different meanings within the different text of each author's work. The director's *oeuvre* can produce a different view from the force of the author's preoccupation rather his obsession with the figure of the woman, as was in the case of Mirza Mohammed Rusva. In fact, the film 'Umrao Jaan' constructs "a visual and musical treat through its social tapestry, lavish sets, personalized star appearance, romantic drama and pathos" (Rajadhayaksha and Willemen 421). Muzaffar Ali, however, did not remain totally faithful to the original story, though he moulded and translated the story into a visual form, which made it the quintessential courtesan film of Indian cinema.

Umrao Jaan who was called Ameeran as a child, lived in Faizabad in her childhood. She was the daughter of a *Jemadar*, an Indian Officer in the Sepoy Army and head of a body of police and of servants. She had a younger brother who was so attached to her that he wouldn't leave her for a moment. She had doting parents and led a blissful childhood with them. As long as she lived with her parents, she did not know any sorrow. At the age of nine, she was engaged to her father's sister's son whose family was pretty well off. Her parents were planning to get her married soon and were in the process of collecting a handsome dowry to be gifted to her at the time of her marriage. However, the twist of fate upset her whole life and pushed her to the path towards leading a courtesan's life. Dilawar Khan one of their neighbours who lived at a short distance was in the league of dacoits. He had a strong grouse against her father as he was arrested on his testimony and sent to prison. He nursed that grievance in his heart and decided to take revenge. It is Ameeran who becomes the helpless victim on account of his rage and is kidnapped by him. Along with a friend Peer Baksh, he sells her off in Lucknow. It is the woman who becomes a victim of patriarchal revenge through mercenary exchange. She is kept hidden at some Karim's house where she meets another helpless victim like her viz. Ram Dei, the daughter of a Hindu trader of a village near Sitapur who is fair and petite and has lovely features. They spent a few days there together and were separated with each getting sold off. Ram Dei is sold off as a maid to a Nawab's begum who has a son called Nawab Sultan. Ameeran is sold off for rupees one hundred and twenty five in the *chowk*, the prostitute's quarter to the establishment of Madame Khanum Jaan. This is the place that gives a turning point to her life and as she said to Rusva in conversation with him, she was to get her due from the world both honour and disgrace, fame and notoriety, failure and success.

Khanum Jaan was nearly fifty then. A well dressed elegant woman, she wore a pair of loose pyjamas made of gold thread and covered her head with a dupatta of finely crinkled muslin cloth. Surprisingly she had a dignified bearing and an air of authority about her. She had a daughter called Bismillah Jaan who was to become a friend of Umrao's later, alongwith Khursheed Jaan and Ameer Jaan. Ameer Jaan was taken in the care of noble hearted Hussaini who brought her up with care and affection and she called her aunty. Her name was changed to Umrao by Khanum and when she grew up, she took her place among the courtesans of Lucknow. Whe she began to write poetical verses she added the pseudonym "Ada" (nuance of a style) and came to be known as Umrao Jaan Ada. However, Khanum always called her Umrao and Hussaini addressed her as Umrao Sahib. Her days and nights were then filled with dancing and singing, shows and concerts and fairs and picnics in pleasure garden. No form of luxury as such was denied to her. There were musicians, servants and full fledged courtesans as friends around. They all had their little court of admirers who kept them flattered and wanted. Khanum's house was like a fairyland ringing with sounds of mirth and laughter song and music all the twenty four hours of day. The ambience of it is beautifully evoked on the celluloid with the grandeur of sets, costumes, jewellery and in the setting of the kotha. Umrao Jaan had a natural aptitude for music and her voice was melodious and suitable for classical singing. After she mastered the scales, she started on with the compositions under the tutelage of an ustaad (master) under the watchful eye of Khanum. Khanum was pleased with Umrao Jaan's eagerness to learn and took a lot of interest in her coaching of singing and dancing. She was also trained in a school alongwith the other Khanum's girls where she was taught to read and write under the supervision of Maulvi Sahib.

Maulvi Sahib paid special attention to her studies and taught her with greater affection and care than the other girls as a result she was chiselled and better trained. He gave her the confidence to speak in cultured company. He taught her books of elementary Persian like *Kareema*, *Mamakeema, Mahmud Nama* and taught Saad's Gulistan. She learnt Arabic grammar from him and fostered her interest in poetry till it developed into a passion. Education gave her the power to transform her life into a meaningful existence. Her passion for poetry not only gets translated into a commodity for her living but its also elevates her into something of her being and vehicle to advance her very existence. It empowers her to chart the journey of her anguish, existence and obsession with poetic ideas which manifest in her growth and maturity both as a poetess and as a person. It helps in diverting her to higher realms and compiling poetry of great depth and lets her to develop a counter culture for herself. Rather it helps her to groom and enhance her personality as a singer and to integrate her expressions with her visions. When one is posed with questions like is there a feminist aesthetic? Silvia Bovenschen answered it as yes and no both. She said, "Certainly there is, if one is talking about aesthetic awareness and modes of sensory perception. "Certainly not, if one is talking about an unusual variant of artistic production or about a painstakingly constructed theory of art." (Bovenchem136). In fact the echoes of contradictions are specific because of two fold pressure, a simultaneous pull in opposite directions. One of it is being, "the affirmative action on behalf of women as social subjects, on one front and the negativity inherent in the radical critique of patriarchal bourgeois culture on the other". (Bovenschen 119). This can be explained to the context of what Umrao Jaan was alleging to speak in her verses which could both negate or objectify her through her presentation.

In the *mise en scene* of her debut *kotha* appearance as Umrao Jaan, she is constructed as a spectacle. Traditionally, the woman figure displays a functional role on two levels, "as an erotic object for the characters within the screen story, and other as erotic object for the spectator such a device that allows the two looks to be unified technically without any apparent break in diegesis. A woman performs within the narrative, the gaze of the spectator and that of the male characters in the film and neatly combines it without breaking narrative verisimilitude. For a moment, the sexual impact of the performing woman takes the film into woman's land outside its own time and space." (Mulvey 61). Such an impact of Umrao Jaan's persona has and earns for her a coterie of admirers when they see her performing and hear the rendition of her impeccable singing in her sonorous voice, of her self composed poems. Her provocative flirtatious style, her voluptuous gestures and her bewitching smile all have a devastating effect on the male figures. With the determining male gaze projecting its fantasy onto her, her female figure carefully styled accordingly. In the traditional exhibitionist role, she is looked at with appearance coded for strong visual and erotic impact, which Rekha as Umrao Jaan delivers with aplomb.

The element of spectacle gets inter-twined with the narrative in the process. The effect of the costume, jewellery, make-up and set props are used to heighten the grandeur of the visual extravaganza. In the cinematic presentation on celluloid with the help of soft fawn of lighting, proper care is taken to project her sensuality, focusing her as a fetishist character. The patrons of the courtesan want her to fall in love with them, as she is being fetished as an object d' art. The courtesan, aware of this desire, quite coquettishly swears allegiance with her vivacious, saucy and winsome ways. Umrao Jaan had a pseudonym 'Ada' which means style when translated from Urdu into English. It was her *Ada* (style) for which her patrons who were also connoisseurs, acclaim her. She holds the look in a red flaming dress, which signifies and exudes passion and evinces the male desire for her. The pearl ornaments are symbolically used as a metaphor to the innate pristine purity of her youth and beauty. The glowing lamps lit all around heighten the erotic spectacle. Muzaffar Ali, as the director aesthetically combines the potent impact of the spectacle and the narrative. He enhances the narrative of the literary work by her visual presence.

Rekha, as Umrao Jaan, is simply alluring and her dance and gestures keep pace with her sensuous look. Her natural persona, her body language and her almond shaped *kohled* eyes add impetuosity to her expression, coupled with her impish petulance. As Umrao Jaan, Rekha uses this 'encoded' appearance as a weapon for a portrayal of self-affirmation. However, these traits can be intercepted as a subversive device when correlated with Khanum's appearance. Shaukat Azmi as Khanum sits in the center dressed up in all regality displaying the grandeur and style of the *kotha*. She is in charge of herself and is a representative part of the patriarchal system, which endorses such a courtesan culture. The pride in Khanum's appearance is the pride of patriarchy perpetuated and reflected through her in the upkeeping of such an establishment. An entire population depended on such courtesan establishments as that of flower sellers, *paan* sellers, instrumental accompanists, *tabala* and *saraangi* players and even the *ustaads* from whom courtesans acquired their '*taleem*' (education in the learning of music and dance). Their condition is financially and emotionally interwoven with each other in a mutually nurturing pattern. Muzaffar Ali handles and shows all these aspects deftly with great sensitivity, inspite of using the clichéd symbols of the courtesan culture. The internal hegemony in which cultural forces emphasize, "the wholeness of the process, may be perceived as the lived dominance and subordination of particular categories". (Bathla 66). The category here is that of a courtesan who is doubly oppressed first on account of gender and then as an outcast by her virtue of gender. As, "the other woman she comes from outside to disrupt the home ... is the mistress, the rival, the sexual threat", to the figure of the wife. (Michie 57).

Muzaffar Ali at times uses the flashback manner used by Mirza Rusva, with situations and incidents moving through the stream of consciousness in the inner recesses of the mind of Umrao Jaan. The past is seen either as an object of nostalgia or as an object of despair, testifying to the fact.

"Flashback is a narrative device used in the film (as in literature) to go back in time to an earlier moment in a character's life and/or history, and to narrate that moment. Flashbacks are the most clearly marked subjective moments within the narrative. Flashbacks are a cinematic representation of memory and of history and ultimately of subjective truth". (Hayward 133).

Even though Umrao Jaan soon forgets her former existence and learns the techniques of being an accomplished courtesan yet, she gets reflective at times and remembers her relationship with the men who came in her life. They had all been different in character and from diverse backgrounds. Gauhar Mirza, a harlot's son and a resident pimp, courts her but Umrao loses her heart to Nawab Sultan Sahib, who is rich, handsome, cultured, and well mannered. Gauhar Mirza (Naserudin Shah) has been her adolescent love and had even managed to seduce her; yet, he remains her constant admirer through out her life, though without a sense of commitment. However, her romance with Nawab Sultan Sahib is short lived as he gets married to a girl of his mother's choice and Umrao Jaan feels desperately desolate and disconsolate. Then there is Faiz Ali, the generous hearted highway robber, who is smitten by her with whom she elopes, but he is killed on the way, and Umrao slowly makes her way to Kanpur. In the novel, Rusva Mirza mentions a vulgar *novueau riche* and rustic outsider called Rashid Ali who is fooled into paying for Umrao Jaan's entrance into the courtesan's profession, not knowing that Gauhar Mirza has already stolen the honours from him. Then there is the sanctimonious lawyer's attorney Akbar Ali Khan, in the novel, who spends his days in coaching false witnesses and the evenings in prayers. The most moving depiction is that of seventy year old henpecked Nawab who engages Umrao Jaan, only just as a matter of pride. To have a courtesan as a mistress was in vogue among the *noblesse obligé* of the Lucknow aristocracy. However, Muzaffar Ali narrows down the men in her life to three for the film on celluloid i.e. Nawab Sultan, Gauhar Mirza and Faiz Ali. The interesting aspect in such a depiction of relationship is not what happens in her relationship with all these men, or her external behaviour with them all. Her inner feelings in her relationships with all of them are tackled with a rare aesthetic insight along with a humane touch. Though, she is displayed as a sexual object or the leitmotif of an erotic spectacle, the sensitivity of her soul and her loving heart craving for genuine love, is beautifully evoked. In the novel, Umrao herself tells Rusva that in their hey days,

> "courtesans were like goddesses at whose alter worshipper brought themselves as offerings for sacrifice. And like goddesses they treated everything haughtily with disdain. Of course the worship is of youth and beauty. Men need her, love her, worship her but they do so in relation to their own selves." (Ruswa 78).

Like in the Indian aesthetic theory, the man bows before the woman who represents the goddess *Urvashi*, the '*diva*' of erotic love. She flits from one lover to another either for monetary gain or for emotional support. There is no scheming design in any of her relationships. She tries to be true and honest in every relationship, even if she is jilted by her lovers or let down by fate. In the novel Mirza Rusva narrates the biography of Umrao Jaan actually from her own point of view. The reader is given to believe that she's going down the memory lane and at the same time introspecting objectively the journey of her life. When it is transformed on the celluloid by Muzaffar Ali, even though she undoubtedly, remains the central character and is shown as a woman of culture, with great class of manner and gentility; yet, the focus is on her body and the male gaze and the director with his rootedness in a sensibility of androgyny which, includes both the male and female perceptions in him, transcribes the novel on the celluloid. "To the man the pursuit of love is a quest of pleasure. To a woman, the pursuit of love is the quest of pleasure as well as of security". (Ruswa 92).

This sense of security eludes Umrao Jaan all throughout the film. She is kidnapped as a child and thus uprooted from her moorings. She grows up with a sense of loss of such a security. In the house of Khanum, she is gliding through life with élan. Good food, clothes, jewellery and admirers are at her beck and call. Yet, the overpowering sense of pain and anxiety persists within the four walls and makes her feel claustrophobic even when she is surrounded by opulence and luxury. A brief romantic interlude with Nawab Sultan gives her a deluded sense of the ecstasy of love. The Nawab is a man of generous temperament and his bearing, almost with a devotee-like admiration, impresses her. His declaration of love seemed genuinely heart-felt to her. Every sentence he speaks to her is interspersed with couplets of love composed by him, which makes her feel elated. Her sincerity of purpose in love for Nawab Sultan comes across convincingly. The Nawab himself is so smitten by her poetical verses, "*In Aankon ki Masti Ke Maastane hazaron hein*", translated "the magic of these winsome naughty eyes have intoxicated thousands", in her sonorous voice, that he feels compulsive desire to keep coming back to her. In the *mise en scene* when Nawab Sultan comes to hear her, is a spectacle of an epicurean erotic life set in '*sringara rasa*' with extra ordinary refinement. "One of the great attractions of Hindi film is provided by showing spaces usually associated with transgressive (non-marital) relationships. The most celebrated of these is the courtesan's house, sumptuous and elaborated furnishings". (Dwyer and Patel 68).

Umrao Jaan who dreams of everlasting love corresponding its ecstasy, is devastated and is shattered when Nawab Sultan chooses to marry a girl of his mother's choice. The revelation to her sensitive poetic soul that she is fit only to be exploited and is fetished to become a victim of the desires of the male gaze rather than having access to espousal respectability, makes her defiant. Aware that her physical purity is tarnished and that she is bound by her body all along, she gets ready to be set free through her body. Umrao Jaan realizes that she's merely an appendage to the man, the wielder of power. Hence Umrao with an air of defiance in her elopes with Faiz Ali, one of her patrons from Farrukhabad. Faiz Ali has not only been generous towards her but had made her feel like the mistress of her own fate. She is, no doubt, touched by his love and concern for her. However, it is coupled with a purpose to have a sense of freedom, which lures her to elope with him, thus rebelling against the tenets of the *kotha* entrapment. This act is like severing the umbilical chord from her very oppressive existence as an object d'art of the male gaze. Her rebelliousness is not so much as a transgression against Khanum's authority and the *chowk* culture of the prostitutes; it rather, has a special significance as an urge to define a new relationship with her ownself. Even when she is separated from Faiz Ali, as he being a bandit the police apprehends him and he is finally shot, she moves on to establish her own *kotha* in Kanpur. This establishment is more an assertion of her selfhood besides being a source of a livelihood. It leads her to a situation, which signifies, "the ability to see and describe one's own reality. It is a significant step in the long process of self recovery though it is only a beginning." (Hooks 25).

Umrao internalizes the idea that develops her to give a comprehensive understanding of her own reality. Exploited earlier by those representing the power of patriarchy on account of her state of a being a female, be it Dilawar Khan or Khanum, she realizes that the hegemony continues being an oppressive one. The realization that dawns on her is that she could break the pattern of domination. She continues with the very profession of dancing and singing, which had earlier oppressed her but now becomes instrumental in liberating her. She becomes a feminist in the sense as Michele Le Doeuff defines "feminist is a woman who does not allow anyone to think in her place". (quoted in Kemp and Squires 142). She does all the thinking for herself and charts out her own destination. She enjoys being her own mistress in her independent set up with her economic self-reliance and a sense of self-defined identity.

Umrao even has a coincidental meeting with her ex-lover Nawab Sultan during this period, when she gets invited by his *Begum Sahiba* (Ramdei) on her son's birthday for an exclusive *mujra* (dance performance) for the females of the household. In the ancient times, the dramas called *Rupakas* were enacted which had sub types called *prakarna*. In these dramas, it was said that the heroine might be of two kinds, the highborn wife of the hero or the lowborn courtesan. Highborn women were supposed to remain indoors and the courtesan outside. It was affirmed that the two should never meet. However gradual changes were introduced in these dramas for the variable characteristics of the heroines.

"The *prakarna* became of three kinds: *Suddha* with the wife as heroine, *Vikrata*, with the courtesan and *Sankirma* with both. This mixed variety (*Sankirma*) was supposed to be about the rogues". (Gupta Chandra Bhan 116).

Umrao however is unaware of the real identity of Begum Sahiba, who is a beautiful woman with a straight nose and mouth like a pink rosebud is Nawab Sultan's wife. Umrao Jaan takes a liking to her as she notices that Begum Sahiba knew how to combine decorum with utter lack of formality and dignity which was so becoming of her. Both Begum Sahiba and Umrao Jaan develop an instant rapport and even recognise each other as the long parted friends who had a shared common features of togetherness when they were both kidnapped by their oppressor and Umrao Jaan then Ameeran was sold off. Begum Sahiba, then Ram Dei, was sold to the senior Begum, the mother of Nawab Sultan whom she eventually married. Thus Ram Dei got the 'kothi' (Haveli) and Ameeran got 'kotha' (house of courtesan). Their positions were an honest appraisal as a twist of their own condition in this society which permeably leads people out of logic. Nawab Sultan who had been away from the house for a couple of days meanwhile arrives then and is startled to see Umrao Jaan in his house. They both feign ignorance of each other when introduced by Begum Sahiba but pose old familiarity of sorts when her performance begins. This is perhaps to accord respect to Begum Sahiba who was so lovely and adorable to both of them. They both meet as strangers but their silent gaze is made quite eloquent by the strategic positioning of all three in the mise en scene, a scene beautifully portrayed by the director with great sensitivity. Two lamps with green shades were placed in front of the carpet, with Begum Sahiba in the center and Umrao Jaan on her left side and her husband on the right. Nawab Sultan gives surreptitious looks and Umrao Jaan returns the gaze from the corner of her eye. Although neither of them say a word, their eyes speak volumes. All the lovers plaints, grievances secrets and allusions get conveyed to each other by their glances. The gazal rendered by Umrao Jaan is laden with soul stirring words of her loneliness. The verse "Umar ka lamba safar tay kiya tanha humne" translated "the sojourn of life has been traversed by me all alone without a befitting companion by my side", conveys to Nawab Sultan her feelings of being left alone, desolate on the cross roads of life. She seems vulnerable in her act of performance, yet she articulates her strength to go through life with all the adversities she has to face. A certain subtleness in their understanding coupled with the equipoise of gender relations between them, helps them in mutually understanding the stark facts of human existence. She deciphers the gaze of Nawab Sultan as that of a real beloved but at the same time she realizes that it was wise to show restraint lest her childhood friend Ram Dei takes cognizance of their relationship and notices it and feels hurt inadvertantly. However Begum Sahiba realizes as she perceives intuitively that she is the lost love of Nawab Sultan but as a mark of respect to both, she dismisses it off gracefully. Moreover, culturally too the acceptance of the courtesan in the society and the lives of Nawabs was the lot of the Begums too.

We live in a world in which, gender constitutes social relations and in which gender is also a relation of domination. As a result therefore, "both men's and women's understanding of anatomy, biology, embodiedness, sexuality and reproduction is partially rooted in belief which reflects and justify pre-existing gender relations". (Flax 177). Gender relations are beautifully conceived in the relationship of Umrao Jaan and Nawab Sultan with reference to the fact that she is just not an erotic persona of his male gaze like she was to the other patrons, but he has loved her with all the sincerity of a poet's heart. However, he could not transcend the barrier and defy the norms of the society to own up the true love of his life Umrao by getting married to her. From the perspective of social relations, men and women are both prisoners of gender, although in highly differentiated but interrelated ways. "That men appear to be (in many cases) the wardens or at least the trustees within a social whole, should not blind us as they too, are governed by the rites of gender". (Flax 175). Emotions in gender relations will always remain and no class caste conflict can defy the power of love. At times, the film comes across as a stereotypical tale of any courtesan film as, "the romanticized apostrophe to woman as the pathetic, impossibly innocent 'other' waiting to be rescued from the penumbra of social opprobrium". (Rao To be 242). According to Yash Chopra a sensitive filmmaker, "between the creator and his creation stands only his perception of the world around him. This is what each director has to depend on; the rest is *shringaar*, a decoration an embellishment to his presentation of such a love and no more". (Chopra 8).

However, "every group, every culture living by its own code, its standards and value carries on a ceaseless campaign to perpetuate them, every culture is partly its own cheer group–which is probably a condition of survival". (Pole 237). Suffering, however, gives Umrao insight and integrity. She has now the confidence to face and catch up with her past. She realizes that both her present and past comprised two different worlds. She does not actually belong to the traditional family of courtesans (*tawaifs*). Yet she gets apprehensive about the fact whether her family would care to mix with a courtesan like her.

Umrao goes to Faizabad, her childhood hometown wherein her roots lie, on an invitation to sing. She, however, does not even remember where her parent's house was but she could recall that it was outside marquee under an old tamarind tree somewhere very close to where she was performing. Large motley of crowd, both men and women has gathered there. The men are seated facing her and the women are seated behind the screens. There is something about the place that haunts her and makes her reflective while rendering the *ghazal* for the people gathered there. She sings a befitting *ghazal* "Yeh kya jagah hai doston, ye kaunsa dayar hai" translated as, "what is out here that is so specific which allures me to be here". After she finishes her performance, she peers in at the door of a house across, which she intuitively senses as her childhood home.

It connects the figure of the dancer with rendition of the ghazal which has a motivated shot in the ambience and the place it is set in. It overplays the notion of rigid, social cultural control from which Umrao cannot find respite. She comes to accept the uprootedness of herself and has to accept the ways of being she was thrown into. There is a quasi-mythological dimension to it. She is like the Karna of the Mahabharta who has no birthright to her own home. She is brought up like him in a set up away from where she does find herself but loses out on her right rather her birthright to be an acknowledged member of the family. The most complex use of dance and gazal is made by combining the aesthetics of the image to show a shrewd twist in the plot, though subtly. The choreography of the dance on gazal presents a particular challenge for technical mastery and organization of disparate elements. It involves the moving character of Umrao who's trying to reach out to her family.

Umrao Jaan feels dazed as if in a trance, her feet dragged her, making her walk unsteadily as if she was drunk on reaching the house. There is a purdah, a curtain kind of partition, kind of device symbolically used to separate the private sphere from the public sphere, basically to separate the males and females as if to safeguard the contamination of the purity of the female sphere. She is made to wait in the outer courtyard as an outsider or an outcaste. She wants to rush inside and has an urge to throw herself at her mother and clasp her to reach out to a source of maternal kinship. It is then that an old lady comes and stands in front of the purdah and asks her name. She feels like telling her, her real name Ameeran yet she replies that her name is Umrao Jaan. However on being asked whether she was from Lucknow and belonged to a family of courtesans, she just can't contain herself nor hold back her tears and confesses that she was born there and was rooted exactly where she stood. The lady standing across the curtain feels assured and certain that she was her own daughter Ameeran. She shrieks at the discovery with excitement and clasps her in a tight embrace moving across the purdah and they both weep aloud, portraying a moment of female bonding that is so therapeutic and enervating.

The scene has been tackled with a rare sensitivity, which evokes a sense of pathos that signifies an androgynous directorial touch as he captures the feminine sensibility so palpably. Meanwhile her brother arrives and Umrao is accused by him for bringing shame on the family and is castigated for enhancing the family's reputation negatively, in the novel. However, in the film, the director very effectively brings a rare touch of dispassionate feeling shown by her brother towards her. He accentuates the effect by showing not a single exchange of word shared between the brother and sister. He uses the device of flashback where Umrao as Ameeran in her childhood is shown caring for her brother with a maternal instinct and teaching him to learn talking. The director very subtly yet pointedly conveys that Umrao Jaan as a child prepares her younger brother to face the world by helping him to develop his communicative skill. It reflects upon their childhood days where she is shown touching his tongue to mould it into forming words so that he can speak clearly. On the other hand, in the present time he quietly moves away from Umrao, taking his mother along with him, leaving her desolate to face the world alone. Her brother behaves like an heir of his predecessors who lead life according to patriarchal strictures. "Essentialism in the end always plays into the hands of those who want women to conform to predefined patterns." (Moi 127). It is after all patriarchy, which has, "always believed in a true female/feminine nature. The biologism and essentialism lurk behind the desire to bestow feminine virtues on all female bodies". (Moi 127).

Umrao Jaan's mother could have been the anchor of Umrao's life, a bridge to her past life to help her comeback again to her roots, but she gives in without a protest of word with total submission to her son's will. She is unwittingly under the grip of patriarchy represented by her son and is declined the authority to care for her daughter. The scene lingers on in one's psyche as Umrao looks at her reflection in the mirror and the doubling of her image metaphorically symbolizes her identity as an alienated persona. Indeed, mirror imagery is abundant in the courtesan film, giving, "an added dimension to the metaphor of woman as essentially 'split' (virgin/whore) and as the looking glass held up to man as women have served all these centuries as looking glasses for men". (Garga 271). The camera looks into the audience in the last scene as if it could imbibe the sense of hurt in Umrao's bruised psyche. One can feel a certain sense of discomfort, with the depiction of Umrao's battered psyche, conveying a disquieting loss of coherence in the last scene. Umrao is left alone desolate by her own family, with an air of callous indifference to chart out the journey of her life, all over again.

The entire dynamics of circumstances surrounding Umrao progress to articulate the system that she is trapped in. She seems to be hoping for an escape from it but the futility of her attempt is portrayed. The director's sensitive attention to the implications and nuance of such a delicate situation is aesthetically presented in an evocative *mise en scene*. Umrao's passionate urge to get connected with the family and her seeking the fold of her mother's refuge, symbolically, conveys her desire to get back into her womb in order to be protected. Her platitudinous conversation with her mother pleases her immensely; yet, once the relationship is snapped off, the same can't be refurbished ideologically. Both the reader and spectator recognize the genesis of such limitations, even as her brother is overtly symbolic of a patriarchal regimentation.

Technically and visually, the film is outstanding and the artistic eye of the sensitive director Muzaffar Ali takes into account every minute detail including the ambience of a *kotha* set up with a genuine setting used to heighten the environment of aesthetic authenticity. Ali shows an understanding in the symbolic use of space and understood the importance of visual art and organizes his shots well. Muzzaffar Ali takes care in projecting other courtesans and their elegant boudoirs. His art director Bansi Chandragupta specially designed the sets, costumes and jewellery. Workers were sent to Calcutta to learn the art of jewellery making and costume design. Bismillah Jaan Khanum's daughter enacted by Prema Narayana wore his own mother's real life jewellery for authenticity. Some of the costumes worn by Umrao Jaan, Bismillah Jaan and other courtesans in the film are almost hundred years old. There is, however, a historical and cultural background to the whole story and for Muzzafar Ali, this film is a confirmation of his cherished desires. It is like filling a void of bygone aristocracy and trace of his ancestry as one who has grown up amongst the ruminants. The song *'in aankhon ki masti ke"* was picturised in Lucknow in the palatial *Baradari* (a room with 12 doors) with great authenticity. To lend a flavour of genuine ambience he even contacted descendants of the Nawabs' families to be part of the mehfil for the song, *"in aankhon ke masti ke"*-a fact which was corroborated by Nawab Jafar Mir Abdullah, a direct descendant of Nawab Asaf ud Daula in an interview with me.

Dr. Yogesh Parvin, a historian from Lucknow, who was also the coordinator in the making of the film *'Umrao Jaan'*, also commended Muzzaffar Ali's commitment to authenticity. Muzzaffar Ali, during the making of the film consulted him and crosschecked whether Umrao Jaan was a fictitious character of Rusva's novel. However they both went to the *kabrastan* (cemetry) where Umrao was buried. There was an epitaph on which is inscribed, *"Umrao jisse farishtey farsh se arsh ki aur lene aaye"* translated as "Umrao for whom the angels descended from heaven to liberate her and fetch her from this earthly existence to the celestial heaven".

For Umrao Jaan to get her biography written by Mirza Ruswa, was perhaps an emanicipatory promise or just an essentialist illusion. It signifies a process to understand her or reflect back upon her sojourn of life. Though Umrao herself had acquired fame for her composition of poetry yet, by urging Ruswa to write her biography, she perhaps entangles herself in the phallocentric discourse. Through it one recognizes the trajectory of the inner recesses of her thought processes and in listening to her story, he becomes a close friend and he dons the role of being a comrade who shows a true understanding and friendship. In getting her biography written by Mirza Ruswa, she presents herself as a woman of remarkable will power, who is forced to find not only her destiny but also finds her own voice as a poetess and courtesan and indirectly as a writer. Since her conservations with Mirza Rusva are a kind of personal narrative, her biography becomes a collaborative product of both Rusva and her own discourse of life.

In the novel she goes on narrating various anecdotes of her life to Rusva Mirza, and refers to instances of an affair with an attorney, her adoption of a girl child and an affair with a rich younger patron too. However, she confides to Rusva Mirza that women's real life lasts as long as her youth and wishes that life should end when youth ends. She also confesses that no man in his senses would fall in love with a courtesan because he knows that a courtesan belongs to no one. She, in fact, says a few words of advice to women of her profession as to be never under the delusion that anyone will ever love them truly. She justifies the gift of true love eluding a courtesan because of her own fickle-mindedness towards her lovers. One can actually accredit Umrao Jaan for having admitted such an inconsistency on the part of the courtesan or perhaps it is redefined by Mirza Rusva's own perspective about courtesans while writing her biography. Muzaffar Ali however sensitively wriggles out of such a situation by ending the movie where Umrao Jaan is left desolate and alone by her brother and mother, to face life on her own.

Umrao Jaan besides being rated, "as the quintessential courtesan film of the Indian cinema" tackles gender relations with a rare insight. (Gokulsing and Dissanayake 101). Umrao is portrayed as a victim of men's lust and she evokes the viewer's pity. Through, "the spectator text relation, the spectator feels positioned alongside that characters' subjectivity and so identifies with that character". (Hayward 375). Muzaffar Ali depicts not only the Lucknow culture visually with a certain nostalgia but took care of heighten it alongwith the beautiful Urdu lyrics of Shahryar our topmost poet today, visually along with the lilting music the timbre quality of set by Khayyam. The use of Urdu language in the dialogues written by Shama Zaidi, Javed Siddiqi and Muzaffar Ali himself is used as the part of the Hindi Muslim unity also which is so symbolic of Lucknow culture and the Indian cinema too. Muzaffar Ali did not use the 19th century Urdu poetry but the ghazal form was used in the film with a more contemporary style. According to Maithili Rao, "this literary sleight of hand however in no way diminished the haunting quality of the film's music". (111). The beautiful photography of Pravin Bhatt, lyrics of Shahryar, music of Khayyam, the authentic sets created by Bansi Chandra Gupta and Manzoor, costumes designed by Subhashini Ali and the choreography of dances so effectively done by the masters Gopi Krishna and Kumudini Lakhia raises the film to the rich genre of a courtesan film that has ingredients of an art film. It has "a luxurious vein of melancholy, druggingly sensuous music, runs through the film that made Ali famous" (Rao Maithili Rebels 111).

The film has been acclaimed as the best narrative of the life and culture of Lucknow. Like in the novel we get in the film too, a flavour of all that was Lucknow with its tradition of refined poetry and music and the ways of life of its citizens, their relationships, in a fascinating manner. Each person that Umrao encounters leaves an imprint on her life and contributes to her understanding of her times. Each person is not only a colourful character but also a type, a representative of the social class. It is through her poetry and *ghazals* that these experiences and encounters are transcended and translated into expressions of beauty. Umrao Jaan yet plays on the popular theme of distress, isolation and pain hidden under the outward veneer of grandeur of a courtesan who is at once an object of lust, awe and compassion. Though critics came down heavily on the film, "for its extravagance and its songs and dances which tend to detract from the main theme", yet, the audience voted it as a box office success. (Garga 266). Nonetheless, 'Umrao Jaan' is definitely a woman's story set in a complex narrative that conceptualizes as a cinematic spectacle to haunt the Indian consciousness, since courtesans occupy a special, though a separate place, in Indian culture and consciousness.

RUDALI

'*Rudali*' meaning 'The Mourner' was released in 1992. The film is about a social ritual, which evolves into a profession for the main female protagonist, leading to her self-empowerment. It is imbibed from a concept that is "culture and gender specific practice that can be seen in India of a professional mourning woman called 'Rudali' ". (Chatterji Shoma Sound 183). The film is based on the short story written by Mahasweta Devi in Bengali and the story has been adapted for the celluloid as a film by Kalpana Lajmi. Though the profession is dying out, its pathos comes across strongly in the film 'Rudali'. Kalpana Lajmi also happens to be the niece of the great director, actor Guru Dutt, a known sensitive *auteur*. Kalpana Lajmi had been making documentaries and television serials before she started making films. She had been a discernible filmmaker and was appreciated for her directorial venture in *'Ek Pal'* (One moment) in 1986 before she made *'Rudali'*. The film is a proof of her desire to paint, "for the first time in Indian cinema, a completely different portrait of an Indian woman, who is capable of expressing her sexuality without regret." (Thorval 205).

With 'Rudali', Lajmi established herself as the filmmaker of meaningful cinema who proposes to espouse woman's cause. The way a female director portrays the lives and experience of women from her own perspective, needs to be looked into. In fact, it is always indisputably argued that even the most liberal minded and well meaning of the male directors in India, "still display some residual patriarchal leanings." (Gokulsing and Dissanayake 181). So it is interesting to examine how a woman filmmaker explores the complexity in relationships. Lajmi conceives through cinematic narrative, an adaptation of the story by Mahasweta Devi of a bitter lonely woman oppressed and beleaguered by social customs in a most effective manner. Hence the choice of this film is one of the strategies to see a work of literary art by a woman writer adapted for cinematic representation by another woman, with a remarkably sensitised perspective that is grounded in a female sensibility. The question of women's self-expression and communication of literary content and values may be surmised as an, "act of re-vision", a term borrowed from Adrienne Rich. "Re-vision is an act of survival, refers to the project of reclaiming vision of seeing difference differently". (quoted in De Lauretis Aesthetics 34).

Mahasweta Devi shies away from being labelled as a feminist herself. She sets the story against an exploitative system and the issue is that of woman's survival. "Rudali is about 'how to survive' bread and mouth. It is very important in my story. The whole system is exposed through this. I write as a writer, not as a woman," said Mahasweta Devi in an interview to Anjum Katyal.[6] (Devi and Ganguli 116). Mahasweta Devi has been widely acknowledged as one of India's foremost writers and has won recognition in the form of Sahitya Academy award in 1979, and the Jnanpith Award in 1996. Padamshree has also been bestowed on her in 1996 for her activist work amongst tribal communities. In fact, Mahasweta Devi herself claims that her work as a journalist, creative writer and activist overlap. Spivak feels that Mahasweta Devi's writing and her activism reflect one another; they are precisely, "a folding back upon one another's reflection in the rooted sense". (Spivak Imaginary preface). Devi sees her story 'Rudali' in the context as an integrated part of her activism, which finds expression as a piece of fiction.

The text of '*Rudali*' perceives an evolution or a metamorphosis polemical as the central characterization of the female protagonist Sanichari. However, at the end of the story she emerges as better equipped to adapt, survive and manipulate the system that she is trapped in. A subaltern, her life has not been a benevolent one at all as she's been battered by the system. The term "subaltern", according to the definition provided by scholars, "denotes a people defined by their subordination in terms of class, caste, gender, race, religion, and so on". (Bhatia 8). A major concern of Mahasweta's text is to establish itself as an articulation of the muted discourse reality of subaltern voices and not fiction. According to Spivak, subalterns are non-elite or subordinated groups. They are,

> "at the regional and local levels, the dominant, (indigenous groups)… if belonging to social strata hierarchically inferior to those of the dominant all Indian groups acted in the interests of the latter and not in conformity to interest corresponding to their own social being". (Spivak Can the 284-85).

Mahasweta Devi tries to situate Sanichari in a socio-economic context by employing the method of historicization, showing her as a part of the community suffering on accounts of its economic backwardness. Her multi-stranded agenda in writing a work like "*Rudali*" is an exposition of the class/caste conflict. It details real characters with real life histories. She shows the harsh face of stark poverty and the threat of exploitation followed by death with all their attendant degradation as targeting the female protagonist, Sanichari. She is born on Saturday or *Sanicharvar*, hence takes her name from that week of the day. She was considered the unfortunate one and doomed to suffer as a result of it. Her father died at her birth and as a child she had been abandoned by her mother, who had run away with an itinerant troupe of performers of *nautanki*. She belonged to the low caste of *ganju* and suffers because of her being low born. Right from the beginning, she is historicized by the author who emphasises that her problems are those which are common to people of her class, caste and gender. The events in Sanichari's life one after the other show her as a victim of an oppressive system. In fact, she's a stereotypical victim of society. She loses her brother-in-law, sister-in-law, mother-in-law and husband one by one. She loses her only son eleven years later and with every loss that she has suffered, she gets increasingly clammed up, wherewith she cannot give vent to her suppressed rage at human and divine injustice.

Sanichari, always blamed for the misfortunes, thus suffers at the hands of her mother-in-law through the worst form of the patriarchal malpractice perpetuated by her. Her husband died of cholera after drinking contaminated milk donated to the Shiva idol by the rich landlords and Majahans. Since he passes away in the next Tohri village, she had to pay for his last rituals to the priest of that village. She is made to pay again for his last rites to the priest of her own village Tohad as he taunts her and scoffs at her that such a 'kriya' (last rituals)[7] of her husband couldn't be performed by a neighbouring village's priest. Hence to appease him she repeats the offerings as a result of which she is placed under debt. She leads a hard tough existence, as her husband was the only provider in her household. She is subjected both to religious and economic exploitation, thus. Sanichari does not cry even when her husband dies. She is however shown breaking her bangles just purchased by her at the fair, evoking a symbolic state of her widowhood. Impoverished, she fails to react and the whole village looks upon her as a cold and unfeeling insensitive woman, incapable of crying. Meanwhile, she becomes friends with Bhikni who comes as a 'rudali' to the village and shows inordinate caring towards her. Sanichari invites her to share her little house as she would give her company and Bhikni would get a shelter to stay in. In the process, what emerges is the closeness between them and both Sanichari and Bhikni develop a genuine female bonding and become friends. In such a state, they shake loose from the male gendered moorings, basking in their female friendship. "The image of these two friends making their quick business like preparations and striding off to work side by side is perhaps unique in Indian literature and vividly captures the essence of an unusual relationship". (Devi and Ganguli 21).

However, in the adaptation of the story for the celluloid, Kalpana Lajmi, the director makes changes, which can be accorded to her own shift-in perceptions. To Mahasweta Devi, her text is a part of the discourse of the class/caste conflict, rather than simply, a gender question but Kalpana Lajmi adds a gendered perspective to the story also. The story in the text explicates various strategies of survival employed by the subaltern Sanichari as an individual and as a part of the community. The situations of her life, her solitude, her companionship with Bhikni and her finally adopting the profession of *rudali* and the realization that life has to go on inspite of all odds, gives her the strength to survive. A major concern, however, with Lajmi, is also to keep clear of overtly feminist thematic overtures. Her film is a departure from feminist rhetoric which can be almost as tyrannical in its stereotyping as the old feminine variety. Rather in her own inimitable style, "she brings an operative flourish to a resonant narrative that details the arid life and dried up dreams, like that of Bertolt Brecht's Mother Courage". (Vasudev Frames 254).

Lajmi's main focus of interest has been Sanichairi, who gets constituted as a set of meanings through the process of cinematic signification. 'Rudali' is a woman's film though not so in the Indian traditional conventional sense. Yet the cultural rootedness is of the female protagonist. She closely adheres to the cultural ideology of the ages it was set up in and is steeped in it. There are no romantic clichés in Mahasweta Devi's story. Mahasweta Devi tells the story of Sanichari who becomes a *rudali* going through the arid journey of her life. Sanichari was a poor lower caste woman who lives alone in her house in a village of Rajashthan. The symbolic metaphor of dry, sandy area unnavigated, unwatered, is symbolic of the sterility prevailing in her life. The water in the form of flow of tears through her eyes as a *rudali*, offers a metaphorical redemption as a person. She emerges from a weak exploited, impoverished woman to a strong matriarch as the provider and decision maker in her home more strongly than before. Her relationships through the journey of her arid life, her friendship, her aborted love affair follow through the various meanderings of her hopeless life, wherewith she has reconciled to the hopelessness of her situation.

Sanichari's lyrical talent for singing is an aspect and a mode of showing that there is more to her than brown warm alluring eyes, which makes her an object of eroticism for the male gaze. The basic sense of warmth in her temperament and her kindness and generosity gets shrivelled and dried up within her due to her compulsive circumstances. Her suppressed rage gushes out like a geyser, an outflow of her inner self, in the climax scene when she becomes a *rudali*. It is then that the true characteristics of her temperament also emerge to show that she is a person who has an indepth perception.

The characterization of Bhikni is also different in the story and is altered by Kalpana Lajmi in the film. Kalpana Lajmi, rather patronizes and romanticizes these women at some point. In the novel they are two withered women, who have borne the ravages of time during their youth, sharing their anxiety for mutual experiences. They both get together and ruminate over the times bygone. According to Judith Mayne,

> "one of the most basic connections between women's experience in any culture and women's experience in film is precisely the relationship of spectator and spectacles since women are spectacles in their everyday lives". (Citron *et. al.* 115).

Hence, there is something about coming to terms within, from the perspective of what it means to be an object of spectacle. Lajmi makes the film in a manner that a woman viewer can identify with the trauma of her female protagonist. She decodes the socio-moral codes that have been used and carried along as a part of patriarchal system and which have been internalized by the women for ages. "Most Indian films are about the exotica where the real people are missing. The novel is a landscape of mind whereas the film is a landscape of action, with dialogues. Since the film medium is larger than life". (Malhotra 3). However, it is necessary to see works of literature from a gender sensitized orientation and not to adhere simply to a critical literally tradition laid down by stalwarts of criticism. For the woman, "film is dialectical experience in a way that never was and never will be for a man under patriarchy". (Thornham Feminist Film 115). It is hence necessary that a gender sensitive approach, which is more humanistic, be adopted. It leads to a better perception of the dilemmas and paradoxes posed before, created out of fact by the fiction. The adaptability of such works of literature for the celluloid brings in a different point of departure and prevents male misreading. What it does above all, "is to reverse the usual situation in which the perspective of a male critic is answered to be sexually neutral while a feminist reading is seen as a case of special pleading and an attempt to force the text into a pre-determined mould" (Culler 49).

In Mahasweta's story, Sanichari and Bhikni are supposed to be childhood playmates who rediscover each other as ageing lonely women when they meet each other accidentally at a fair. However, in the film Kalpana Lajmi adapts their relationship as a mother-daughter duo with Sanichari unaware of the fact that Bhikni is her mother until Bhikini dies. In Mahasweta's story the character Bhikni is like "a major fictional strategy used by the author to inflict a whole gamut of signification" (Devi and Ganguli 19). In Mahasweta's story, they both meet at the local *mela* for the first time. Sanichari has lost every member of her family, her husband, her son and her daughter-in-law. She is free of all other ties and relationships. Bhikni is also abandoned by her son and hence has left her home but with no plans and nowhere to go. Both of them strike a friendship, rather a female bonding. Compared to Sanichari, Bhikni is more of a dare devil type and rebellious. When her son refuses to help her pay off the debt, she had incurred in order to arrange his marriage, she sells her goats and takes to begging as means of livelihood.

In the story, they both become *rudalis*, women who act as professional mourners at the death of the rich. Being a '*rudali*' is a profession, wherein an organized band of women comprised of the marginalized and outcaste women, put a solemn act at the death of the rich where they rant loud cries to portray grief and get paid for it. In the story the social acceptability of the profession of *rudali* is high and is not a matter of a concern, even when outcastes like prostitutes do it too. It is rather looked upon as a job. In the story both Sanichari and Bhikni work as a professional team of *rudalis*. Bhikni who is more positive and adaptable settles to the idea of their becoming a *rudali* whole-heartedly. They shake loose from the male gendered moorings and together, they intervene to subvert the solemn hypocrisy of an occasion, which is a metonymy for a patriarchal exploitative system. What the author is in effect, doing is transforming a woman intensive casual labour sector into an organized sector– a conceptual twist significant in feminist terms, in terms of financial agency. In the story Dulan initiates Sanichari for taking up the job and quietens her misgivings about being a *rudali*. In the film, it is Bhikni who prepares her for it. Bhikni is already a *rudali*, when she comes to the village as she is hired to cry at the death of the local landlord Ram Avtar who is gravely ill and is on his deathbed. Bhikini stays with Sanichari while she is waiting for the landlord to die. The two women become close and Sanichari unburdens her soul to Bhikini, something that she has never done with anyone, before.

In a flashback, she tells her all about her life and sufferings. She tells her that she cannot remember ever having shed tears. Bhikini who is a professional mourner is amazed at Sanichari's inability to shed tears but declares that she will make her a '*rudali*' yet. She makes her realize that such a profession would not only empower her, be a source of her livelihood but give her strength to fortify herself against their oppressors who include landlords, mahajans and all high caste born men. She is, in fact, quite a contrast to Sanichari in appearance too. In the story, the author does not individuate Sanichari. Her physical appearance is not an attractive one, nor is she shown psychologically sensitized in the way Bhikni is shown in the film. In fact, Mahasweta Devi de-sentimentalises her text and is concerned with the problematic of the survival as a more deep-rooted issue. Bhikni is also supposed to be plain looking and both are supposed to look like ordinary tribal females. Dimple who enacts the role of Sanichari, is basically shown attractive in places where she catches the young landlord's eye in her youth. However, she's shown ageing as a middle-aged woman in the film. During that process, harsh reality of poverty and tragedy in her life are shown to take a toll on her beauty as she dispenses away with the adornments too. She looks too plain sans make up, sans jewellery. To adorn herself is not just a thing of *shingar* for Indian woman's feminine attribute, but is considered to be her sacred duty too.

In the *Ramayana* too, when Sita takes off her jewellery to accompany Rama to the forest, the palace women do not permit her to do so. She is advised that as a married woman she must not give up flowers, jewellery, cosmetics and bright clothes. Even a poor woman is expected to make herself pretty in the Indian culture in whatever way she can afford and bright bangles, silver anklets and *kajrari* nayan i.e. kohled black eyes, comprise her *shringara* (adornments)[8].

> Bhikni on the other hand, supposed to be Sanchiari's mother in the film who had abandoned her as a child, is shown to be still a luscious beauty. With all the adornments of jewellery and natural glowing looks, her beauty is highlighted all the more. In fact Kalpana Lajmi through the two contrasting characters displays two kinds of female sexuality. Raakhe as Bhikni is shown as sensuous in her appearance and outlook. She's not the essential melodramatic self-effacing stereotype of the Indian woman. She forsakes her motherhood for the love of wandering adventure and for the lures of good life. Sanichari, on the other hand, represents the prototype of the stereotypical sacrificing Indian woman. She does not forsake motherhood, even for the promise of a rosy life and romance with the younger landlord. She lets the opportunity bypass her, fearing the threat of a social scandal and stigma. In fact, by projecting both Dimple and Raakhe as two diametrically opposite women in their attitudes to life, Kalpana Lajmi shows *Rudali* as, "a ballad that mourns the tragic out come of these contrary impulses. There is an underlying play on existential binaries– the lure of nomadic existence and the rooted ness in one's own soil". (Vasudev Frames 254).

Bhikni, even as the mother figure is shown in stark contrast to Sanchari's enforced self-abnegation with her spirit of gay abandon and in animated pursuit of pleasures. She is yet led onto a life, which is not of fulfilment as she has to take up the job of a rudali to earn a livelihood eventually to survive. In crying over the death of the rich, she degrades herself for her existence, though she tells Sanichari that she uses it to empower herself. The camera captures the look on her face, which is meant to prove that she might be the incarnation of satanic evil. She has a joyful demeanour and devil may care attitude about life. She carries no baggage of being anybody's wife, mother or daughter-in-law. She is shorn of all roles, which burden the self-imaging of a person. She is self assertive, unlike the self effacing Sanichari. She is no embodiment of a woman's noble sacrifice. However, she is shown to be fond of domestic work in Mahasweta's story. Indulging in it, she finds happiness and in caring for Sanichari too. It is perhaps on account of her guilt complex of a lost motherhood that she showers affection on Sanichari which is beautifully evoked in the scene in a courtyard of Sanichari's house. At dusk, Bhikni cooks for Sanichari and makes hot *chappaties* on the *chullah* and serves her. A caring like attitude this was never a part of Sanichari's fate as she had been fending for herself since her childhood. After dinner, they both lie in their charpoys together and Bhikni oils and combs Sanichari's hair with loving care. She lulls her to sleep in her lap as a mother rocks her baby to sleep. For the first time, Sanichari is shown to be vulnerable with a cocooned childlike innocence, basking in the warmth of love, and not careworn as the director generally shows her. Her warmth and care for Sanichari forges them in a stronger bond which is so humane. Bhikni herself looks very vulnerable with an equally childlike Sanichari in her lap looking into the camera sensitively. It may be interpreted as an impalpable mutation, a feeling to which hitherto both of them were oblivious, yet it is a bond forged as an expression of their humanness. Here the director shows an idealistic vision of human yearnings, which touches what is noble in our souls.

However, Bhikini has to leave the next day, as the man for whom she had abandoned Sanichari as a child, was on his death bed breathing his last. She promises, though, to Sanichari that she would come back soon but she does not. Sanichari learns later about Bhikni's death and also that Bhikini was in fact her own long lost mother, who had abandoned her as a child. Meanwhile, the ailing landlord Ram Avtar passes away for whose mourning Bhikini had come to the village as a *rudali*. When the message for a *rudali* to weep at landlord's death reaches Sanichari's house, where Bhikni had been residing with her, it transforms Sanichari into a *rudali*. She herself goes as a *rudali*, as a replacement of Bhikini. Her sorrows, which were held in check, just gush away surging forth torrentially. In a daze, Sanichari stands paralysed as she realizes the weight of her loss on Bhikni's death, which ironically, facilitates her transition to the state of being a *rudali*.

Mahasweta Devi feels that her story, "could especially be identified with women in anyway since gender is subsumed into the discourse of class. To emphasize the former at the expense of the latter is a denial of history as she sees it" (Devi and Katyal 17). Since Mahasweta Devi is an activist for the tribal cause, her writing is an instrument or a weapon in her battle against their exploitation. At the level of social consciousness, she is up against the male/capitalist/traditional order. The *Vedas* and *Dharmashastras* have laid down a set of rules, the observance of which results in the maintenance and well being of a social order with fixed castes and sub-castes and the duties and roles allotted accordingly to maintain that social order. Every individual, whether a male or a female, according to such an ideology has to play his/her role steadfastly as a vocation of *Dharma* depending on the set of rules the caste he/she is born into. The codified area, which seems so well defined, entraps the mindset of both males and females to confirm within the predetermined circle a class/caste as a traditional cultural norm. The structure upon which the Indian society rests, has its roots in ancient India, hence the society is based on the caste system. The transgression of such a system leads to caste and class conflict. In the hegemony of the caste system, at the top hierarchy is the *brahmin* and bottom is a *shudra*. The class conflict is established accordingly between the haves and have-nots. As a result of the caste discrimination, class hierarchy also sets in the name of order or balance to be maintained in a society, so that at the outset rebellion is suppressed.

Sanichari born in the low caste is as much victimized as any male of her community, according to the original story. However, Kalpana Lajmi highlights that her gender oppresses her still further. Amongst the poor, all exploitation is vertical. Mahasweta Devi shows class solidarity as the norm, both poor men and women of the lower castes and classes are helpful and supportive to each other. Dulan, the male protagonist in Mahasweta's story personifies the same phenomena as a head of the community to which Sanichari belongs. In the story it is the voice of Dulan, the male protagonist which condemns and criticizes the upper classes and highlights their greed, hypocrisy and moral corruption. In the story, Sanichari and her husband are shown as partners working together for the upkeep of their home and livelihood. They are supportive of each other and have mutual understanding towards each other. Sanichari's son Budhwa is also shown as sensitive, thoughtful, gentle and caring towards her and is a genuine source of support of her life when her husband passes away. However, in the film Kalpana Lajmi makes a departure from the storyline. The very tone of the characterization of her husband and son is changed. She has a wastrel of a husband who rather being her equal partner is indifferent to her. Her son is a vagabond given to wanderlust. They both epitomize the values of an oppressive patriarchy, yet she is committed to them.

Lajmi makes such a shift deliberately in the film, making departure from the fictional caricatures of Sanichari's husband and the son with a purpose, to highlight Sanichari's strength. She works hard as a maid in the house of the Thakur to supplement the household income. She feels often muted as she is treated as an inferior commodity both at work and at home.

She's an archetype Indian woman in her placid stoicism, which is vulnerable to all sorts of oppressions, religious, feudal and patriarchal and within a general framework all of these are modes of oppression and collude with each other. In the film, through the flashback device, Sanichari relates her story of misfortune right from her birth onwards to Bhikni. She confesses how she rejected the promised fulfilment of genuine love from her lover for the commitment towards her husband and the family though they are all indifferent to her.

In Mahasweta Devi's story, there is no such hint of a pastoral romance. In the film, the director perhaps wants to highlight and accentuate the 'ray of fate' in the life of Sanichari. She has a point to make that so overridden is Sanichari by her life of misery and so sterile is her life that even her dreams have dried up. She is not ready to accept even the warmth of love extended towards her by the younger Thakur who happens to be village landlord's younger brother. He is however married and has a wife devoted to him. Inspite of that, he is charmed and allured by her deep brown eyes and earthy looks. It is a point cinematically highlighted through camera's eye, which focuses on the actress Dimple's kohled brown eyes as expressing untold profundity and sensualism. Kalpana Lajmi looks at Sanichari through the camera lens of the male's gaze, as to how Sanichari is looked at and viewed by the Thakur. Even when Sanichari walks on the sand, she is viewed through the camera from the high point of camel's back on which Thakur sits and views her. Sanichari herself is aware that the ray of love ensuing from Thakur's love is like a silver lining in her dull mundane loveless existence. It is like an oasis in her arid life. It is a counterfoil to her psyche, which is, as gritty as sand and has almost become a part of the desert's harsh beauty. The younger landlord's attraction for her defines her in terms of her visibility. She carries her self-image as a function of her being for another. It is in fact, a subject/object look "which may be experienced as mutual as a process, a fulfilment in a relationship," (Kaplan Looking xvi) which she has been deprived of ever since her birth. However, Sanichari is so driven by her humdrum existence in her struggle for survival that she lets it pass and rejects the hope of love offered to her. The young landlord undoubtedly is consumed with his own anxieties, which are inevitably intermixed with desire for Sanichari. Though Sanichari herself is not a passive object to such an arousal of the young landlord's desire but she suppresses her passion and resists it to lead a life of austerity. However, she gets a small house bequeathed by the older landlord on the request of his younger brother Gopal Singh, as a reward for the rendition of a song at a gathering in the 'haveli'. In fact her captivating song lends a kind of melodrama; a sense of poignancy to the romance that is so short lived or rather nipped in the bud, which had been a rejuvenating replenishment for her dull existence. She is so used to self denial of herself in going through the grind of her existence that even a hint of excitement, of fulfilment through romance seems unrealistic to her.

Lajmi very effectively creates the ambience to set the tone of promised romance in the rich folk tunes and songs of Rajasthan through the sonorous music of Bhupen Hazarika's music. The trend of basing film music on folk songs reappears with fresh sounds and vigour. That is the strength of folk melodies of any culture in the world. "Hindi films have played a very significant role in the integration of Indian folk music. They have helped to bring together the folk music of different regions into the mainstream". (Gulzar Music 273). People have started recognizing the melodies of different regions, and their cultural images. The backdrop of beautifully filmed Rajasthan with its portions of vibrant and rich landscapes and colourful location lends a very contrasting aura to Sanichari's sterile life.

The story can take a myriad dimensions in the hands of a highly imaginable director. "It can even be romanticized and invested with the vision of a desirable or a lost utopia" (Nandy The Secret 11) which could be recreated. The director's vision expresses a yearning or a desire to reconstitute humanity beyond the trappings of a system, into a homogenized society with a new world order of equations, be it in caste, class or gender. In fact Raj Babbar as the young landlord, is shown capable of being compassionate, unlike his tyrannical hypocritical brother or Sanichari's own husband. Like Dulan in Mahasweta's story, even though, the young landlord is not from the same community as of Sanichari, he speaks to her, as one of her own. There is no aura of authority surrounding him nor does he have any condescending attitude towards Sanichari. Lajmi supports her narrative with dream like visuals of their togetherness and his repudiation of her reserve when she alerts him that she is from the lower caste. The *mise en scene* during the song "*Dil hoom hoom kare, Ghabraye*" translated "my heart goes dizzy and I get apprehensive and feel scared", evokes in its visual form their suppressed fantasies which Sanichari is too apprehensive and scared to live out and fulfil. In fact the state of hopelessness in her life makes her look up to the realm and hope of love also stoically in the eye as she abstains from feeling regaled in it with flourish and ease.

Years later, when they have both grown old, they meet again in the *haveli* on the occasion of the *Thakur's* impending death. She tries to elude him as she had in their youth. Yet, he tries to seek her out for a brief conversation and lets her know that he still admires her. She realizes that she had always put a premium on herself for community's approval or disapproval and rejected the promise of genuine love in life. Trapped as a woman she makes her own history even though she's driven to conditions not of her own choosing. Various issues of psychological and moral value tussle together in the women protagonist consciousness. Lajmi very strongly, invokes a feeling of desperate hopelessness in the condition of a woman, whether it is the Thakur's wife, high born, or that of Sanichari. The state of hopelessness of being a woman overwhelmingly comes through when the former concedes for Sanichari singing in the haveli on her son's nuptial ceremony. In fact, there is a kind of ambiguity in the young landlord

Gopal Singh's relationship with Sanichari. Even though his romantic attempt gets foiled, there is no bitterness or cynicism in his attitude towards her, nor a sense of authoritative attitude, determinism exemplary of the feudalistic forces he is supposed to symbolize. What happens when a male looks at a female and that too when he is hierarchically on the higher status and when his look is reciprocated even though with apprehension, is elaborated here. Just as Gayatri Spivak asked "Can the Subaltern Speak?" (Spivak Can the 271). Ann Kaplan questioned, "Can the Subaltern look?" (Kaplan Looking 4). She herself answers it by saying that "like everything in culture, looking relations are determined by history, tradition, power hierarchies, politics, economics. Mythic or imaginary ideas are in turn closely linked to class politics and economic relations. Looking is power". (Kaplan Looking 4). The Thakur understands that he has the power to look on account of his gender and status and even if Sanichari wants to look back, her class, caste and gender will not let it sustain, so he has to let her go.

Kalpana Lajmi very realistically portrays through such a state of affairs that an ideal sensitive reciprocation of love in the man-woman relationship is the prerogative of the upper classes or between men and women of the same class. In the *Vedic* times, the maid who works in the household was called a '*dasi*' (a servile person). According to the *Natyashastra* such a maid is called, "an '*anya*' heroine. An '*anya*' heroine could be a maiden or a married woman who belongs to another. Love for a maiden or '*anya*' could be represented in connection with the principal or subordinates sentiments but love for the married '*anya*' woman should never figure in a principal sentiment". (Gupta Chandra Bhan 92).

Sanichari's becoming a *rudali* is not so much of a poetic revenge as she trades her tears in an unholy bargain with the oppressive feudal forces, as Mahasweta Devi connotes in her story. It is, in fact, an upsurge of her pent up feelings of a life time. Similarly in the film she collapses, racked by in a paroxysm of grief and pain, as she becomes a *rudali*. Her cry articulates a heart-rending grief, a cry connoting her re-birth, of her very being or her existence. In the film, Lajmi very effectively shows it in the form of a dance, a ritual of crying and ranting performance which Sanichari indulges in as she dances away as a *rudali*. The dance is beautifully choreographed and evokes all the nuances of her birth as a *rudali*. It becomes a metaphor for life through re-birth after death, for life's sustenance and also destruction. In this unique theatrical dance with loud cries ranting all over the place, it creates a well-synchronized mosaic. It is both lyrically haunting and self-explanatory, evoking mourning with complexity, loaded with layered inferences. Actions speak with verbosity and a hypocritical ritual for the sadistic celebration of the dead is created to elevate the status of a dying person, along with music and soulful strains, which elevate the very spirit of Sanichari as a *rudali*. Sanichari's life which has been so full of sorrow, betrayals and the parting, finally snaps the umbilical chord on her rebirth as a *rudali*. "The poignancy of a barren earth mother runs like a lyrical under current through *Rudali*". (Rao Maithili To Be 255). Sanichari achieves the highest level of female independence, which gets manifested on her becoming a *rudali*. It is like an empowerment of Sanichari, which is beautifully evoked by the figures surrounding in flowing dresses, letting her go. It is pertinent to take note that,

> "Dance is a richly polymeric and common occurrence throughout the history of cinema, used for widely different reasons by filmmakers. Dance may be a single image in a shot, a motif, theme, a trope, a recursive figure, a complex configuration or an isotope which integrates itself into narrative programme". (Laing 130).

As a professional mourner, Sanichari draws on her own pain and grief to earn her livelihood as she gives vent to her own sorrows to empower herself. She, who had never shed a tear, sheds tears for the first time in her life and by becoming a *rudali*, does not only earn a way of livelihood but also gets connected to life. Her rejecting the adornments denotes a gesture of protest against the patriarchal norms of feminine adornment and so also her rejecting the love of younger Thakur which could have been a boon for her, and her shrivelled up life, as she rejects and renounces life symbolically. But in a becoming a *rudali*, there is acceptance-acceptance of life, and sorrow, to which she had become indifferent making her stronger to face the worst eventually. By not valorizing her silence, Lajmi refrains from perpetuating an aura of the imagined mystique created earlier.

Sanichari's relationship with Thakur, the younger landlord in not seeing the light of day, was a part of silence. That deliberate error of the rejection of love as Bhikni called it, was a device employed to strengthen Sanicahri as a whole self-assured person. Such apparent denial of self-assertion manifests counter productively in her self-empowerment as a *rudali*. Jn fact, "there are lessons to be learned from other history's of sexual identity, not only the unacknowledged histories of the subaltern sexuality in our own cultural context." (Bharucha 124).

Lajmi tells the story of Mahasweta Devi sans the clichés of popular cinema aesthetically, intersecting with lilting tunes and songs of Bhupen Hazarika. The song sung by him for the film in the background score also elevates the story of Sanichari into higher planes of being a spiritual quest. It reflects the deep down yearning of Sanichari for a balm for her restless soul, which has been subjected to excruciating suffering.

Lajmi makes creative use of sound by detailing its social and aesthetic elements. Bhupen Hazarika's soulful music invested with rhythms, communicates the passion of romance. It strengthens the film in its terms of its forms and content. Though the film appropriates the folklore to its own purpose of entertainment, yet, the music and songs are unique in their cultural implications. According to Harihar Swarup, "his compositions for 'Rudali' won him recognition across the subcontinent and made him a legend in his lifetime" (13). The folk music of Bhupen Hazarika inspires and co-ordinates with the kinetic visuals of cinema employed by Lajmi in the progression of a heart-rending tale about a beleaguered survivor.

The picturesque locales of Rajasthan against the sand dunes, the dry arid tone of the atmosphere heightens the haunting and touching tale of Sanichari's struggle. The sets of earthy mud houses lend a rooted-ness to the story set in soil and to the character of Sanichari who herself is rooted in tradition. In fact, the writer does not fall into any easy ideological slot as such and the cultural ambience is set as grounding, a kind of launching pad for Sanichari's empowerment and emancipation through and intrinsic sense of self with her selfhood relationship result. Mahasweta Devi tries to raise our self-consciousness through her story. Lajmi, through the film conscientizes the viewers by questioning, through psychological and moral values, raises our consciousness on the relevant issues drawing us to empathize with Sanichari's sufferings. Sanichari metamorphoses herself, which leads her to become a *rudali* and helps her to realize her own strength in the process. It is as Judith Butler points out that,

"every subject position is the site of converging relations of powers that are not unequivocal; in other words, no identity affiliation upheld by even the most marginalized of minorities can fully describe those it purports to present." (Butler Bodies 229).

The film speaks of Sanichari's inner resilience and strength that paves her own resolute way through an exploitative, sexually discriminatory world serving as an inspiring symbol of hope and endeavour. She emboldens both the director who portrays her strength and integrity effectively and the viewer, alike, to endure and prevail.

In all the three films discussed in this chapter, none of the films has a traditional happy ending. There is no meeting of the soulmates to live on happily ever after even if they've met and understood each other's craving for an ethereal blissful state for each other. The poignant *'birha ras'* (separation) of the Indian *Rasa* theory has been the pervading factor in the life of the main protagonists. All the three female protagonists Hirabai, Umrao Jaan and Sanichari in *'Teesri Kasam'*, *'Umrao Jaan'*, *'Rudali'* hale from the depraved section of the society and they are a marginalized lot and hence suffer more than their male counterparts at separation. They are oppressed, not by their gender alone but by class and caste too. Their position in the social code is problem ridden as that of a muted group in the hierarchical of power of structure relationships. It is the subordinate group's different social experience that constitutes their different relationship; yet Hirabai, Umrao Jaan and Sanichari all manage perfectly well to survive and move on in life without the male cudgels. They are alive, vibrant women and as Toril Moi says "We should be alive to the dangers of fetishization" (Moi 159). All three of them are aware women and they have seen the contradictions inherent to the domain of privileged reason, lucidity and unity belonging to the masculine figure.

They have all perceived the differences and similarities in the language used in speech and nonverbal communication which the medium of cinema heightens through expressions and gestures in all the three films. The language used in literary texts arrests our attention while reading, but cinematic language as a mode of expression enhances it even further.

Happy endings however are presumed to belong to the realm of fantasy. If a film or a novel has a closure, the most different things in life can be neatly wrapped up as gift package. According to Pico Iyer,

> "when the ending of a film is spiked with just a little sadness or uncertainty we can convince ourselves that we are being served a more grown up fairy tale in which romance has been served with a pinch for realism". (Iyer 6).

All three films are not an escape from reality in that sense. Even if all the three female protagonists feel that they are rejected yet they do not feel completely dejected and consequently themselves reject the power and presence of the male protagonists in their lives. All three of them, transform their very existence into a more fruitful way of life, transforming the very concept of the power unto them. This is in reaffirmation with what Toril Moi has to say about the relevance of feminism. "Feminism is not simply about rejecting power, but about transforming the existing power structures and in the process transforming the very concept of power itself". (Moi 147). Every group, every culture lives by its own code, its standards and values and carries on a ceaseless campaign and perpetuates the social attitudes, which are consequently mirrored in the minds of the individuals. In the *Bhagvad Gita* it is said that,

> "those people who are free from pride and delusion with the evil of attachment conquered, ever dwelling in the self with desires completely receded, liberated from the pairs of opposites known as pleasure and pain and undiluted, reach the eternal goal." (Jayanti 311).

In the Indian cultural ideology, there is a frequent reference to the lofty nature of the final destination in the goal of journey. This co-relates with the ideal of ascent of the doctrine of the vedic mystics. Shri Aurbindo writes, "the image of the sacrifice is sometimes that of a journey or a voyage; for it travels, it ascends; it has a goal, the true existence". (Jayanti 281). It is perhaps this kind of true existential bliss that is being sorted out by Hirabai, Umrao Jaan and Sanichari in all the three films in keeping with Indian cultural ideology. Such an ideology gets internalized in the consciousness of the writers and filmmakers in India, finding projection in their works. The cultural codes are strongly embedded in Indian literature and hence get enunciated, condoned or denounced in the film adapted for the celluloid. What is interrogated in these films as well as in the literary texts from which they are adapted, is loss of faith in inter-personal gender relationship.

It is perhaps on account of such cultural ideology that dominant male patriarchy gets perpetuated to victimize women. Equations in gender relations may, however, not be there even in happy endings too but for the reconciliatory process of acceptance of their position vis-à-vis each other is an accepted bygone factor. Due to the lack of progressive views and individual travails in the case of the male protagonists in psychosocial terms, they are not able to find solutions to seek meaningful gender relationship. They possibly can't transcend the rigorous realities they are trapped in, inspite of their sensitive disposition, which they feel. However, all the three filmmakers develop their own aesthetic dynamism with a degree of autonomy to achieve a device to portray the same cinematically. The problematic of gender relations as a class, caste divide get looked into in a bold and a more realistic manner sensitively.

In each of the three films, all the three female protagonists emerge as great survivors. They look at truth in the face, yet, at times they retreat and cling to the trappings of cultural ideology. Alternatively, they celebrate newer elements of 'New Cinema or Parallel cinema' in a bold and hybrid manner through cinematic narrative. There is in their psyche a pronounced desire for emancipation and a liberal attitude to ease conflicts in gender relations. All the three directors, two males, Basu Bhattacharya and Muzaffar Ali and one female Kalpana Lajmi reject the ideal of romantic love though they show all the three female protagonists emotionally vulnerable. They are not female stereotypes trapped in the Sati Savitri image to simply satiate the male super ego.

Yet somewhere, they are entrapped by the Indian cultural ideological image of the Radha figure. Radha, who in her love for Krishna, broke all the rules, does not appear in both the epics *Ramayana* and *Mahabharta*. In the *Mahabharta* she appears in scattered references in the folklore and poetry from as far back as the sixth century AD. It is only in Jayadeva's 12th century poem 'Gita Govinda' that she is finally brought center stage. She is the love interest of Krishna but is not married to him hence theirs is an illicit love. Similarly, all the three female protagonists Hirabai, Umrao Jaan and Sanichari are also not married eventually to their love interests and rather have to part from their lovers whom they whole-heartedly love. In the chapter 'Seeing Radha/ Being Radha' the first essay in book 'Researching Indian Women,' Vidya Rao talks about the day she began to learn *thumri*. Her guru, the famous singer Naina Devi told her, "Sita, Lakshmi, Savitri, these are held up as role models for other women but we are singers. We are different. To sing *thumri* you must understand Radha. You must become Radha." (Rao Vidya 380).

Every interpretation of Radha, even when she is not named, is unique in its own way, the quest to understand Radha gives many answers as it helps to comprehend the *Leela* (divine play) that is both unseen and seen. In Indian mythology,

"God is *Leela* and leads us on to *maya*, (illusion) but in the western myths, the gods invariably are caught in the web of *maya*. Krishana, representing the soul, enters in to play or *leela* with Radha who is mortal and longs for the divine." (Gandhy 103).

The *leela* syndrome yields many answers to historical, social and even personal problems faced by the Indian women, trapped by cultural ideology, "To become complete, Radha must become self contained. In other words, the beloved is only a reflection of the self, that is Krishna is only a mirror, revealing her own soul and love force." (Gandhy 109). Even when the two part physically, they carry the image of the other within. Hence, in actuality they never part from each other as each lives within the other.

All the three female protagonists in the respective films do not enact meaningful role models that one finds in the scriptures of cultural ideology in every day life. They do not conform to the role models reminiscent of Sita and Draupadi from Indian mythology. None of them is a stereotypical heroine of Indian cinema who has, "often been projected as a cross between the one who goes through trial by fire to prove her chastity and the other who triggers off the *Mahabharta*." (Somaya Sex Symbol 393). However the three male protagonists in the films are not Krishna archetype as conventional romantic hero, admirable and desirable. The female figures also are not heroines but mere survivors. Home, a place where all journeys begin and culminate, is a cocoon not for them or for their noble quest and respectability. Forbidden love is their fate and the noble quest for harmony, which signify darkness, is an ignoble obsession for them in gender relations.

It does seem as if these women have done nothing wrong in stepping out into the limelight as if to make a spectacle of themselves and each one portrays herself as a, "female grotesque...making a spectacle out of oneself seemed a specifically feminine danger. For a woman making a spectacle out of herself has more to do with a kind of inadvertency and loss of boundaries." (Russo 53). However, an ideological analysis shows that these woman figures parade themselves as an object of a spectacle to challenge the canon of cultural worth being an exclusive match preserve. According to Gledhill,

> "the notions of cinematic voyeurism and fetishism serve as norms for the analysis of classic narrative cinema and the early cinepsycho analysis found it difficult to theorise the feminine as anything other than 'lack' 'absence' 'otherness'". (Gledhill Pleasurable 167).

She argues that since the narrative organization has been patriarchal, the spectator constructed by the text is also masculine. The patriarchal subject is constructed as a unified consistent but illusory identity. As a result, for patriarchal subjects, the difference of gender, sex, class, race, age and so on are alienated as 'otherness' and repressed.

The repressed figure of the women threatens to make resurgence however, through the process of the 'unconscious' Le Doeuff focuses on the constancy with which women have been figured as 'other' and she claims that women are valued in marginalized ways. She proposes that, "phallocentric imagery about women and femininity usually betrays a theoretical weakness, a difficulty that has been unable to overcome." (quoted in Deutscher 63). She argues that marginalized imagery is felt necessary to be present in films or philosophy and that women as lovers, daughters or disciples were felt necessary to be really present as such and are just not incidental[9].

All the three films emphasize that the woman does not need a man to fight her battles in confronting life. Each of the three female protagonists Hirabai, Umrao Jaan and Sanichari never lapse into self-pity. There is, however, a haunting pessimistic atmosphere in the films markedly of melodramatic strain, a relic from the literary tradition.

"The melodrama is an oxymoronic in that it has to produce dramatic action whilst staying firmly in the place; this gives it an inherently circular thematic structure, hence often the recourse to flashback" (Cook 80).

It is one of the inherent factors in any literary themes that get transported into the cinema. The flashback device has been used in a very compelling manner in the narratives of the films and all the three Hirabai, Umrao and Sanichari never lose their spirits completely and survive the most compelling circumstances.

The third chapter thus focuses on the representation of woman as a survivor figure who embattles and contests a set of deterministic socio cultural conventions in order to emerge as a strong and self reliant person who can survive the odds of life with tenacity and resilience. In all the three films there is a reversal of gender role rather to the extent that male figures or protagonists are subsidiary and act more or less as an appendage to the women characters. "Cinema has been sensitive to the constraints that individuals have felt in realizing their aspirations in the various social categories to which they belong." (Das Gupta Susmita 375). On the one hand, cinema has seen the individual as the reason for the system; on the other hand, it has also seen the survival of the system as a reason for the individual's freedom. Cinema's strength lies not in conventional narrative, something which literature or even theatre can do better. Cinema rather attempts new ways of tracing the flow of characters, thoughts and replaces logical expositions with collages of fragmentary images, complex allusions and multiple points of view. At the same time, art cinema equals other arts in seriousness and depth.

All the three directors explore the cinematic language and explore the conflict and contrast in the lives of the main protagonist in all the three films, respectively. All the three female protagonists who emerge as survivors are immensely affected both emotionally and psychologically. The fundamental form of Indian cinema is argumentative. The characters argue about a situation and its constraints and discuss how to transcend the same. This very argumentative characterisation of Indian cinema gets drawn from the country's tradition of epics and forms of its classical music. In either case, the central theme meanders through interpretations and re-interpretations. The female protagonists may have been shown in the Indian cinema stereotypically and silently succumbing to oppression. Yet Indian cinema has also portrayed women who can survive the most compelling circumstances. Even, if Hirabai, Umrao and Sanichari in the three respective films, discussed in this chapter, are an object of sexual desire yet they pass the acid test of endurance, sacrifice and emerge as survivors. Inspite of the deterministic code of moral conventions, they seek strength through their self-determination to face the eventualities of the life. Their grimaces and gestures convey their stoic forbearance enhanced through their acting skill on celluloid. In all three films, the directors portray their tenacity and inner resilience through the nuances of their directorial skill.

They emerge as survivor figures, self-assertive women having been through the journey of life without any hopes or fears to live up to role fulfilment set up by the trappings of cultural ideology. They are rather liberated from such trappings of conditioned rootedness in tradition and can perhaps find new avenues of self-fulfilment and can do without models, standards or examples. It is tempting to read all the three films as a progression in feminism as all the three female protagonists emerge more self-assured by the end of all the three films. All the three actresses Waheeda Rehman, Rekha and Dimple as Hirabai, Umrao and Sanichari respectively provide riveting performances with a realism and truth unsurpassed in modern Indian cinema.

The story of all the three films has enduring themes and characters. All the three female protagonists try to break free from the constrictive mould of their designated stature in life through their brief hoping for spasmodic and spiralling ascent into fructifying avenues of aborted longings and aspirations. They are not attuned to fight the system; however, they rescue themselves from the state of the victimization syndrome even if they have to face the alienation and suffer on account of the conditioned theoretical culture. Although they have to exist eking out their living in a patriarchal set up which oppresses them and restricts them from finding their happiness, yet, all three Hirabai, Umrao Jaan and Sanichar survive. All the three female protagonists are the controlling force of the narrative. Throughout the narrative they interpret the world through a feminine alternative for self-expression. They access forms of representation of their own that leave space for the feminine. They almost all function, "to cast *phallocentrism, phallocratism*, loose from its moorings in order to return the masculine to its own language, leaving open the possibility of a different language. Which means that the masculine would no longer be 'everything'. That it could no longer, all by itself define circumvent, circumscribe the properties of anything and everything. That the right to define every value-including the abusive privilege of appropriation– would no longer belong to it." (Irigaray This Sex 79-80).

In order to return the masculine to its own language they open the possibility of a different language, which means the masculine would no longer be everything. The final image in all the three films is not of fulfilment of gender relation with the men in their respective lives. They all in a way seem to compromise, yet their experience of loss is rather overwhelmingly played out in the realm of the respective survivor spirit. One way of reading these three films with reference to cultural ideology is to expound the non-conformist figure of all Hirabai, Umrao and Sanichari and then the point of view of their pride becomes comprehensible. They are all interesting figures, sometimes simply used as a pawn and have to yield to the trappings of cultural ethos or so called cultural ideology.

One way of looking at the memorable expression of their sorrows and joys, desires and fears even if they become the object of hostility, is their moral integration and there is a germ of truth in them. Yet, they are dreamers and have aspirations and are worldly wise. They all share a genuine mutual love with the male protagonists in the respective films, which have all the traditions of romance steeped in antiquity of cultural ideology. The language of love can be described as the mystical love of inward joy in harmonious relationship. Their categorization on account of their caste and class also transcends the boundaries. The dramatic and emotional scenes between them owing to the literary sensitivity of the writers' are portrayed with great precision and understanding. However there is a sense of pathos, which occurs due to the lack of commitment of loyalty by the respective male protagonists in the films on account of the rigid trappings in the name of tradition of cultural ideology, inspite of the reassurances of their understanding. It makes the male protagonists appear harsh, inspite of the emotional undertones evoked in their characterization.

All the three films evoke a strong visual quality and the women in the narrative show sudden changes of emotion, as moments of hope and joy of triumph in their relationships are followed by one of sorrow and separation leading to 'birha ras' (poignancy of separation). The romance element in all the three stories and films finally vanishes as all three female protagonists are connected with the elements of caste, class and community. However, their transition from marginalized figures to being survivors is an intense affirmation they acquired through their fortitude and helps them emerge as strong women. In a way the power to survive inspite of their sufferings helps them for their edification and does not destroy them from self-abnegation or annihilation. Their sublimated passion leads them to the way of life of shedding of the need for romantic theories by striving towards the ideal inexpressible barriers between desire and into fulfilment beyond the loss and separation.

All three earn their own livelihood and are self empowered through the same and not dependent on men to attain a sense of purposefulness in their lives. Though, they all have to devise and adopt unconventional ways ascribed for Indian woman as norms of feminine conduct; yet, they succeed in articulating a sense of self-realisation. They, however, do not suffer from a persecution complex; instead they are all left to fend for themselves to work out their own liberation, holding onto their self-esteem in their own genuinely integrated way of living.

NOTES AND REFERENCES

1. According to Imelda Whelhan, "in the narratological approach to adaptation, the process of presenting a literary text on film is one in which the stock formal devices of narrative—point of view, focalisation tense, voice, metaphor must be realized" (Whlehan 9).
2. "Nautanki is the folk dance of this region. The songs and main theme are recited in operatic style which are accompanied by the drums and music". (Narayan 93).
3. Ardhinareshwar: half-male and half-female form of Shiva and Parvati. In "the divine play of the union of opposites; transcendence; the merging of the male and female polarities within us; all boundaries fall away and we transcend time and space. In the world of myth this experience was understood as a spiritual experience". (Gandhy 244). When Shiva was separated from Parvati, Kama, the god of desire tried to enrapture him through his arrows. He however, turned his anger on Kama and burnt Kama to ashes.
4. Habib Tanvir, the doyen of Indian theatre of 'Charandas Chor' fame' the man who metamorphosed the face of modern Indian theatre, as a movement of human theatre feels that people are not caring towards folk theatre and have misconceptions that theatre belongs to the elite. He strongly believes that, "the villagers have natural sense of culture whereas the urban elite is very far it. The villagers are culturally rich as they have the art of singing openly, can do *'abhinay'* (acting) with an open heart and they have the *Samskar* (legacy of traditions) that matters". (Gokhale: "Art is Always Anti-Establishment" *The Hindu Magazine*, Sep. 26th, 2004 p. 2).
5. All subsequent citations are followed by page numbers in parentheses from the text by Ruswa, Hadi, Mirza. *The Courtesan of Lucknow Umrao Jaan Ada*. Trans. Khushwant Singh and M.A. Husaini. New Delhi: Hind Pocket Books Ltd., 1970.
6. All subsequent citations are followed by page numbers in parentheses from the text by Devi, Mahasweta and Usha Ganguli. *Rudali from Fiction to Performance*. Trans. Anjum Katyal Calcutta: Seagull Books, 1988.
7. Customs/rituals are used as proscriptions and exploitation of the individuals. The author shows how the religious rituals as a cultural/ideological trap which get reinforced to victimize her.
8. "An Indian woman is rather supposed to draw on almost all *solah shringar* i.e. the 16 love charms taught by Mahalakshmi herself which are bindi, kajal, perfume, flowers, pretty, hair pins, bright clothes, ear rings, nose ring, toe ring, finger ring, bracelet, armlet, anklet, griddle, necklace and scented supari to keep her lips red, breath fresh and stain free all of it is mentioned in the Kamasutra". (Singal 37). The concept of the beauty myth and beauty is a pre-determinant of being feminine within the Indian cultural context.
9. According to Le Doeuff, "the theoretical devotion of a woman is very comforting for someone experiencing his own lack. How can it not be gratifying to be seen as a plentitude when one is oneself caught incompleteness and disappointment." (quoted in Deutscher 63).

$$\boxed{4}$$

The Conflict Within and Without

All films are particular ways of seeing the world and have a relation to that dominant way of seeing the world in which is enshrined the ideology of an age. "The emblems and icons and the cinema stereotype say much more about the social history of our times than any other genre." (Kazmi Fareed Foreword). Rather, they represent the very moods of an evolving society. They also focus on the burning issues of society at a given specific period in the history of a nation. Historical sources in a film can be used to construct the cultural climate as a link of the past and in appropriating it with the present. The writing of history has had a continuous interface with literature and with historical sources being constructed into fictionalized narrative, such like narratives, which get interwoven into fiction, contextually, are derived from particular cultural underpinnings. According to Romila Thapar, "It is not necessary, to authenticate a story as history, for a story to remain fictional. But it can reveal perspectives of a time and a society". (Thapar Sakuntala 12). The concept of culture in relation to the history of any nation implies intersecting of disciplines.

Both literature and cinema do not simply reflect the social world, but they also construct coherent versions of social realities within which ideological tensions are contained, understood and at times resolved. Despite the belief of "the existence of kitsch of inanities and apparent irrelevancies, cinema can be deadly serious". (Kazmi Fareed 15). Political cinema can be ideologically loaded, as its raw material is always congruent with the divergent ramifications of the socio-cultural reality. The ideas, ideals perpetuated during the nineteenth century, those of nationalism in India, have become an integrated part of our cultural ethos. Nationalist discourse, at any given time has moulded and fashioned our cultural fabric. These ideals are also present in Indian cinema, "routed through familiar, if modified as cultural and narrational reference points." (Vasudevan *Making* 116). Even though the movement of nineteenth century nationalism in India was considered to foster a precarious balance between tradition and modernity, however, at the same time, newer, broader class, gender codes were also being forged.

At the outset, nationalism was seen as an all inclusive and liberating force, the world over. Its appeal was popular and democratic with its ideological foundation in anti-colonialism. It attacked feudal practices and oppressive imperial tyrannies and proclaimed the sovereignty of the people and right of all peoples to determine their own destiny. "It broke down the various localisms of religion, dialect, custom and clan and helped to create large and powerful nation–states". (Smith D. 1). The question of the relations between the issues of gender and nationalism was pursued with very different assumptions and methodologies in different countries. According to the masterly survey carried out by Sylvia Walby, "in the older nations of the West, the formation of nations was long drawn out and women's emancipation came very late in their 'rounds of restructuring': whereas in the new state of Africa and Asia, women were accorded full citizenship rights with independence." (Walby 91). However, she asserts that, "indeed the granting of full citizenship to all was one of the ways in which previously dominated colonies could make a claim to nationhood." (Walby 91).

The nationalistic ideology in India also had an impact on questions of gender and the role of women in our freedom struggle and nationalist movement in the era of colonialism commanded significant critical interventions. In the Indian society, which had almost patterned along caste/class formulations that were highly hierarchal, the concept of equality based on gender or class, had been an alien one. However, the exposure of western educated Indians led to liberalism and helped to pave certain changes leading to certain social reforms. As a result, removal of certain practices and customs against women were championed by people like Raja Ram Mohan Roy, Ishwar Chander Vidyasagar, Keshav Chander Sen, Ranade, and Karve and by various other like-minded men. The record of reforms they undertook to achieve, "spanned action to abolish the practice of *sati*, the custom of child marriage, the custom of disfiguring widows, the ban on the re-marriage of upper caste Hindu widows and a host of other evil practices that affected women". (Chitnis 84). However, the British government ruling over India then, did not back these reforms vigorously, as they feared that tampering with tradition would make them unpopular and destabilize their rule.

The nationalist movement for freedom did pave the way for the advancement of the status of women in the Indian society, inspite of the factionalism operating therein. A conservative segment of the nationalists did look upon reformers as traitors for the cause of freedom in India, as they felt that this process of emancipating women was an imitation of western ways. However, Mahatma Gandhi who emerged as the country's political leader played an eminent role in helping the women to evolve and bringing them in the mainstream of public life, as well as in the eradication of untouchability against the lower castes. Through the idea of involving the entire population in the non-violent struggle for freedom, he felt, it was imperative to involve women in the mass movement. The concept of *Stree Shakti* i.e. the might of womanhood took hold and the struggle for freedom movement propelled the women to be treated as equals in political life. As a result, the women of India plunged headlong into the struggle for Independence from the British in 1947. The emergence of a nation obviously requires a re-negotiation of gender equation and identity formulation. The culture of any nation is not merely a blind adherence to tradition or what is inherited from the past. It also includes modern values and new ideas that get integrated into the substance and quality of life. Much of the study of culture can be sorted out if culture is examined vis-à-vis the interactions between people. However, freedom also led to a partition of the country into India and Pakistan. It is said that, "the political partition of India caused one of the greatest human convulsions of the history". (Butalia 3) As a result of the partition, as many as ten millions of people on religious lines had to exchange their homes and countries in the space of a few months between the new, truncated India and Pakistan. Communal riots were triggered off between Hindus, Muslims, and Sikhs, which led to a kind of catastrophe and loss of life. They had to face fear, uncertainty while fleeing from their original homesteads to safer havens.

The community called the 'Nation State' is a modern phenomenon, for it is promised on participation of a kind that is impossible in either feudal or absolute regimes. The dominant root metaphors of the Indian nation state, beside the tradition of caste-system, are those of anti-colonialism along with the metaphor of ancient and glorious civilization, which India has had. The mobilization of the women, lower castes and minorities and their participation in the freedom movement informs the Indian cultural tradition. Thus, gender relations need to be looked into and perceived in the backdrop of the freedom movement too. The manner in which gender relations got disturbed and affected the man-woman relationship in the process is an aspect; I am going to look into the films adapted from the literary texts, based on evoking those epoch times. The films, chosen in this chapter are based on fiction *'Ghaire Bhaire'* written by Rabindra Nath Tagore, *'Gaban'* by Premchand and *'Train to Pakistan'* by Khushwant Singh. The directors are Satyajit Ray, Krishan Chopra/Hrisikesh Mukherjee and Pamela Rooks, respectively. Each film is different from the other in its tone, texture and temper, but the mood and theme captured therein is of men and women set in the backdrop of the different phases in the emergence of the nationalistic forces. There is a sense of emancipation and awakening, at the same time there is a conflict within and without which correlates to the national upheaval and communalism in the contemporary pre and post era independence. Each film text resonates with an incisive insight as every director probes into the fictive narrative to convert it into a profound and telling film narrative.

GHAIRE-BHAIRE

Rabindra Nath Tagore, a versatile genius, is the most outstanding name in modern Bengali literature. In fact, he was the one, who first gained for modern India, a place in the world literary scene. The nineteenth century is one of the most eventful formative periods of the history of India. Rather, it was the period, which saw the birth of modern India and the beginning of a series of movements, both of development and reformation, with far reaching consequences. The award of the Nobel Prize for literature to Tagore for "*Gitanjali*" was also the beginning "of a drama of reconviction on a global scale to which there cannot be many parallels in literary history". (Iyengar 99). He belongs unquestionably to Bengali literature but he has affiliations with the tradition of Indo-Anglian literature too. In fact, he has an inter-connectedness with the entire nation of India.

Nineteenth century was an age of all round awakening and progress in Bengal and this was amply reflected in contemporary literature, providing a window through which one can look at its cultural developments. Tagore portrayed the modern trend of modern thinking in India in his works. He was a poet, dramatist, actor, musician, painter, novelist and short story writer and a critic of life, par excellence. Tagore belonged to one of the most extraordinary families in the cultural history of modern India. His father Debendranath Tagore was one of the pillars of Raja Rammohan Roy's *Brahmo Samaj*, the Hindu reformist movement which was to be crucial to the formation of both modern Bengali middle class *bhadralok* (literarily, 'civilized person' or 'civil person') and of secular India. *Brahmo Samaj* was founded in 1830 and was, "a monotheistic Hindu society implacably opposed to the ubiquitous idolatry, rituals and belief in caste. For the *Brahma Sabha*, idols, rituals and caste were blasphemous at least in theory" (Robinson and Datta 28).

Rabindra Nath, like his father, also revered the *Upanishads* as the summit of Indian philosophical thought, but he found them incomplete in their answer to the complex longing of the human soul. *Brahmo Samaj* movement had a young activist Keshubchandra Sen who formed his own separate movement in 1866 in contrast to the high church of Debendranath. Tagore was influenced by his father but also became more and more radical in his belief. Tagore and modern Bengali literature were, "reinvented to represent the unbroken tradition of religion and wisdom, rather than being situated in the modernity and middle class culture to which both belonged". (Chaudhuri, Amit 28). Tagore delved into the subconscious of the middle class as secular Bengali psyche and a liberal philosopher, a kind of a prophet, whose fecundity and vitality were amazing. Above all, he was a practical idealist, too, who had the ability to turn his dreams into reality with great integrity and the establishment of *Shantiniketan* is a proof of his relentless strive and quest for the sense of knowledge. *Shantiniketan* was supposed to advocate a new experiment in living, wherein the culture of the East was supposed to find its own soul. Tagore was, "a reconciler of East and West", according to Mulk Raj Anand a well-known novelist and critic. (Anand 185). He believed in merging the dichotomy between the two into a creative unity, to help achieve a broad base of human understanding and purposive activity. The manifold avenues of Tagore's creative mind led to a regeneration of the progressive outlook in several parts of the country. His writings permeated deep into the soul, nurturing the consciousness of modern India, thus making him a cult figure.

Tagore has remained not only the supreme literary figure of our land but was also a great modern humanist. He was imbued with a sense of history like all India's political leaders during the struggle for Independence of the country from the British. Alongwith Bankim Chandra he felt that our country, "having a history of her own must hunt up material from forgotten or neglected indigenous sources and record it in a spirit of constructive national service". (Mukherjee 12). In fact Bankim Chandra Chatterjee wrote· the novel 'Anandmath' which was published in 1882 and portrayed the revolutionaries sacrificing their lives for the motherland. Bankim's emotional hymn "Bande Mataram" "Hail to the mother" became famous throughout India. This call to save the Motherland was not just a call to women to join the political movement but rather a linking of idealized womanhood with nationalism. Nira Davis-Yuval in a thought provoking and a systematic survey applies, "a deconstructionist analysis to the relationships between gender and nation, and includes the ideological and symbolic modes of locating women as vital components of cultural reproduction" (Smith D. 207). She believes,

> "that women, are often constructed as the symbolic bearers of the collectivity's identity and honour. A figure of a woman, often a mother, symbolizes in many cultures the spirit of the collectivity, whether it is Mother Russia, Mother Ireland or Mother India". (Yuval 45).

When the centrality of what may be described as the 'women's question' arose to the entire gamut of educated middle class religious and social reform movement in 19th century Bengal Renaissance, "the reformist liked to call it a movement for *Stri-Swadhinta*". (Sarkar Sumit 2). In 1905 when the British partitioned the province of Bengal, women joined the men in protesting this division by boycotting foreign goods and buying only 'Swadeshi' goods i.e. (local goods) goods made in Bengal itself. Women took a vow to devote themselves to the motherland and same women even gave their support to the revolutionary organizations. They sang in praise of Mother India and posed it as regenerated Indian womanhood. Mahatma Gandhi who returned to India in 1915 as the hero of the South African struggle felt that India needed women leaders who were "pure, firm and self controlled like the ancient heroines Sita, Damyanti and Draupadi." (Gandhi 4-5).

He evoked the cultural ideology and extolled the women with the virtue of Sita the heroine of the great legend Ramayana who followed her husband into exile suffered abduction and underwent an ordeal of fire to prove her fidelity. Damayanti, the faithful long suffering wife of Nala was able to recognize her husband in any guise. Draupadi, the wife of five Pandava brothers in the Mahabharta India's other great legend, was ordered to strip by Duryodhana her new master when she was lost in a dice game by Yudhistra, the eldest pandava. However, Lord Krishna to whom she prayed and beseeched for her protection recognized her chastity and innocence and saved her from digrace by covering her by yards of sarees which couldn't be undone. According to him all these heroines in the Indian culture context had suffered at the hands of men but survived with dignity. He urged the women to wake up and recognize their essential quality with men. He felt that, "only when they appreciated the strength of their ancestress would women comprehend their right to freedom and liberty". (Gandhi 4-5).

S.K. De points out that the literary movements in Bengal had perforce been closely bound up with political, social, religious and other movements. "Every great writer of the Renaissance in Bengal during this period of transition was out of necessity a politician, a social reformer or a religious enthusiast". (De, S.K. 51). The period of Renaissance or re-awakening in Bengal may have reverberated the history of the influence of European ideas on Bengali thought. Whereas early authors like Bankim Chandra Chatterjee represented past learning and the heritage, writers like Raja Rammohan Roy, Akhoy Kumar Datta or Ishwar Chandra Vidyasagar were considered from the English school, though they were no less proficient in Sanskrit learning and equally influenced by it. In fact, the early nineteenth century, particularly in its first half, was marked by ideological conflict, cross currents and contradictions. Rather, in different spheres of life, there was a certain amount of inconsistency and this was reflected in literature. Even in the early part of nineteenth century, the conflict around woman question loomed large. "In fact it was not a question of what do woman want but rather how can they be modernized."(Forbes 16) The British regarded their domination of the sub continent as proof of their moral superiority. In British terms, social reform became such an important issue that accounts of Indian women suffering because of sati, child marriage, widowhood, polygamy and prohibition of education, were often embedded in the discussions and writing of nineteenth century reformers and writers. As Lata Mani writes,

> "Tradition was thus not the ground on which the status of woman was being constructed. Rather the reverse became true. Women in fact became the site on which tradition was debated and reformulated". (117).

Inspired and influenced by western ideas, reformers like Raja Ram Mohan Roy, Pandit Vidyasagar, Swami Dayanand Saraswati and many others who were also trained in Hindu classics of Sanskrit language, tried to recover Indian women from a dark age. There were also discussions of the ideal relationship between men and women. James Mill, after having learnt about Hindu society through Halhed's code of the 'Gentoo Laws' translation of the code of Manu and some religious works, condemned the habitual contempt and degradation, which was entertained towards women in the Indian society. In his influential history of British India, he had argued that women's position could be used as an indicator of society's advancement. The formula was simple, "Among rude people, the women are generally degraded, among civilized people they are exalted." (Mill 309). Colonial domination, thus, set the change in motion and reshaped the imported ideas and institutions thus to fit the society and cultural milieu. Gender relations were being thus re-defined and a new progressive ideology was emerging. The works of Tagore represented the apex of the nineteenth century renaissance in Bengal. The many dimensional character of his artistic mind helped him in utilizing his creative necessity along with social necessity in his works. His writings permeated deep into the soul of new India emerging not only making him a supreme literary figure but a great modern humanist too. Where a number of intellectuals praised their own culture's treatment of women, it was felt that female education and female emancipation was the first steps towards progress. He like other progressive thinkers was convinced of the need for reforms for women, which "extolled gender relations and shared an ideology, later linked to the nationalist project that separated the home from the world". (Ray Rajat 3).

Tagore wrote '*Ghaire Bhaire*' in 1916 in Bengali which became 'The Home and the World' in its English translation. Of Tagore's full-length novels, only three appeared in as approved English version in his own lifetime, of which '*Ghaire Bhaire*' is one of them along with '*Naukhabandi*' (1905), which appeared as '*The Wreck*' and '*Gora*' (1910) which retained the same title in English also.

Tagore was basically a prolific writer and by the time he was fifty, he had already a staggering output to his credit and thrilled people with excitement and exploration of his works. In 1913 he was awarded the Nobel Prize for literature for '*Gitanjali*'. He was also the national poet of Bengal and was admitted and idealized and placed on a pedestal almost as an idol. Tagore left behind an immense mass of prose writing in Bengali as well as in English. There are novels, plays, short stories, poems, lectures, essays on a variety of subjects ranging from works like '*Gitanjali*', '*The Gardener*', '*The Fugitive*'. '*The Post Office*' alongwith his "*Collected Poem and Plays*", which appeared in 1936 are infact to mention a few of his compelling laudations.

Satyajit Ray, one of India's best-known film makers who got recognition in the international world of cinema with his '*Pather Panchali*' (1956), wanted to strike a balance between commercial and art cinema and for that he needed some knowledge of the basic Indian art which lured him towards Tagore. He left crowded Calcutta and arrived in mid 1940 to study fine art in the stillness and space of *Santiniketan*, Tagore's place, his Abode of Peace. Satyajit Ray had a penchant for adapting good literature for the celluloid. His first film *'Pather Panchali'* was adapted from the short story by Bibhuti Bhushan Banerjee. Over the years, Tagore and Ray have become indissolubly bound. "If non Bengalis got to know Tagore it can be attributed mainly to the virtue of Ray's interpretations of him in his films". (Robinson 47). He adapted some of Tagore's works and it is said that a path taken by Satyajit Ray in the revival of Bengali cinema, is directly in the line with the role of Rabindranath Tagore in the Bengali cultural revival. "Both of them came from a dynasty of intellectuals, musicians and teachers of the cultivated upper middle class owing their allegiance to the reformist *Brahmo Samaj*." (Thorval 238).

In fact they both thus shared an affinity between them which has the deepest of the cultural roots. Both of them were recognized in Bengal and abroad. Some of Ray's finest films are based on Tagore's writings and adapted for films. One of them was 'Charulata' made in 1964. It was based on Tagore's novella *'Nastanirh'* ('The Broken Nest' 1901) 'Ghaire Bhaire' written in 1916 became the ('The Home and the World'). Three short stories of Tagore in *'Teen Kanya'* ('Three Daughters' 1961) were three powerful and brief portraits very different amongst themselves. They were 'Post Master' ('The Lost Jewels') *'Monihara'* and *'Sampati'* (The Conclusion).

Both Satyajit Ray and Rabindranath Tagore are two of the prominent Bengali artists and intellectuals who have been seriously concerned with the constricted roles that Indian women have had to play in Indian society and in Bengal in particular. A great deal of writings were done during the social reformation in Bengal by Raja Rammohan Roy, Ishwar Chandra Vidyasagar, Bankim Chandra Chatterjee, Sarat Chandra Chatterjee in literature art and religion. According to Ashis Nandy, a sociologist, "womanhood as a symbol and womanliness as a subject of study have been center pieces of creative conscious in different sectors of Bengal life", although he felt that some of them, "tried to redraw traditional definition of women and identity trying to introduce into its new elements drawn from reinterpreted tradition". (Nandy Woman 77). However, the Bengali revival led to acquiring education and hence enlightenment even though by a section of the elite belonging to upper middle class. It rather became a key not only to their personal freedom and emancipation but also their participation in their struggle for national freedom.

With the international recognition of Satyajit Ray's *'Pather Panchali'* in Venice (1956) Indian cinema entered an age of liberation and awareness. *'Pather Panchali'* was greeted with the accolades, which put it in 'world class' category. With it, "Indian Cinema entered an age of liberation and awareness, Indian Cinema became aware of itself its Indianness". (Nihalani Talking xi). This awareness evolved into a greater and wider perception in a cinema as an art form with its power and potential as a communicator of ideas and as an experiential media that provides a vital debate on issues concerning us at large. After being hit by the Ray sensitivity, filmmakers like Martin Scorsese commented, "images of Indian culture we had were usually through colonialiast eyes. With Ray's films one became attached to the culture through the people, their customs and began to realise that there are other cultures in the world". (Scorsese 65). A film like 'Ghaire Bhaire', like other films of Satyajit Ray, generated an awareness that films could be made outside the pale of the traditional commercial structure of film making, prevalent in the country.

Satyajit Ray's *oeuvres* portrayed the plight of women functioning within a patriarchal society with great sensitivity. Ray had a peculiar ideological stance and felt strongly that an authentic Bengali/India filmmaker, "must face the challenge of contemporary reality, examine the fact, probe them, sift them before he transforms into cinema without the trappings of mythology or any social melodrama". (Ray Satyajit 41). Satyajit Ray's career in filmmaking from 1960 to 1985 shows his feminist sensitivity in portraying gender relations. He embarked on a series of woman-centred films during that phase, which are laced with a historical insight, too. His perceptions reflected upon the state of affairs which are culturally coloured and the, "trapped journey Bengali/Indian woman had to make under patriarchal gazes and threat of a conspicuously Bengali/Indian masculinity". (Cooper 5). Most of his films were in Bengali which includes *Pather Panchali, The Apu Trilogy, Devi, Charulata, Ghaire Bhaire, Ganashatru, Shakha Prosakha, Sadgati, Aaguntak, Jal Sagar, Jana Aranya* etc. but for a Hindi movie *Shatranj Ke Khilari.*

Ray was, from the beginning, a believer in the uniqueness of the individual and did not have to struggle with the pressures of socialist collectivity. From Apu to Agantuk, he saw the ethical development of the individual, the importance of good means to achieve good ends, as the key to social regeneration. "This was most clearly defined in 'Ghaire Bhaire'. His mentor was not Marx but Tagore. The heritage he upheld was one of the Bengal renaissance and the *Brahmo* movement beginning with Rammohan Roy and culminating in Rabindranath Tagore". (Das Gupta 8). The ideology that Ray internalized and expressed in his cinema is of this reformist movement, striving to reconcile religion with modern science and western democracy on the basis of an Upanishadic, rationalist monotheism. Even before directing 'Pathar Panchali,' Ray had already in mind the adaptation of 'Ghaire Bhaire' translated in English as 'The Home and The World'. However 'Ghaire Bhaire' was made in Bengali in 1984, twenty years after 'Charulata' was made in 1964, which it recalls in many ways. This time Satyajit Ray returned to Tagore, in colour, adapting a controversial novel that had increased in stature over the years. 'Charulata' is set in the Calcutta of 1879, the period of Bengal Renaissance. 'Ghaire Bhaire' is set against the background of the terrorist movements following the first communal partition of Bengal in 1905. The novel tells a triple story, interweaving the diaries of the nationalist *zamindar* Nikhil (Victor Bannerjee) with the story of his wife Bimal (Swatileka Chatterjee) and of their guest, the fiery activist Sandeep played by Soumitra Chatterjee. The action of the novel is set with the partition of Bengal in 1905 in its backdrop, which was like a precursor to the partition of India in 1947.

The nineteenth century reform movement and the national movement for independence saw the beginnings of women's activism in politics and visible public presence, in entirely unprecedented ways. In the light of such a great historical break there was a tendency towards change. Like all the young educated men of those times who had the ability to absorb and even accord position of honour and prestige to women, Nikhil becomes a representative figure. Raja Ram Mohan Roy had been the first to claim in public in 1818 that women could perfectly well adapt themselves to conditions other than domestic tasks with their mental and intellectual calibre. After him in each subsequent decade, fresh generations of reformers reiterated this claim. Missionaries in the 1820s, the Young Bengal group of the likes of Vidyasagar in the 1840s and 1850s and Keshub Chandra Sen in the 1880s with their suggestions debated on *Strisiksha* which gathered new strength and bitterness too as it led to division of view between liberals the young group of students of Derozio, an anglo-Indian called the Derozians and the orthodox. The Derozians were radical and iconoclastic enemies of orthodoxy. Their journal, *Jnananveshan*, not only mocked the prohibitions against *Strisiksha* but linked it with pleas against child marriages too. It was felt by people like them that the mode of education should ensure to help the Hindu woman to freedom with aspects of constrictive domesticity.

Satyajit Ray, to a large extent remained faithful to the adaptation to Tagore's novel, which focuses on Nikhil's and Bimal's story. Their autobiographical narratives intertwine to make the novel cohesive along with Sandip's story. Ray however, focuses more on Bimal's story with a rare insight of feminine sensibility. He uses the flashback device in the narrative, which makes us see the film from Bimal's point of view. The action of the novel 'Ghaire Bhaire', 'The Home and the World' (in English) and even the film itself is set in the revolutionary Bengal of 1905, and begins with the depictions of the 'swadeshi' movement and the recourse to Bankim Chandra's fiercely activist notion of "Bande" through the renting of the battle cries "Bandemataram". For Lord Curzon, the then Viceroy of India, the partition of Bengal in 1905, was a cause to celebrate as he took the opportunity to 'divide and rule' the Bengalis both comprising Hindu and the Muslim population. Before partition, there was a boycott movement for the foreign made goods (*bideshi*) in favour of Indian made (*Swadeshi*) substitutes. However, Hindus could withstand the boycott but the poor Muslims could not.

Nikhil is the idealist husband, who, with the impact of English education and western learning, has two characteristic features which are patriotic feelings, along with national sentiment and humanism. He is emancipated enough to lead his wife Bimal, who happens to be educated but with a traditional mind set from the *Ghaire* i.e. the home across to the *Bhaire* i.e. the outer world. She had not set her eyes on a man outside the domain of her house for almost nine years after her marriage, and hence had no idea about conducting an interaction with any man besides her husband as such. She rather makes a note of this in her personal diary, which she keeps almost as a record of her life's sojourn.

Bimal has such a deep-rooted traditional mindset that she would take the dust of her husband's feet every morning and would fill the partition in her hair with vermilion mark, a symbol of the married women. In fact, her husband dissuades her from following such traditional norms set by the cultural ideology of Indian culture; yet, she would touch his feet on a sly quietly, when he was asleep. She thus practises a tradition as a deterministic norm of being servile, subservient. She notes in her diary that thus she avoids, "the shame of being detected by him lest he suspect her trying to earn such a merit secretly."[1] (Tagore 51). Trapped by the cultural norm, she feels that she must worship her husband in order to love him truly. She, infact also writes in her diary that her father-in-law's house which signified the dilapidated grandeur from the days of the kings, had manners of the *moghuls* and *pathans*, yet, some of its customs were those of the conservative and chauvinistic ideologues of Manu and Parashar. Nevertheless, her husband was quite modern in his attitude.

Nikhil, her husband, was the first inmate of the house to go through a college course and take his M.A. degree. Because of his education, he has an egalitarian outlook and overstepped the ancient usages by virtue of which the wife ought not to be treated with subjugation, nor did he expect absolute devotion. He introduced her to the modern age in its idiom and language. He believed in gender equation and she mentions in her diary that her husband used to say, "that man and wife are equal in love because of their equal claim on each other". (Tagore 14). Because of his modern outlook, Nikhil was very keen to take his wife out of the binding customs of *purdah*, which was a reductive domestic designated for the seclusion of the *zenana* i.e. female company. When even Bimal would show her disinclination to move to the outside from her home he would persuade her by saying, "that the outside may want you." (Tagore 18) Nikhil feels that he should have his wife Bimal more fully initiated in (*Bhaire*) the outside world and until then they were still in debt to each other for deriving fulfillment from their relationship. He wants her to come to the heart of the outer world and meet the reality head on.

Nikhil does not want his wife Bimal to be trapped by the household duties, living her life in the world of household conventions and drudgery of its chores. He strongly felt that only if both man and his wife came to understand and recognize each other in the real world, outside the domestic sphere then their love could blossom fully. Bimal world brush away such offers of shaking off the tradition cultural world of moving to the outer world (*Bhaire*) and pose questions like whether there was anything wanting in the love they both shared at their home (*Ghaire*). However a turning point comes in their lives when Bimal decides to take a step outside. Bimal, who had till then, not budged despite her husband's persuasion and entreatments even to be present when he had particular friends to dinner, she wants to invite his friend Sandip for dinner and attend on him, which surprises her husband no end.

Sandip is a college mate of Nikhil's and had come to their neighbourhood along with his followers to preach practices of *swadeshi* (i.e. use of local goods) and the boycott of foreign goods. Nikhil had been helping him with vast funds of money for his ventures. Bimal used to vex her husband then and felt that Sandip was exploiting Nikhil and taking the advantage of his friendship. She had earlier seen a photograph of his and was not impressed by him. She felt that though he had a splendid handsome face, the light in his eyes did not shine true. However after she listens to his fiery speech and sees him across the screen sitting along with other women, she gets thoroughly mesmerized by him. His triumphant shouts of '*Bande Mataram*' thrill her through and through to such an extent that she impatiently pushes away the screen in front of her and has her gaze fixed upon him though none in that crowd is paying any heed to her doings.

Mary Ann Doane, who questions the legitimacy of conceptual gaze for the woman says that she, "may exercise an 'active investigating gaze', only to end after all as victim, only to be punished for such transgressions". (Doane 139). Having caught his sight, she feels elated as if she was the sole representative of Bengal's womanhood and he was the champion of Bengal. The wooden partition across which Bimal views Sandip signifies the nuance of the reversed image of 'feminine voyeurism', inviting a contemplative experience of the outer world. When her husband Nikhil accedes to her desire to invite Sandip for tea, Tagore sets out to portray maturity of a western educated and broad-minded male like Nikhil, who wants to break the fetters of the proscriptive chauvinism. Satyajit Ray, to a large extent, while remaining faithful to the adaptation of Tagore's novel, which focuses on Nikhil's and Bimal's story, focalizes the narrative as being centred around the female protagonist Bimal. The story unfolds right from the beginning from her point of view[2] through a flashback narrative device. In such a case, "the woman cannot function merely as passive spectacle or no narrative would be possible." (Thornham Feminist Media 219).

Nikhil is averse to the hypnotic paranoia generated by patriotism and is a spiritually and intellectually evolved person. Sandip calls, "such hypnotic texts truth and any means are permissible to attain it." (Srinivasan 100). However, both Tagore and Ray try to trace Bimal's evolution to a quest for self-identity through the psychic recesses and physical gestures manifested by feminine sensibility. Bimal is no longer willing to be a Sita figure alluding to the mythical tales that bind her to shackles. Until now she has led the sheltered life of a typical Hindu wife. Nikhil, on the other hand who is an idealist and a benefactor at heart, inspite of being a well off *zamindar,* he does not take this *zamindari* as a field, or a fiefdom but as a family to be taken care of. He belongs to a class of Hindu intelligentsia and resents the flare of terrorism in the garb of the nationalist '*swadeshi*' movement. Bimal though, notes that it was not that her husband refused to support *swadeshi* or was in any way against the cause, but he had not been able to accept the spirit of *'Bande Mataram'* whole-heartedly.

Bimal may be considered as a prototype of scores of Indian women, who swore by the *swadeshi* movement. They wanted to achieve *swaraj* and improve the women's status, by and large. The first step to *swaraj* was the education of women to create an awareness of their double oppression as colonial subject and inferior sex. Bimal, who has been eulogized as the 'Queen Bee' and 'Mother Goddess' by Sandip, thus falls under the hypnotic spell and his brand of patriotism. Sandeep and Bimal gradually become involved with one another and she feels liberated during the process, while being inundated with national fervour. A Bengali revolutionary, Helena Dutt said that, "we were liked caged tigers," in explaining how she and other girls her age had leapt into education and politics. (Dutt 121) As a result, women, single and married, young and old, from liberal homes came forward and joined the struggle against colonial rule. Though their number was not large yet women's involvement and participation called the British rule into question. It not only legitimized the Indian nationalist enterprise but also got an approval from the Indian men.

In fact, Sandip symbolizes the intoxicating outer world of *Bhaire*. Bimal is just not infatuated by Sandip but wants to move out of the domestic *Ghaire* to the outside world of *Bhaire* epitomized in the construct of the 'Nation,' which offers her new possibilities of self-affirmation and fulfilment. "The idea of nation as an imaginary construct opens up a space for thinking." (Kaplan Looking 46). Wrapped up in the cocoon of her inner world of *Ghaire,* till then, Bimal has been contented and complacently smug about it. However, on moving over the threshold towards *Bhaire*, she feels so enthralled by it that she is mesmerized into total liberation by the outside world of *Bhaire*. Ray beautifully evokes the confused consciousness of Bimal with great sensitivity. Ray puts, "Bimal is in the same position as Tennyson had put Guinevere in the Idylls of the King. Nikhil is the Arthur figure, the noble zamindar that, by his lofty ideals, sets up different standards of morality in devotion, behaviour and motivations. Sandip is the Lancelot figure bringing temptation, heat and colour into Bimal's life making her illicit Eros glitter in the dark. Nikhil creates a tiny Camelot for Bimal and himself like Arthur, Nikhil displays unstained virtues". (Cooper 92). In the end, Nikhil is able to accept his wife's newfound sense of individuality while Sandep is shown to be an opportunist. On celluloid, Ray plays down the novel's political overtones in favour of a straight love triangle, enacted in a meticulously researched period setting. The novel *'Ghaire Bhaire'* written by Tagore in 1916 and which Ray had intended as his debut work does recall *'Charulata'* in many ways but by the time Ray re-wrote and shot the film in 1984 it had become somewhat anachronistic. Ray's son, Sandeep Ray completed the postproduction after Ray suffered his first heartbreak.

Satyajit Ray beautifully evokes in the film in his narrative manner with his eye for detail, the obviousness of the meaning conveyed through mise en scene. Ray, however, very cleverly shows the thought process of Nikhil also when Bimal is humming an English song taught by Miss Gilby (enacted by Jennifer Kapoor) who she was lured by Nikhil himself to teach Bimal the English language, songs, manners and etiquettes. Bimal sings the song which conveys the meaning that she's been waiting to be wooed. *"Let me forget that, so long you have wooed"*. (p. 42). Nikhil gets apprehensive and a trifle stands cautioned about Bimal's state of mind. However in the novel, no such device of Bimal's infatuated state before meeting Sandip is mentioned. The song has been used as a clever strategy to project Bimal's infatuated attitude even before meeting by just casting a glance over Sandip's photograph.

In the novel Bimal just reproaches her creator for not making her surpassingly beautiful enough to steal a man's heart. She is apprehensive of her plain looks which may not impress Sandip Babu lest he just takes her to be another ordinary domesticated woman. That morning she takes special care of her looks and hence scents her hair. She drapes in a gold bordered white sari with short sleeve muslin jacket, also bordered with gold in keeping with the view that the myth of beauty is a deterministic citation of a woman's being. Her widowed sister-in-law called the 'Bari Rani' (the older daughter-in-law) gives her a meaningful smile which angers her. As a result of it, Bimal feels like putting on her everyday clothes. But she justifies her style of dressing up to her ownself by reasoning out that women are of ornamental value to society and her husband himself would approve of presenting herself beautifully clad in front of his friend Sandip Babu. She even declares to him that she envies Draupadi in the epic of Mahabharta who was the joint wife of five Pandava brothers. Inspite of professing to emancipate his wife Bimal from the *purdah* from the *Zenana* in order to herald her to the outside world Nikhil himself is surreptitiously trapped in a mind set that his wife should love him like the dutiful Sita. In the novel he does say so, "my heart has become all eyes the things that should not want to see these I must see". (p. 42). He realizes the conventional right he could claim over his wife Bimal and pride in her being his possession was taken for granted by him. His endeavour to have Bimal with him in the Bhaire i.e. the outer world was a trial which he had put himself into. However, Bimal's hero worship of Sandip did pain his heart. In the film, the connotation of his feelings speaks volumes through his expressive eyes eloquently and through a grimace of his facial expression.

Nikhil had earlier urged her to leave the *Zenana* or women's quarters to move in the outer world and meet reality and develop her personality. Bimal herself confesses at one point that she had read in books that women are called caged birds but she felt contented in that cage of her according to the tradition of purdah. She had then felt that there was no room for such a thought in the universe for her nor did any such urge then. But Bimal who has lived the sheltered life of a traditional Hindu wife from 9 years now suddenly hears the call of the *(Bhaire)* outside world in the form of Sandip, ever since she set her eyes when he came to preach Swadeshi in the neighbourhood. However she's encouraged by Nikhil to explore the *Bhaire* the outside world and crosses the threshold of the house Ghaire and is led by him both literally and metaphorically to the outside world Bhaire. She is introduced by Nikhil to his old classmate Sandip, a revolutionary who happens to be a bachelor. He puts forth a fact about Sandip before their meeting that he had many affairs of the heart in the past. He had been acclaimed as a lady charmer and women both *Videshi* and *Swadeshi* easily get enticed by his charms.

Sandip has been portrayed both in the novel and on the celluloid espousing radical ideology propagating Swadeshi goods. His triumphant shouts of 'Bande mataram' thrill Bimal and it seems to her .... "as though the skies would be rent and scattered into a thousand fragments". (p. 27). When she hears him giving a fiery speech the first time across the screen, the mise en scene is used as a clever device by Satyajit Ray to introduce both Bimal and Sandip surreptitiously to each other for the first time. She sees a mythological pattern in his fiery speech after she feels he had caught a sight of her. He was like, "the Indra's steed in the Hindu mythology who refused to be reined in". (p. 29). She has the vision of herself as the 'Shakti' (divine energy) of womanhood incarnate crowning Sandip with her presence. When they finally meet Bimal is clad in gold bordered sari and he provocatively addresses her as the 'Mother Goddess" or 'Queen Bee'. He flatters her by saying that the gold border of her sari was her own inner fire framing self out and twining around it. He infact imposes a kind of narcissism and dual personification of feminity as the powerful 'mother' as he flatters her addressing her as Mother Goddess and queen Bee who can preserve and nurture. During the tea sequence Ray establishes in mise en scene Bimal's growing attraction towards Sandip in which she is shown as becoming the sexual object of his gaze. Ray registers the mise en scene evocatively by a careful arrangement of tracking shots and slow zooms that first draw Bimal's eros to the surface and then target it on the man as a sexual object. When Sandip gets up abruptly to sing a stirring patriotic song, Nikhil and Bimal are sitting on the sofa. As he sings, the camera is focused directly on Sandip from behind Nikhil's head tracking it side way, until it rests behind Bimal's head. Moreover Ray conveys subtly the distancing of Bimal and Nikhil as Nikhil is often seen removing his glasses and wiping them. According to Cooper, "such an action brilliantly registers the gradual loss of the wife from the husband's gaze, whereas the repeated zooms seem to bring Bimal and Sandip closer together in the implied spaced from which Nikhil has been evicted". (Cooper 95).

Tagore had artistically presented with his pen-picture the impact of changing forces on everyday life in the obscure *zamindari* in Bengal. What is remarkable is the contemporaneous quality of the novel, which is thought provokingly highlighted on the celluloid by Satyajit Ray. The aesthetics *mise en scene* set up of the household, and the crossing over of the threshold of the *Ghaire* to the *Bhaire*, through the long never ending passage of a gallery leading onto it, is heightened with a cinematic projection that is so penetrating, yet enervating. The changing relationships of all the three protagonists and the conflicts going in the inner recesses of their mind are effortlessly portrayed through the expressions and with the help of props, like a caged bird desperately seeking freedom; yet, complacent in its cage, which is symbolic of Bimal's state of mind.

In Sandip's narrowly focused vision, Bimal is basically an emotional woman reduced to functioning as a sexual prisoner. In fact Sandip flatters her no end and places her on a pedestal as 'Goddess' so convincingly that she loses her own self in the outer world (bhaire). A 'feeling of personal liberation from moorings, gnaws at her heart as the stance of her support for swadeshi now get interspersed along with an attraction for a man i.e. Sandip other than her husband Nikhil. Sandip not only proves to be an opportunist and entices her to satiate his own sexual longings but even extorts her for financial gains in the name of swadeshi and liberation for the motherland. He rather smirks at Nikhil's ideal emptiness who had wished to emancipate his wife from the isolation of Ghaire. He had cherished the belief that the harmony of the home with the outside world could co-exist and would be perfect for her. Sandip on the other hand hankers to see her as the mythical Radha in the Krishna Radha legend. The songs of love of Radha-Krishna which have remained in mortal in Bengali literature for aesthetic and poetic beauty are unequalled in any literature. The view, "of {of *Parakiya,* Radhika as the married consort of another is introduced by the Bengal school of Vaisnavas and this view is established and defended in Caitanya Caritamrta of Kaviraj Gosvamin". (M. Jayanti 312). Accordingly Sandip expects Bimal at any moment in her trance world, burst in to sing the Vaishnava lyric song, "for my lover will I bind in my hair, the flower which has no equal in the three worlds". (p. 167). Moreover he tries to impress upon her that she's debarred from offering her heart at his feet which he has managed to drive her to do by his flattery. She feels obliged to pay him the sum of Rs. 50,000 demanded by him. Unwittingly Bimal is actually reduced to becoming a thief as she steals the amount of money to give to Sandip which Nikhil had put aside by, for his sister-in-law Bari Rani. However when Amulya, Sandip's misled follower brings about the revelation of Sandip's greed and penchant for good living, the reality of Sandip's true characters dawns on her.

She realizes that she has been deluded by him through psalms of her praise which he so devotedly sang. Enraptured by the vision of heaven on earth by him she realizes that it was all dust after all. From a king of heart he falls to the level of a boor. She realizes that Sandip had no strength of righteousness, unlike Nikhil. She feels guilty of the fact that she had believed that he had "the unfailing quiver of the Gods, but the shafts in them are of demons". (p. 200). Her guilt makes her lose her peace of mind. Earlier she wanted to keep running to Sandip to hear his song of endless praises for her. The 'Bari Rani' her sister-in-law had many a times taunted her for such escapades to which she had boldly become indifferent too, so smitten she was with Sandip then. At heart deep down she is basically a conventional God fearing woman trapped by the cultural moralistic ethos and feels that she will be punished for her transgression for having an affair with Sandip. She now realizes that it is Rudra the Terrible, a name of Shiva in the Hindu mythical legend who is the Lord of Chaos who destroys their bonds. Though she was allured by an immense attraction towards him and he had irresistibly drawn her towards him by manipulation and got hold of her. She realizes that it was the virtue of righteousness which Nikhil possessed and not Sandip.

Sandip however still tries to seduce her with his flattery and when he fails after Bimal gets a hang of his real designs and intentions, he shamelessly walks into the 'Ghaire' the inner chambers and privacy of Nikhil and Bimal's bedroom. Rather than being apologetic of such an action towards them, he very blatantly accuses Nikhil that if one rule can be broken by him then the other can be broken by him i.e. Sandip too. The mise en scene device used by Ray says a lot poignantlhy vis-à-vis the startled reaction of Nikhil and Bimal on Sandip's transgression into their private chambers in his cool defiant attitude and the helplessness of Nikhil and embarrassment of Bimal. Bimal clings on to the rod supports of the bed; Nikhil has a non-plussed look on his face. In the emancipatory mirror offered to her by Nikhil we see her reduced as a puppet or an object d'art for Nikhil. In fact, Nikhil earlier had taken pleasure in dressing her up with fancy western over coats, educating her, in western manners, language and songs. In fact, it is an adventurism of sorts for him, the way he loves to see Bimal adorned with distinctively coloured garments of modern fashion. In the process Bimal had even aroused the jealous wrath of his sister-in-law the 'Bari Rani'.

Bari Rani, who was Nikhil's elder brother's wife was widowed at a young age and had been a childhood companion of Nikhil when she came as a young bride to the household. Nikhil really cared for her, hence would accede to her demands. She would rather taunt him at times in his enthusiasm for his dressing up Bimal. She in fact provokingly asks him once that hasn't he got tired of this childhood game of playing with dolls yet. She feels that Bimal is symbolically a fancy doll of his childhood days. In his emancipatory attitude he leads her across the threshold over to the Bhaire. However when Bimal's growing attraction towards Sandip is noticed by 'Bari Rani', she is upset for her concern for Nikhil's well being. Bari Rani had been his childhood companion, hence a kind of a soul mate and so she could understand the hurt and pain of Nikhil's heart too. Nikhil in his magnanimity, even reconciles to Bimal's fondness for Sandip and even thinks it's inevitable as Bimal had never set her eyes on any male in last nine years. At the same time, he does not fail to remark to the Bari Rani that if it has happened then perhaps she (Bimal) was like that and there's no point regretting the freedom he gave her. In fact, such an attitude brings out the nuances of his character too. He absolves himself of pushing Bimal into quandary of such a state of affairs. He very conveniently professes his openness of mind on account of emancipated outlook which compelled him to give her the exposure of the 'Bhaire' the outer world. Little does he realize that this magnanimity of his has proved to be disastrous for Bimal in the sphere of her emotional psychological and spiritual well being.

The effect of the episodal sequence of the first meeting of Bimal and Sandip brought about by Nikhil is to encourage the audience to place the main three characters in relation to each other, and to judge the nature of the dilemmas they face in the context provided. In this way the film helps to connect up in such a single frame, the separate parts of the system existent in the society which was still in the process of dealing with the position of the women in the Bhaire, of which the drawing room is a symbolic space and metonymic semblence—the awkwardness of Bimal, the apprehensive uneasiness of Nikhil and brashness of Sandip ready not to understand the inter transitory image. It was a trying time. Satyajit Ray thus positions his heroine, "between the mirror of one man's ineffectual enlightenment and another man's sybriartic sexual politics." (Cooper 4). Bimal who had adhered to a traditional set-up right from childhood, now encouraged by her westernized husband is out to explore and execute his new ideas not only in dressing her up in western styles and attitude but her being led to the *Bhaire* hitherto unknown to her. She is literally led out into a trap unwittingly from the cocoon or her cage of *Ghaire* to the amending vistas of *Bhaire*. Caught between tradition and modernity, she becomes a puppet whose strings can be pulled by Nikhil and Sandip alternatively. The meanderings of her soul are beautifully evoked through the acting prowess of the actress Swatilekha's expressive eyes and her gestures. The price that Bimal has to pay for her so-called liberalization because of her husband's emancipatory stance, leads her only to a mental turmoil, which has to be borne by her single-handedly in seclusion. She is basically a conventional woman who has feelings of guilt gnawing into her and feels that God will punish her for her affair with Sandip. She not only emerges from the traditional constraints of the trappings of the cultural ideology but also finds no fulfilment for herself, even in the *Bhaire*. In fact, she feels burdened with guilt after she acquires the discrimination to see the difference between Sandeep and Nikhil who has the innate strength to face a crisis.

Sandip, in the meanwhile not only stirs up trouble, for his personal and political gains, between the Hindu and Muslim community, leading to rioting but even takes to his heels the moment problems arise. Nikhil, on the hand tries to interpose between the antagonistic forces, losing his life in the process. Bimal is reduced to widowhood and Ray through his filmic presentation visually captures the nuances inherent to the image of a widow. In a powerful but pathetic cinematic presentation, Ray portrays Bimal in the position of widow with shaven hair, a plain *saree* and an unadorned self through three dramatic dissolves of her appearance. From the rich wife of a *zamindar*, bedecked with luxurious hair, expensive clothes and jewellery, she is reduced by these three cruel dissolves device, to a weeping widow in keeping with the Hindu forces of her age as informing cultural practice. The woman figure, shorn of all her adornments, looking like a recluse or a very phantom of herself, reflects on the price a woman has to pay, a price for her induction into the outside world and whether the man leading her to it has to be the empathetic sacrificial lamb, is, however questionable.

It would be debatable to take into account the views of C.S. Lakshmi who believes that when the film begins with a flashback shot of Bimal talking about herself, the viewer is given to believe that her eye is going to be synonymous with the camera eye. However, it is not so, "since when the film unfolds she is not the narrator anymore. The camera represents the director in terms of the knowledge it is imparting." (Lakshmi 220). Lakshmi feels that if the film had been from Bimal's point of view, then one would perceive how the world seemed to her when she was in the confinement of the *Ghaire*, the household and later how did the world seem at the magic moment when she stepped into the *Bhaire* i.e. outside world. No such emotions of Bimal or her feelings are portrayed from such a point of view in the film. Apart from showing the flashback from Bimal's point of view, the narrative is woven around what Nikhil and Sandeep see or fail to see. The audience follows Nikhil's growing uneasiness and Sandip's voyeurism blatantly as he defiantly woos Bimal. He has chosen to be a successful revolutionary with all the attendant possibilities of pursuing the means to the end selfishly. Yet one feels that Ray works through the maze of Bimal's emotions and manages to show her emotional upheavals effectively through her facial expressions. According to Andrew Robinson, 'The Home and the World' is high tragedy, its ambit is of much greater complexity and shorn of easy romance, its characters are forced to confront the wider effects of their own deficiencies.

"However the vision of Ray is deeper, maturer and darker. There is a kind of tension in the film you know everything is going to fall apart. The movement and growth of character and relationship is important to him than what's happening on the surface and develops using a musicality that brings to mind the late Beethoven". (Robinson 272).

Even though, the problematic "relation of 'woman' to nation is often overlooked in discussions of nationality and nationhood." (Kaplan Looking 47); yet, it is not relevant to ignore this representation. Bimal's moving out from the *Ghaire*, the home to the *Bhaire*, outside world reflects startling moments of insight experienced by her as in a way it implies,

"a displacement, leaving or going up a place that is home (physically, emotionally, linguistically and epistemologically) for another place that is unknown and risky, that is not only emotionally, but conceptually, a voice of discourse from which speaking and thinking are at best tentative uncertain and unguaranted". (Yeatman 139).

Bimal is placed in an unenviable position as she is taken to the 'Bhaire' by Nikhil and wooed by Sandip with his public oratory skill for the *swadeshi* cause. She is both manipulated and manoeuvred by both of them. One sees her seduced by two different worlds in which her liberation is promised but never delivered. Both the men try to impose their own version of the ideal Hindu woman they want Bimal to be. Each world and culture which *Ghaire* and *Bhaire* i.e. Home and the Outside World embodies, becomes in the film, a strategic mirror in which the ownership of both the males on Bimal is determined as they both manage to mould her to their attitudes. The mirroring device becomes the film's central motif and Ray uses it masterfully to chronicle the painful odyssey of a woman, whose image is never fated to be her own. Both displacements, the personal and conceptual, are painful and she has to work out her salvation through tribulation and experimentation and suffering and disaster. In fact, both Bimal and Nikhil suffer since Sandip conveniently exits and leaves the scene, as he has no more pound of flesh to be extracted.

Nikhil pays the price with his life by getting killed during the communal riot but it is Bimal who is ultimately victimized and punished. She had felt pangs of guilt as a conventional woman for indulging in the affairs of heart and going against the cultural ideology. In fact her image of widowhood shorn of all the adornments now is like that of the *Bari Rani,* her sister-in-law who had been widowed earlier. In a similar process, Bimal is emptied of her essential female selfhood of the way married Indian woman sees herself decked up with all the essential adornments, which declare her marital status, which is highlighted as a contrast by Ray earlier in the movie between Bimal's and *Bari Rani's* appearance. This is attributed as essentialism as a belief of a true female/feminine nature of an Indian woman. In the novel, her waiting for Nikhil who has gone out to interpose between the two antagonistic forces riot stricken Hindus and Muslims seems like turmoil to her which could be put to end by her death. She feels that so long as she was alive her sins would loom large intrinsically as an integral part of her being. Her very existence would gnaw at her guilt for the destruction she brought upon herself. In the novel, however, Bimal is redeemed with the cathartic purification of Nikhil's funeral pyre. But in the film Satyajit Ray leaves a starker, stamped expression of Bimal cinematically in her imagery of widowhood with her physical purity tarnished. Earlier Bimal had fears about the impending threat of punishment, which might be meted on her on account of her nature of illicit relationship with Sandip. Bimal suffers from a guilt complex that she is not supposed to desire any other man in her life. By her act of desiring Sandip she has terminated her need for her husband Nikhil. Since Nikhil dies leaving her a widow it proves to be a logical culmination. In a way by reducing her to a state of widowhood Tagore affirms the view of the threat of widowhood for the educated woman, which, though, was rooted in a kind of superstition then. Her love even though misguided for Sandip gets seen as a transgression and symbolically cancels out Nikhil her husband.

Widowhood for Bimal can be seen as a physical embodiment of the emotional consequence she has to face for it. It replicates, farce written in the connection between adultery and widowhood in 1897 by S.P. Pal in a play whose title 'Meyeder Lakhapara, Apna Hath Dube Mara' may be translated as "educate the woman, and you are digging your own grave; educated woman first turns to adultery, and then murders her husband". (Sarkar Tanika 158). Unwittingly, both Tagore and Ray replicate the traditional imagery of the widowhood in 'Ghaire Bhaire'. Ray accentuates it by cinematically reducing Bimal to a stark look of widowhood on the celluloid. Both, thus put a question mark on the meaning of women's education and on the social reform in this sphere. To the orthodox Indian male patriarchy, the figure of the wife has to exercise a total and unmitigated commitment to the husband. To the emancipated, liberal, western educated man, the education for the wife was to mean a better order of conjugality. Yet, somewhere both Tagore and Ray seem to grapple with these contradictions and there seems to be an apprehension about it. Bimal is considered no longer chaste by Bari Rani and also by her husband Nikhil. His desire to meet her as an equal in the Bhaire; rather, indicates the repudiation of the fatal course. Her yearning for Sandip has the images of an allusion clearly derived from the references to the Indian scriptures such as the representations based on illicit desire like the sacred liaison between Radha and Krishna. Fascination for Krishna actualizes the popular imagination by Mirabai, the famous 16th Century saint poet of India. "It is symbolic of the dual aspect of reverence and repression latent in the Indian tradition". (Kishwar In Search 29).

Mirabai belonged to the traditional royal family of Mewar and she was married at an early age, much against her wishes. However she refused to mould herself in confining role of a wife and daughter-in-law. The 16th Century Bhakti movement of social and religious reform provided Mirabai as it did many other women of that period with a way of defying and stepping out of the oppressive social obligations imposed an women of her caste and class. For this, she had to face tremendous persecution at the hands of her husband's family including attempts to poison and kill her. Yet until today she is remembered as part of popular folklore not only for her beautiful poetry but as much of her ability to resist and challenge the tyrannical power of her oppressive family. Many such women emerged during the 19th Century Social reform movement as well as during the national movement.

The narrative fluidity of the story is interesting and lucidly expressed in the film as it captures the subjective consciousness and the interior life of the main protagonists Bimal, Nikhil and Sandip. In the first stage, when all three Nikhil, Bimal and Sandip are shown in one frame in the celluloid medium that they look startlingly static together, though it is a heavingly loaded charged scene. Bimal keeps looking away offscreen and seems uneasy in the set up initially, though as she gradually seems to settle down even enjoying being in Sandeep's company, the Bhaire. Nikhil who has been a go-between in getting Bimal and Sandip together in the Bhaire in the long run gets reflected as the lonely outsider surprisingly. The mise en-scene rather shows Nikhil's psychological discomfort while trying to strike up an attitude of benignity in getting Bimal to the *Bhaire* to meet his friend Sandip. The camera moves and counter moves from Sandip standing a little away and to Bimal and Nikhil sitting together on the sofa and points to a syntax of exclusion versus inclusion giving the viewers a spectatorial position. The visual interference of the artifacts lying around in the rooms that are aesthetically set up, enhances the *mise en scene* device. They correspond, however to Nikhil's presence, as he seems to be being excluded even though unwittingly, with Sandip and Bimal developing a rapport and feeling of congeniality with each other. The sound play variation signifies inclusion of gaze away from Nikhil towards Sandip. Sandip's persistent gaze at Bimal and Nikhil's thoughtfulness constitute the defining concept.

Nikhil, a young upper caste liberal minded *zamindar* influenced by western education, feels the need to emancipate his wife Bimal who is taught to sing English songs and play the piano and dress up in the English kind of blouses with the Bengala kind of sari she wears. *Bari Rani* represents the orthodoxy in the novel and in the film as such which represented on accord of by her scathing comments about Nikhil's exposing Bimal to the western influence. Like the orthodoxy she feared social ostracism, threats of excommunication and of losing their caste. Bimal too, earlier is of a similar mind-set and is apprehensive about Miss Gilby and is unsympathetic towards her when she is attacked by a stone pelted on her by one of the revolutionaries for freedom movement. Nikhil's role is that of the western influenced male who offers emancipation to his wife and in a way becomes a suggestion of the role which he assumes in the relationship of his role as the Sahib vis-à-vis the woman, represented here by and Bimal as that of the Indian woman who stands in the same relation to the Indian man as he was vis-à-vis the colonial master. The relationship between both is the relationship of colonization, of the colonized and colonizer. To possess her and mould her to his thought process was to feel like a man in the colonized country. *Bari Rani* feels that Nikhil is weaning Bimal away from past rich cultural traditions and by aligning her to new western rules he would corrupt her ultimately. Nikhil was out to create an authentic, autonomous new female selfhood for Bimal. Bimal under the influence of ancient laws that she had imbibed as a part of cultural ideology believes that it is her destiny to accept subjections under her husband. Gradually as Bimal moves out from the threshold of the home (*Ghaire*) inspired by his liberalism and his attitude towards reformation, she sees the *Bhaire* (outer world) as a means of liberating herself from the claustrophobic *Ghaire* (household). Little does Nikhil realize that his masculine identity primarily in terms of his power over Bimal would be threatened with the emergence of Bimal as an autonomous person. The *Bhaire* (outer world) no longer lets her be the repressed one, and destabilizes the culturally ordered balance of power in their gender relationship. There is a feeling of loss, of her beloved devotion towards him and her innocence is no longer based on ignorance but experience, which she acquires in her interaction with the *Bhaire* in the form of the other protagonist Sandip.

There is a wealth of meaning in the story and the film adapted for the celluloid. There is however, an easy kind of polemical point that Bimal, "was merely a dupe of a liberal mirage brought along with in light eminent knowledge systems". (Chaudhuri 153). In 'Charulata' based on the novella 'Nashta Nir' (The Broken Nest), the traditional role and status of woman is questioned, as Charulata suffers claustrophobia even in her materially comfortable and socially prestigious marriage as she looks through her binoculars into the outside world from her home's balcony, which in a way symbolizes freedom and happiness. She is an aware educated woman who admires the writings of Bankimchandra. Her husband Bhupati, is an editor and publisher of an English political weekly, The Sentinel. He is a modern intellectual and is much influenced by liberal western thought, but with very little time for his wife Charu whom he indulges rather than understands. She spends her days in isolation, reading novels and working on her embroidery in the Ghaire (her household). It never occurs to her husband that she needs to interact with the life in *Bhaire* (outside world). In fact he gets his younger literary cousin, Amol to interact with her in the Ghaire itself which leads to her falling in love with him. It is only in the end when Amol leaves to get married to a rich heiress in England instigated by Bhupati that he realizes that Charu had seen him as a companion for her lonely moments and intellectual discussion.

By making 'Ghaire Bhaire' after 'Charulata', Ray, infact naturally follows the course of a situation, which could inevitably occur if the wife moves from the *Ghaire* to the *Bhaire*. The film justifies in a way a natural progression of events that perhaps Tagore was in a way apprehensive about, as he set the story of 'Charulata' in the Calcutta of 1879 and the story of 'Ghaire Bhaire' in 1916. In the adaptation of the novels for celluloid "Ray not only depicted the Indian woman's wilful and radical participation in a revolution to gain her emancipation, but also focuses on her attempt to force the Indian man to acknowledge her equality to provide her with necessary opportunities to be a woman and to view her femininity as an essential part of her personal identity". (Cooper 79).

The patriarchal hierarchy led to insensitive gender organization of the family, the condition of widow's relationships of power was the world that reformers sought to change. Nikhil a progressive idealist, thinker of his times, defies those reformers in the older world, which kept men and women in their separate domains of *Ghaire* and *Bhaire*. Nikhil too like many liberated men of his times, wanted to see his wife Bimal, in the *Bhaire*. India was moving through various socio-economic and political stages, a colonized country towards struggle for independence. It was also one of those transitory trying times in the journey from segregation of the *Ghaire* to the outside world of the *Bhaire*. The transitory change of those times to move away from the *Ghaire* to *Bhaire* was a great challenge for women of her kind too. To peep into her world and look into the inner recesses of her dilemma could be luminous, however, which just can't be portrayed by a male justifiably. Even if Tagore was writing Bimal's diary, it is immensely difficult to project the complex reality of her living.

Nationalism involved the acceptance of liberal western ideas and paradigms of literature along with the revival of Sanskrit poetics. However, the acquisition of western knowledge was also acquisition of the means of social climbing. The account of the rise of English was in the context of the colonizers-colonized relationship. Nikhil the main protagonist, wanting his wife Bimal to learn to play the piano and learn to sing English songs, is acquiescing to the western influence. Perhaps somewhere Tagore is apprehensive about the colonial experience, which affected the Indian perception of many western influenced liberated men. It was one of the transitional changes for the western educated liberated youths and in the conditioned cultural values rooted in his mind as an intrinsic part of tradition. Somewhere he was trapped in his mind eventually on account of it. The Indian Renaissance and the Indian nationalism had tacitly accepted cultural amnesia as an indispensable condition for progress. In a way it reflected of the Indian capacity to accept cultural duality, which was finely sharpened by the colonial experience. However the fear psychosis and the sense of crisis and tension caused in being torn between westernisation and trappings of cultural ideological tradition gripped the psyche of the Indian male. It led to the sense of crisis of the transitional period, which was rather irreversible as a never-ending transition.

The concept of *'Ghaire Bhaire'* i.e. the home and the world, was only a nineteenth century invention. It is more likely that this feudal social life of the property classes of Bengali Indian lent itself to manipulations and adoption by elite male proposals for the construction of the nation. This arrangement however was never satisfactory nor fully accomplished or perhaps be conclusive even logically, inspite of the growing western influence. Rabindranath Tagore's novel by the same name, "'*Ghaire Bhaire'*, 'The Home and Outside world' speaks of the ultimately impossibility of such a division." (Bannerji 193). It was perhaps in a way repudiation of the liberated western educated Indian's who wanted to mould their wives for the *Bhaire*. It was also in a way warning to them, that such an act could have the potential in the disruption of their domesticity. The metaphor of *Bhaire* could have all the potential of disruption in the harmony of the gender relations too which pre-existed before the wife moved from the *Ghaire* to the *Bhaire*. In fact,

> "the binary of the home and the world lent itself to manipulation in male constructions of the nation, the home being projected as a repository of spiritual values and the world as the realm of active political struggle". (Chaudhuri and Mukherji 9).

As a result many a women's minds and bodies were sacrificed at the altar of patriarchy. Nikhil's conduct may reflect here the coldness of intellectual husbands who fail their wives and drive them into a kind of insanity because they do not understand them at all. The character of Nikhil has a kind of semi-intellectual tinge to it, or to be more rude 'metaphysical' content about it. Nikhil who is a representative of the modern liberal reforms, little did he realize that modern education and the binary of the home and the world which he was tying to diminish in Bimal's life to see her as an equal partner beyond the *Ghaire* i.e. Home in the *Bhaire* (outside world) proves to be burdensome to Bimal. It placed her like many a Hindu wife who obeyed her husband to be under a double burden of servitude to her deracinated educated husband. It was in keeping according to, "the cultural agenda of white masters who educated Indians to destroy their cultural authenticity," according to Dipesh Chakrabarty. (19). The conflict between bondage and liberation was a major thematic concern of *Ghaire Bhaire*, 'The Home and The World'. "The emotional theme of gender relations i.e. man-woman relationship beautifully intertwined along with the political theme of Indian Nationalism raising women's question too". (Basavraj 39).

GABAN

Gaban (The Embezzlement) can be seen as a middle class film offering a critique of Indian society. In its linear narrative form it imparts to convey the reality of our life through veracity and authenticity, a phenomena, "which is regarded in the west as synonymous with Indian cinema." (Dwyer and Patel 7). It has Hindi film's, "omnibus genre of the social, with its underlying theme of the feudal family romance". (Prasad 118). Munshi Premchand is irrefutably one of the greatest Hindi novelists, who embodies and reflects in his works the entire social stratum of life during the years of pre independence era, during the struggle for independence and non–cooperation movements, a period of stress and storm. He unconsciously took up a position on the social and political problems, which affected the people at that age. His greatness lies in expressing faithfully the frame of mind of the peasants and the outlook of the middle classes at the time of radical changes in the social and political life of the country.

Premchand was the pen name of Dhanpat Rai. He took to writing merely as a hobby but had an insatiable hunger for devouring whatever came in his way without any judicious or critical selection. He was a government servant with a comfortable salary but resigned from the government service and joined the swelling ranks of non–co-operators against the British government in 1920, under the influence of Mahatma Gandhi. After that, he devoted himself entirely to the cause of nationalism and literature. In fact, his creative literature was an outcome of his philosophy and outlook on life. The period (1905-1936) in which Premchand lived and wrote was the transition from feudalism to the bourgeois order. The old foundations of the peasant economy and peasant life went crashing during the period of national struggle against British domination and the advancing wave of capitalism. There was an ancient and ever-growing discontent in the village with the land owning system. All this matured during the political struggles of 1920-22 and 1930-32. As a result, of it there was the emergence of the class of workers, a new force created by the rise of capitalism.

Premchand was born in a village near Benares, the holy-city of India. He lived in the heart of the countryside and was sensitively aware of the social and political changes, which were taking place in the life of the people of his region. Premchand expressed very faithfully and vigorously the frame of mind of the peasantry in his writings along with the outlook of the middle classes at the time of the radical changes in India. He correctly reflected the epoch of his times and saw and understood it with an eye of a sensitive artist. The economic and social factors of his times had a bearing on his works, which had conditioned the psychology and ideology of inner social consciousness and sociological interpretations. Premchand's first book of stories was published in 1909 in Urdu but he turned writing from Urdu to Hindi in the year 1916 because of his belief that writing in Hindi would reach a wider audience. To him, "belongs the distinction of creating the genre of the serious short story as well as the realistic novel in both Hindi and Urdu". (Chaudhuri 133). He drew a vivid picture of the problems and values, which governed the life of middle classes, landlords, industrialists, peasants, workers, untouchables and even the outcasts of society, such as widows and prostitutes.

For Premchand, the geographical boundaries and frontiers did not exist on the map of literature and he admired both Tolstoy and Gorky. Gorky was a people's writer and so was he. He had a deep empathy for man and invariably searched the good and the true and the beautiful in humanity and he felt inspired when he discovered these values in mankind. Premchand also deeply believed in the equality of sexes and expressed great indignation over the injustice practised by men on women. He never had much faith in the worn out traditions of the past. Time, he said, was always on the move and social laws were subject to change. He was essentially a reformer and not a revolutionary. Premchand made his reputation as the father of social realism in the act of, "mirroring the era of social trauma and reform in North India, with its problems of caste, widowhood and the impoverished peasantry by both chronicling that world and transforming it into a purgatorial landscape." (Chaudhuri 34). Premchand's writings are timeless and secular to the core but he was not, at the same time, severed off from the Indian cultural roots. Rather, he upheld the joint family system. He may not have written political history of a nation in turmoil, yet no one wrote more poignantly about human emotions and Indian farmers as he did. He belonged to a progressive social group, espoused a particular standard of morals and used the novel to express his social purpose and social criticism. He was, in fact, the pioneer of the new art form and the novel with a didactic social purpose.

Premchand was a writer rooted in his time; he was a novelist who saw his medium as an instrument of social change. His realistic portrayal of the life and times of India in the twentieth century has an unmistakable strain of idealism. He was the most famous novelist of India of his times and is rightly called so because he was true both to life and art. He started writing fiction at the turn of this century and observed with a keen pair of eyes, the changes occurring in the social fabric of India. He was also aware of the political aspiration of the Indian masses. He chronicled the political and social turmoil in the life of Indians, through the medium of short stories and novels. His first collection of short stories was published in *The Hindu* and was entitled *'Soze-Watan'* (The love of Home Land). For Premchand, literature was not mental luxury or a matter of word play, for he was convinced that literature has a social role and it could remain significant only if it is zealously guarded in its relevance to real life. In this aspect, he was influenced by Tolstoy and later by Gorky, who struck sympathetic chords in his artistic psyche. He never believed in the theory of art for art's sake; yet, he believed that fiction could have an impact on the psyche of the reader only if it had a satisfactory form and a topical theme.

There were several films adapted from Premchand's stories and novels for the celluloid. Satyajit Ray made a film based on Premchand's story titled *'Shatranj ke Khiladi'* which depicts the decadence of life during the regime of the Nawabs of Oudh in which people are more interested in the intricate game of chess rather than vital issues facing life. Mrinal Sen, too, has directed a film based on his story *'Kafan'*. His novels *'Godaan'* and *'Gaban'* have also been made into films besides *'Hira-Moti'*, which presented the glimpses of peasant life by Premchand during the complete tensions and paradoxes of contemporary historical, political, social times. His fiction has an artistic consciousness about it, which has significance and meaning relevant to the vision of life. He, however mainly used his artistic creation as an instrument of social change. His art echoed life in his times and is yet timeless. As a progressive writer, he was handicapped by the limited vision and ideology of his own class. Yet, he was a prolific writer who gives a comprehensive picture of the middle class life and its problems. With an incisive and probing style, he analyzed the diverse problems, which affect the members of the class and gender relations. As a matter of fact he was the first Hindi novelist who has treated the socio-cultural, economic, moral problems in an earnest and sincere way.

'Gaban' which was based on Premchand's novel was co-directed by Krishan Chopra and Hrishikesh Mukherjee, as the former director died during its making and Hrishikesh Mukherjee finally completed it. He successfully patched together this film following the death of the original director Krishan Chopra and it was finally released in 1966. The co-script writers were Krishan Chopra and Bhanu Pratap. Baij Sharma and Akhtar-ul-Iman wrote the dialogues. The lyrics were penned by Hasrat Jaipuri and Shailender and many of its songs went on to become the popular hit songs of their time, set to the music of Shankar-Jaikishan. Since Premchand was a realist novelist, its representation in the cinematic medium was also set along the lines of a realist style, by the filmmakers. According to Fareed

Kazmi, "when a filmmaker decides on a realist style he or she does so to decrease the distance between the viewer and the subject". (Kazmi Fareed 54). The final director, Hrishikesh Mukherjee was also an editor and had worked as an assistant director and editor for Bimal Roy. He was renowned for introducing certain editing conventions, which are basic to Hindi films e.g. intersection shots and acquired the reputation of being able to salvage films that went out of control during shooting. He however continued making films in the vein of Bimal Roy's socials.

The film was set in Allahabad, in the year 1928 during the anti-British extremist movement that was at a peak between the Simon Commission and the Gandhi-Irwin pact (1929). *'Gaban'* in Hindi means embezzlement. The novel was written by Premchand in 1931 and is strictly speaking, devoid of any incident of actual embezzlement taking place in the story. The story deals with a highly interesting problem, which affects the married life of a lower middle class couple. A perpetual want of money on the one hand and a craving for high standard of life, on the other threatens their happiness. Ramnath, the male protagonist of Premchand's novel, is basically a foppish young man, an idler but being the eldest male child in the lower middle class family of the *kayasth*-sub-caste represents the typical Hindu male who gets married to Jalpa, a beautiful young girl who has been brought up on the notion of gaining respectability and opulence through marriage. There is a belief that,

> "marriage brings a qualitative change, a reconstruction of two individuals into a single being, and thus an instance of the temporal in touch with the permanent, the marriage of two mortals recreating the original marriage of the sun with the earth". (Handy and Westbrook 200).

However, just a mere legal procedure does not cause such a reconstruction; a special language is required for it. Similarly, the father of the bride just does not simply tell the groom to take her to be his wife but it is to be solemnized with rituals. *Kanyadaan* i.e. giving away the daughter is the act of handing her over to the groom. It is not a symbol merely but involves the daughter also who acts out her part in the play by leaving the side of her parents and joining hands with the groom and his family to become an integral part of the family too. However, in the story of *'Gaban'* hidden from her is the fact that the groom's family is not as rich as made out by the groom. She is thus unable to accept the fact that she has not been bestowed with a special necklace *'chandrahar'* as part of her wedding present from the groom's family especially when Ramnath, the groom has grossly exaggerated his family wealth. Indian society is characterized and dominated by collectivities of the family as a unit. "Family patterns are cultural patterns which vary from place to place and aspects culture directly define the patterns of social inter action". (Davis 4). A young girl child in India, especially in 20s and 30s was brought up with a vision to be an ideal '*bahu*', wife and mother in the Sati Savitri and Parvati mould. But the female protagonist, Jalpa, the wife of Ramnath, the main protagonist has also been indoctrinated with an inordinate love of jewellery from childhood by her family, relatives, friends and neighbours.

The novel as well as the film strikes the right note in the very first chapter/first scenes of the narration on reel. The cultural atmosphere at the weddings in the display of ostentatiousness of the then typical Hindu Indian family is also established à galore. The young girls are attuned to the idea of the use of ornaments at the wedding and jewellery, which becomes a part of their dreams and desires right from childhood. Jalpa recalls at her wedding the peddler's remarks, who while selling artificial jewellery to her as a child, remarks that she would be married as a grown up and receive a real *chandrahar* of her own. Her mother too tells Jalpa, "your necklace will come from your in-laws"[3]. (Premchand 26). Jalpa embarrassed, runs away, but the words had been engraved on her heart and the idea of her future in-laws house was no longer so terrible to her. In the celluloid version, the script-writer and the director make the heroine sing and dance, "*Aye re din sawan ke*" translated as, "the beautiful days of spring have come," reflecting that a girl is on the threshold of her youth and is singing and dreaming of marriage, the groom and of course the jewellery. The lyrics of the first song sung by the heroine in the film embody the same emotion for love, jewellery, in-laws, groom and happiness.

However, extravagant ostentatiousness and expenditure at the wedding beyond his means, finds a victim in Dayanath the father of the groom, too. He, too, succumbs to his desire for showing off, and this, makes him also a culprit to a certain extent along with his son to all the related problems later on. The novelist, as well as the director of 'Gaban' beautifully depicts this cultural scene. The delighted face of Dayanath comes across on the screen when he sees his friends, neighbours admiring the wedding *barat*, but the audience can also see a twinge of guilt lurking behind the gleeful countenance of Dayanath, at the thought of wasting precious money. Again, the director does a marvellous job of this particular scene. A word here, a sentence there, and the message is conveyed. Ostentatious display of wealth and jewellery and by extension, the society that exaggerates its significance, all this is suggested in the written words and on camera. According to C.G. Jung, "the hypothesis of a collective unconscious belongs to the class of idea that a people at first find strange but soon come to possess and use as familiar conceptions" (Jung Archetypes 205).

Ramnath, as an ideal husband, does not deny Jalpa any money. She encourages him to accompany her to the cinema and thus openly challenges the norms of society. He, however, feels a great sense of pleasure and pride in accompanying her on outings. At one time, he had been a devout follower of *purdah* and when sometimes he took his mother to bathe in the Ganges he would not even let her talk to the *Brahman Pandas*. One of the leading lawyers Pundit Indra Bhushan's wife Ratan befriended Jalpa and sought her out. Ratan, infact, was Vakil Sahab's wife from the second marriage. His first wife has died thirty-five years ago and after her his young son died too. He had got married at sixty years to a young not so good-looking orphan Ratan to beget children. Unfortunately, the doctors had told her that she couldn't have any children yet Vakil Saab was not offended about it and treated Ratan with great respect and denied her nothing. She revered him like God in return. With Jalpa, she develops a sisterly relationship and is very understanding when Ramnath suddenly vanishes, as he fears that the police will catch him for the embezzlement.

Ramanath basically tries to be honest but borrows large amounts of money in order to satisfy his wife's desire for jewellery. Ramnath who has just been employed as a clerk with Municipal board as a new job recruit, is shown getting tips from his predecessor on how to maintain a personal account alongside the company cash box. The cinematic device shows the rascally goldsmith's signboard characteristically, which reads the axiom "honesty is the best policy" in the film. However, he is deeply in love with his beautiful wife Jalpa whom he wants to please but cannot do so because of the lack of *chandrahaar*·in her jewellery. It has been a dream of her to own one since her childhood, spurred by her own parents. His eager desire to see his beautiful wife Jalpa, all decked up in finery leads him to certain misdoings. Jalpa oblivious of it on the other hand feels gratified when she receives *chandrahaar*. Her lovely face sparkles which gives Ramnath a sense of pride. Jewellery is not just a means of displaying wealth in India, but is considered a woman's only legal possession as an aspect of cultural tradition. "The jewellery she is given on marriage is known as *streedhan* (woman's wealth) and it never belongs to her husband's property". (Patel and Dwyer 24). However, Ramnath also tastes the joy of victory as a loving and giving husband which he had not felt on account Jalpa's endless sulking as she had to return the jewellery given to her at the time of her marriage by her in-laws so that they may clear their debts. With the possession of the new *Chandrahaar* she threw her glass *Chandrahaar* away. Its luster seemed dim and dull to her as that compared to the light of the stars next to the clear radiance of the moon then to her. The beautiful rendition of the song *"Maine dekha tha sapnon mein Chandrahaar aaj balam neh mujhe pehanadiya"* translated "I had visualized the Chandrahaar in my dreams, today my beloved has gifted me one in actuality", highlights her sense of ecstatic pleasure. From that day on Jalpa's love for her husband Ramnath is marked by a new devotion. For Ramnath the ornaments that he had brought for her seemed mere trifles compared to the sweet affection she showered on him. As a result, Jalpa who had become a solitary isolated distant woman hanging around feeling crestfallen and hiding herself from social gatherings now becomes very social with the neighbourhood. Her beauty and charm alongwith her attire and new found courtesy and conduct very soon gives her a place of honour among the women in neighbourhood. With her soft sweet speech and her incomparable grace she seems to be the queen of her new circle of friends and she brings new life into local female society. She enters into this society with dignity and her beauty has that austerity, splendour and brilliance which reflects the imprints of a good family descent. The actress Sadhna in the role of Jalpa suited the role totally and carried it with great aplomb.

Ramnath after buying *Chandrahaar* for her finally, gets involved in debts without her knowledge. As he is a victim of middle class respectability and his own egoism, he does not disclose this debt and forgery to his wife who could have easily saved the situation by returning the fatal ornament. This forces him to temporarily 'borrow' government money and gets the police after him. Ramnath flees from Allahabad to Calcutta and when he finds himself in the mire, he gets thoroughly demoralized. Hence he becomes a person who can tell any number of lies, can beg, can turn an approver, a police stooge against the revolutionaries, who were his own college mates once upon a time, to save his skin. According to Ashish Nandy, "The Hindi film has more than its fair share of villains, and of these some are demonic but for that reason all the more assimilable to *rakshas*, the creatures of mythology rather than the history". (Nandy The Secret 237). However, the police force made up of Indians, which is basically a British establishment, alternately bully and fawn over Ramnath and persuade him to give fake evidence against the revolutionaries. It is then that Jalpa becomes the only redeeming feature and a saving grace in his life. As soon as she comes to learn of his financial debt, she sells her gold bangles to clear off his debts and thus represents the ideal of Indian womanhood in the story. Ramnath, however, is unaware of all this fact.

The whole novel in fact is a journey for Ramnath and Jalpa from darkness to light, from deceit to truth. A similar journey is destined for Zohra, a prostitute who becomes a strong character in the novel in the end and also Ratan, a friend of Jalpa who acquires interesting hues as the novel progresses and is a transformed character by the time Premchand draws a curtain to the novel as well as various characters. Surprisingly, but perhaps not so surprisingly, both the characters of Zohra and Ratan do not occupy much celluloid space in the cinematic version of the novel directed by Krishan Chopra and after his untimely death by Hrishikesh Mukherji. The script-writer Akhtar-ul-iman Ali has done away with lengthy characterization of certain characters that occupy many pages of the novel but on the screen, have either a fleeting existence or are absent altogether.

The film script which gets off to a leisurely start with the hero Sunil Dutt as Ramnath drifting from chess board to matrimony which is arranged by his parents. According to sociologists, anyone turning to the Indian family soon encounters a strange paradox. On the one hand, all the manifestations of popular thought disclose an intense and continuous interest in family affairs, yet every short story, film, novel and play weaves its plot around romantic love. However, "solemn books harp constantly on the family's importance in personality development and social well being assuring *ad nauseam* that the family is the most fundamental and universal of all institutions". (Davis 392). In fact, more than Ramanath or Jalpa, it is the society, which has been given undue importance, thus leading to 'embezzle' true self of the main protagonists of the novel/film. They achieve true bliss, salvation and *moksha* only when the shackles of 'embezzler' society are thrown away in the end.

The relationship between both of them is initially based on her love for jewellery and his for her. Out of his love for her, he boasts of an imaginary wealth, out of her love for *chandrahar*, she demands it because of his wealth. Both are initially groping in the dark She is unaware that he has no wealth and he is unaware that she loves him too and not only the *chandrahar*. Ramanath is a weak character and cannot muster courage to face reality, a trait that eventually is his undoing.

Questioning is taking place in the minds of both but the overwhelming emotion is love. Both are on the threshold of their marriage, love is on the horizon, but her obsession for *chandarhar* and his basic meek and weak traits, ordain otherwise-till the course of events begin to change and they both realize their true self. The theme of true love and its impediments is indeed a universal one and evokes the sympathy of its audience. Love's transformative potential lay in the idea that it was an intense passionate relationship that establishes a holy oneness between man and woman. In India it was the medieval *Bhakti* movements and personalities who elaborated a discourse on spiritual love with romantic overtones. The songs of Mirabai express devotional love in a language drawn from the institutions of sexuality, courtship and marriage.

"Gender has never been a stable matter. It has been argued that the meanings of 'female' and 'woman' abound with ambiguity, self-contradiction and paradoxical argument. Gender relies on incoherence of definition". (Deutscher 1). The concept of spheres, the public open to men and the private being women's domain has been a major orienting principle for women's history. However, Jalpa has to shift from the private space i.e. domain of the family to the public space/domain i.e. the society and nation. Even if any given family is connected to the rest of the society in only a limited sense, the family in that sense seems socially unimportant. However, according to sociologists, "it is only the pattern of family relationships and the effect of this pattern in millions of homes that influences the total society at large". (Davis 393). As a result, in any study of the cultural pattern of human society as a whole, marriage and the family cannot be omitted. Their fascination for the popular mind and their identification with morality, both attest their social significance even though it is not the sort of significance that lends itself to being understood by rationalistic social science. Jalpa has to resolve the integration of Ramnath into the family who has moved on a path which takes him away from the family being on the run from Allahabad to Calcutta as he fears that police is after him. He manages to find surrogate parents at Calcutta in Devidin who is a doughty patriot enacted by Kanhaiyalal. He, himself has lost his sons to the freedom movement. He has a dominating wife who not only looks after the tea stall shop and manages the finances of the house but also runs the odd errands and looks after the house efficiently. Jalpa is like Rama, in the epical mythology of *Ramayana* who goes in the search of his Sita as she moves into public space, from Allahabad to Calcutta in search of him.

Ramnath is unaware that Jalpa has repaid the embezzlement money for which he is blackmailed by a repressive police force into being presented as a false eyewitness to give evidence that would convict non-violent nationalists for terrorist acts. Ironically, he is also lured by Zohrabai, who at the behest of police tries to entangle him in love through lust. According to Stevi Jackson, "it is through our embodiment that we recognize each other as gendered beings and engage in sexual practices". (Jackson 142). With all her wisdom, Jalpa moves out of the family paradigm. She takes her younger brother-in-law with her and locates the place where Ramnath had been living with his surrogate parents, endears herself to them and tries to save Ramnath from the grip of Zohrabai and the police finally. She initially even defies her in-laws to move out who finally realize her earnestness to get Ramnath back to the family fold. They supportively endorse her courage, her resolve to solve the problem of the family and of her love and her marriage. She is bold, intelligent and dignified having self-esteem and maintains her individuality and draws respect and admiration from her in-laws contrary to her image of obstinancy of demanding a 'chandrahaar'. Besides being intelligent she is politically aware too and gets actively involved and controls the reins of a vacillating husband bringing him on the right path through her perseverance. Not only does she give up her life of comfort, she even works to look after the revolutionary leader's family who is imprisoned and meets judges to apprise them of the unduress pressure on her husband by the repressive police force to be a false witness in the court.

Jalpa's travelling from Allahabad to Calcutta in search of her husband Ramnath, traces a complex intellectual and psychic journey. There is a linked new consciousness to it. By reversing the male/female role of Rama-Sita in Jalpa and Ramnath in such a subversion of gender roles, she gets signified as an active looking person. As Mary Ann Doane says, "the intellectual woman looks and analyses and in usurping the gaze she poses a threat to an entire system of representation." (Doane 140).

Premchand was a realist novelist and he invariably searched the good and true and the beautiful in man/woman. He felt inspired when he discovered such values. He deeply believed in the equality of the sexes and expressed great indignation over injustice practised by men on women. He never had much faith in the worn out traditions of the past. Being always on the move, he strongly felt social laws were subject to change. He was essentially a reformer. To show the social reality in traditional Indian popular cinema, melodrama is an apt device, "Melodrama as a form, a space as cinematic space and femininity, as a condition are three basic issues at stake". (Biswas 126). Encounters with the past or historical awareness of kind are necessarily tied up for us with realistic modes of culture accordingly. Peter Brooks, in his authoritative study of melodrama has shown how melodrama and realism have been closely inter-linked since the nineteenth century.

> "Melodrama emerged in the nineteenth century as a form which spoke of a post-sacred universe in which the certainties of traditional meaning and hierarchical authority had been displaced. Rather than being two essentially antithetical modes, as our art cinema, each criticism has usually held one and has shaped and deflected the other too". (Brooks Peter 136).

Hrishikesh Mukherjee was one of the few directors who could handle large spaces and his mastery of it grew with each film. *'Gaban'* has a picaresque quality about it with characters on the move from one place to another as the story progresses. The film is swift and beautifully articulated and the atmosphere is both austere and warm. It shows the closed knitted set-up of the community. The film is both a place of judgement and habitat of the infallible human beings. The main focus of interest has been the ways in which Jalpa the female protagonist has been constituted as a set of meanings through the processes of cinematic signification, whereby meanings are produced in the story.

Premchand reveals the cultural values among other things about freedom and virtues. The directors of the film, with the aid of cinematic device make the visible invisible, which the director constructs through its images and narrative structure. Annette Kuhn feels that, "making visible the invisible is an analytical activity that can work at number of levels. The most obvious object of this kind of activity is perhaps the film text itself." (Kuhn Women's Pictures 73). The inclusion of the woman's voice i.e. of Jalpa in mode of her assertiveness is a model of the emancipated woman. The rest of the female characters in the film *'Gaban'* are however stereotypical, e.g. the wife, the vamp, the girl next door, the mother and so on are portrayed in clichéd roles. In the traditional Indian films, which are dramatic narratives, mostly the stories are hero centered and he is endowed with larger than life qualities. In *'Gaban'*, however, the hero is shown as a coward. He is ready to even give false evidence against his revolutionary friends to save himself from the clutches of the police. The film however pays a fine tribute to the spirit of revolutionaries by showing the hero as a coward in the contrast. *'Gaban'* may not have been a path breaking film but Premchand definitely possessed a modernist sensibility. He was one of the realist social writers and could grapple with subjects exploring the vast social change, which was gradually sweeping across modern India, wanting to celebrate the freedom not only of the country but also of the human spirit.

Jalpa is characteristically like 'Mother India', whose idealism is in danger. Her husband Ramnath, has deviated from the path of self righteousness on account of his cowardice. Thus in salvaging his honour she, seeks his redemption. Jalpa, with her maturity operates in the public terrain, moving away from the private space of the family and finally redeems to integrate Ramnath in the family fold and to do away with his isolation from the family and society at large. It is finally the family, according to sociologists, "that helps to meet the needs of the individuals who compose it." (Davis 395). It is the social system that must somehow meet the organic needs of its members not only for the survival of its members but also to motivate them in such a way as to induce them to perform the activities necessary for meeting societal needs. It contributes to the individuals' sexual gratification, psychic security, affection, guidance etc. The heterosexual couple formation and the goal of coming together of the man and the woman lies at the heart of the conventional film narrativity almost globally. In fact, the model of narration in cinema develops largely on the premise of this basic motivation. However according to the film theorist Madhava Prasad,

> "the migration of the familial to the conjugal has remained incomplete in the social reality of our films as the very gaze itself as produced in our cinema should be considered in a different manner. Certain areas in the characters' lives are not visible at all because the private space of the couple does not exist in the modern sense". (Prasad 133).

However Jalpa's obedience and devotion to her husband is paradoxically punctuated by rebellion in the sense that woman's place is expected to be bound within the home. She ventures out to save her husband. Her in-laws however are understanding and liberate her from the private space of the family. Rather than rebuking her into silence, they hear her out. By granting her that freedom, she gets freedom from her own anger and resentment by forgiving her errant husband. "Belittling women in a simplistic way indeed it is. Women's marginality in a male dominated world can indicate not their helplessness but their pent up power". (Guerin *et al.* 216). However, his love is engraved on her heart. Her friend Ratan wife of Vakil Sahib explains her that affection does not come from youth or beauty or money, it comes from affection itself.

When there was no trace of Ramnath since his fleeing away from Allahabad, Jalpa took the whole blame on her own head. She feels that God had punished her for her greed, which made Ramnath squeeze money out of others to adorn her with ornaments. She decides to sink all her ornaments bundled in a pile in the Ganges and lead a new life from then on. She enters a journey from darkness to light, from falsehood to truth. She decides that when her Rama (personal name for her husband) returns she would not spend a single *paisa* unnecessarily nor let him bring home even a single *paisa* unnecessarily. She realizes that love was a thing of heart and not of money. However, when she comes to know through Praja Mitra, a newspaper about his whereabouts in Calcutta, all kinds of reproaches arouse within her and she thinks aloud as to what did he think he was doing sitting there? Was it because he was independent and free? She wonders that if she had abandoned off like that, without saying a word, how he would have behaved towards her. Perhaps he would have come with a sword and tyrannized her or perhaps never looked at her face for the rest of his life. It was like almost opening a complaint office in her innermost heart, as she stands thinking there about inequation in gender relations, an invitation to conformity that she had to adhere to and that she was in way, "standing in feminism's place and receiving as a convenient metonym the attacks directed at it". (Miller 103). She feels it is the tryst with the femininity, which is at a stake in the recovery of their lost time and souls. The anticipation of a female as a redeemer in the cultural domain site emerges here as in most Indian popular Hindi films. However, Jalpa after paying up Ramnath's debts and clearing him of all allegations against him evokes respect and the blessings of her in-laws and she goes to Calcutta with her brother-in-law from the domain of private space of the family to the public sphere.

The complex equation of power relations shows not only a grim scenario of inhumanity but also, states that the only redeeming feature can be the use of reason through a profound understanding of humanity, which should transcend gender, class, caste etc. Ramnath's simplicity and basic goodness enchanted even a prostitute like Zohra who is a police accomplice too. She offers to be helpful when Zohrabai learns about the sacrifice of Jalpa epitomising ideals of Indian womanhood and she restores him back to Jalpa. Zohrabai is impressed by Jalpa's conscientiousness, her true devotion, her unaffected love, her devoutness, her adoration of her husband, her selflessness and above all Jalpa's dedication to service of the nation. Even though a prostitute by profession and depicted as a fallen woman, she is aware of her worldly prospects and that by siding with the police, she may have a motor car, servants, a fine house, costly jewellery she yet prepares to bear great suffering by turning hostile against police. She develops a female bonding with her and realizes that such materialistic joys have no value to the heart of a beautiful young woman like Jalpa. According to Jean Curthoys, "idealization is mostly something that men confer upon women and that women want from men. Its role is a symmetric between the two sexes". (28). This kind of idealization is something they seek for as a form of recognition, which lifts them up from an existence to elevate them from amongst the women too. In fact, even though, women have no reason to idealise men as they have an ability to psyche men out and it is a puzzle why no evaluation of each other be made in non-binary ways where ones worth as a woman is thought not to depend on patriarchal world but, her own, is perplexing. However, Zohrabai breaks such shackles of patriarchal system and realizes her own worth by joining hands with Jalpa. Instead of a typical genre of hero oriented films prevailing then, Ramnath is shown to be a weak character in the negative shade. Through the cinematic device on celluloid Ramnath as Sunil Dutt efficiently portrays bouts of timidity and bravado alternatively through his facial expressions and expressive eyes portraying his mental conflict. His last minute dash to tell the truth into the court seems, though, just a dramatic exigency because he could just have contacted the defence counsel before the proceedings. However, all the court scenes are handled with great restraint. The few shots of patriots who are revolutionaries and their leader's family are wistful but free from sentimentality.

The closing scene, as Ramnath stands alone as the courtroom empties, is realistically portrayed. Sadhna as Jalpa makes an excellent foil to the weak hero. She is at her best in the sadder moments towards the close. Her active seeing attitude is opposed to being 'seen' rather than in usurping the gaze. She thus poses to be a threat to an entire system of representation. It is as if the woman had forcefully moved to the other side of the spectacular. The over determination of the image of woman, "is a crucial aspect of the cinematic alignment of structures of seeing and being seen with sexual difference". (Miller 103). Sadhna makes an indelible mark as a feminist in this film though not overtly. However there is an inversion of gender roles between Jalpa and Ramnath in the traditional set up of the Indian cultural ideology. It is not merely to be seen as a gender issue but an intangible factor, which directly impacts their relationship. Jalpa is not only logical and rational as men are seen but highly perceptive and observant too. She's better equipped with vision and foresight and hence stereotypical perspectives in gender relations get broken. Like Bimal Roy's and Guru Dutt's heroines she is portrayed as a strong character. She may be home bound but has a voice of her own. She creates space for herself inspite of wanting to be an appendage to him and even tries to be his saviour.

According to Michele De Doeuff, "feminist is a woman who does not allow anyone to think in her place". (De Doeuff 143). So powerful was Sadhna's image evoked as a self righteous assertive person in the film 'Gaban' that throughout her career, she got roles portraying her as a thinking person, a rare feat then in the 60s and 70s in Hindi cinema for an actress. Her role as Jalpa was that of a fresh flower blooming with fragrance and radiance with a bewitching smile. The appropriation of the women's body is further complicated in the cinema where the woman is the object of gaze. "The very pervasiveness of it flattens out any epistemological or ontological dimensions". (Probyn 84). Conceived in a pervasive powerlessness in the face of the patriarchal world, her life story is like every other female's life story. This is in keeping with as Judith Gardiner defines, "female identity as typically less fixed less unitary and more flexible than male individuality". (Judith 27).

Premchand as a writer was not severed off from the Indian cultural roots and upheld the joint family system. But as a good writer, he not only rose above ordinary but also possessed the insight to plumb in human depths. Gender relations in his stories are built up on the premise that Premchand himself realized the power and influence of his wife on himself. The coinage to negate him is reflected in the character of Ramnath and his realization of his failings. The cultural ideology for gender relations makes a woman's life script a non-story,

"a silent space, and a gap in patriarchal culture. The ideal woman is self-effacing rather than self-promoting and her 'natural' story shapes itself not around the public heroic life but around the fluid, circumstantial contingent responsiveness to others that according to patriarchal ideology, characterizes the life of woman". (Sidonie 50).

In a typical patriarchal society, women's bodies do not belong to themselves, but to the patriarchal male. In the times set in the novel, couples did not meet each other before marriage and the families of both the boy and girl decided on the choice of partner. In such families, the older members decide what is important for the young woman, "any attempts by her to exercise her own choice becomes a source of family conflict". (Dwyer and Patel 84). The film 'Gaban' uses the cultural ideology to prop up a great theme through this ideological device and sends a message that it intended to convey. The search for her husband (Ramnath) shows her on the lines of the Savitri mould who had fought the *Yama*, god of death to save her husband from the clutches of death. Her autonomy is itself acquired by way of the acceptance of a definite moral position. It is with an objective for that of her husband's redemption and integration reiterating him back into the family.

Jalpa, the wife does not become dishonourable once she moves out of the private space of the family. Premchand's understanding of Jalpa and her objective to be a good wife and daughter-in-law is consistent with recognition even in her autonomous state. Her aim to be a good wife and daughter-in-law is the most significant aspect of Indian cultural ideology, which still prevails as shown in our films. However, at the time when the novel 'Gaban' was published (1931) and made into a film in the 60s, women's liberation movement was at it peak which was being rejuvenated in the USA. Some of the feminists like Shulamith Firestone believed that,

"in a male run society that defines women as inferior and as parasitical class, a woman who does not achieve male approval in some form is doomed. To legitimate her existence a woman must be more than a woman, she must continually search for a way to be out from her inferior definition and men are the only ones in a position to bestow upon her this state of grace". (quoted in Curthoys 26).

Since the woman was rarely allowed to move out of the private family domain of space she could hardly ever realize herself through any kind of activity in the longer society i.e. the public sphere dominated by males. However women were seldom granted the recognition they deserved. Jalpa within the social, and material constraints of her life and her being seeks recognition by redemption of her husband. Both the writer and the filmmaker constantly reinforce positively the paradigm where she works out in the public space having moved from the private domain. Her virtue of integrity, her love and intelligence give meaning to her very existence inspite of the past and present impediments notwithstanding of cultural trappings and overpowering ideology. In the reversal subversion of roles of Rama and Sita, she truimphs like the Rama who got his Sita back successfully from Ravana, here symbolized by the corrupt police. Jalpa is liberated however from anger and resentment by forgiveness of her in-laws who by granting her freedom to move into the public space do so. In turn she grants forgiveness to her husband whom she resolutely helps to get out of mixed situation to achieve his redemption. Having accomplished her task she goes back to the private domain of family, back again from the public sphere to live happily with them. This indexing is what Partha Chatterjee terms the nationalist resolution of the woman question. Partha Chatterjee emphasised the primacy constructions for the family to notions of culture and nation by suggesting that, "the family was not a complementary but rather the original site on which hegemonic project of nationalism was launched". (147). In the aftermath of the colonial encounter the indigenous male made a sustained effort to insulate then home perceived as the repository of the authentic Indianness from the world.

Even though the film has been lost in the oblivion with the passage of time, the songs are immortalized and all the *rasas* and genres are juggled together in the film. The performances seem deeply personal and emotionally evocative in it at the same time brilliantly lucid and accessible. It is a character of role, with which makes an actor grow in stature and power as Sunil Dutt did in 'Gaban' and with every other role later. Sadhna as Jalpa is lovely, glowing, innocent and wise. She is spontaneously feminine without a hint of primness. Kanhaiyalal as Devidin plays a carefree person, is even irresponsible towards the idea of running the tea-stall he owns. It is his wife Jageshwan played by the versatile Leela Mishra who runs the shop successfully. Yet he is a free thinker as he wakes up to the call of the struggle of freedom. Having lost their sons to the cause of struggle for freedom during non-cooperation movement called up by Mahatma Gandhi, Devidin and Jageshwari become surrogate parents to Ramnath. They cajole and lead the errant Ramnath to the path of self-righteousness after dissuading him to be a witness against the revolutionaries. They try to make good the loss of sons they have lost by trying to help him to retrieve as a false witness and back to his family and Jalpa. Both have the earthy sense of wisdom though their manner is hilarious. In their performance is a genuineness, agility and self depreciable humour. They are unlike the parents of Ramnath and Jalpa who live upto tradition bound by conventional values and customs laid by society.

The film shows the images and the class trajectory of a complacent middle class, pleased with conventions and tradition. Jewellery for the bride, is a loop hole gaping loudly in such a conventional set up, leading to suffering and a crack in gender relations which dominate the motif in the film. The set up evokes the ethos of culture with real insecurities lurking around the corner. The film celebrates the freedom of human spirit though in a melodramatic manner, calamity notwithstanding. Premchand was realistic in his approach and he never accepted idealism for the sake of it.

Premchand was a visionary writer and never limited himself creatively. A different ambience and atmosphere gets created in all his novels. However, he talks about issues, which are beneficial for a healthy wholesome society transcending gender, caste etc. He always wrote for the better deal for women spurred with elimination of gender discrimination. He believed in rehabilitation of widows, prohibition of child marriages, sati and the Devdasi system of temple prostitution. His novels like '*Godaan*', '*Gaban*' also adapted for celluloid represent the social reform movement in the Indian cinema.

Hrishikesh Mukherjee, who believed in making 'middle of the road cinema'[4] socials aptly, handled this film too even though, he had to patch up with the earlier part of the film directed by Krishna Chopra. "Even when the *swadeshi* movement frittered away around 1911, its social and cultural influence was to last across and rent into the two decades into the 1930". (Kaul 90). Filmmakers endeavoured to energize Indian society through themes of socio economic and socio-cultural bias in reshaping the society. The novel published in 1931, adapted in 1966, expresses the passionate intensity of the enlightened consciousness of that moment about which both Jalpa and Ramnath had no awareness of, initially. They both discovered themselves and understood their true love and desire to be free through that consciousness. Their inner experiences may appear to be quite mundane but their response is amazing eventually. Jalpa realizes how she has to liberate herself from self-concern and help Ramnath to do the same. Enlightenment of herself and her situation helps in not only liberalizing but discovery of the profound mystery of her own self. Liberation from self concern, her obsession with jewellery and especially *chandrahar* which lead Ramnath to embezzlement and eventually their separation enables them to recognize the true nature as human beings in love. It is one of the miracles to realize that love is not personal and does not have its roots in the personality. Gender relations are inbuilt on that edifice. Love is literally liberating oneself from the depth of understanding of one's being and it emerges out of its own accord. Any man, woman can understand this miracle and their relationship can be fulfilling if they really want it to be. They just have to be willing to understand each other.

The lines that spring from the mouth of various characters in the dialogues of Akhtar-ul-Iman, impassioned but controlled, combine effectively with the lyrics of Shailendar and Hasrat Jaipuri. Their poetry, feeling and argument is heart rendering and set poignantly to the music of Shanker Jaikishan. No doubt the songs went on to become more popular than the film and were at the top of the charts on Binaca Geet Mala played on Radio Ceylon then compered by Amin Sayani then. The visionary and extremely personal expressions of despair, fantasy and social realism which Premchand evoked in his novel got transformed onto the celluloid, rather enhanced through the songs.

The songs were not only hummable but carried the story forward in an effective manner and in a linear progression. They filled up the blanks beautifully amiss the chaos which got created on account of the death of Krishna Chopra after H. Mukkherjee took over after a gap of some time. The songs spoke of the friendship between friends, love between a couple and their separation thus celebrating various *rasas* in Indian *Natya Shastra* effectively. For Ramnath a carefree young boy before marriage whose father was an upright clerk not given to corruption, he depended on his friends for the yearnings of his youthful desires. The love for his friends mattered most to him. Thrown together with friends, he sings about his obligations to them in the famous song, *"Ehsaan mere dil par tumhara hey doston, yeh dil tumhare pyar ka mara hai doston"*, translated "I am highly obliged to you dear friends, as you help me to override my problems, my heart is filled with love for you". Another song on similar lines was filmed on Jalpa with her friends talking about matrimonial love and bliss that she is supposedly going to enjoy after her marriage all decked up in the jewellery and the possession of cherished *chandrahaar* which would be bestowed by Ramnath. She makes a picturesque beautific angel singing song joyously at her friend's wedding later. The love songs which both Jalpa and Ramnath sing then are full of great anticipation which they are full of at the threshold of their marriage. On their *suhaag raat* i.e. wedding night so smitten is Ramnath by her beauty that he considers himself one of the most fortunate guys on the world. It convey the essence of their being two bodies, but one soul thrown together by God's grace. He considers that it might be a one time rare miracle bestowed by God on him. The song is seeped with Sringar rasa, *"Shola Shingar Karke aayee hai raat jalwe tumhare layi hai yet raat ...... Pyar ke malik ne banayi khub yeh raat"* translated "what a beautiful night has come all decked up in its glory embodying fully the beautesous self, cupid the God of love, has been generous enough to grant this night". Then there is a song of separation in *Birha Ras* (song of separation) is in the form of a duet which tells the pathetic poignant state of mind of both Jalpa and Ramnath. *"Tum Bin Sajan barse nayan, tab jab badal barse,* translated "without my beloved my tears overflow like rain bursting from clouds". He answers back singing in the duct in the next frame but from a distance *"Mazboor hum Mazboor tum, Dil milne ko tarse"* translated conveying how helpless they both are and desperate to meet each other".

However it is the song, *"Maine dekha tha sapnoy mein ek chandrahaar, ajj balam ne pehna diya"* is the crux of the theme of the film. She finds herself fulfilled as her love for *chandrahaar* has been fulfilled, and she is overwhelmed with joy. There is an ecstatic rendering of the song translated, "I had dreamt of a *chandrahaar* (Moon like necklace) today my beloved has got it for me. He has bestowed me with new life, new joy so much so that I may go crazy with happiness and my feet do not seem to touch the ground beneath my feet". These songs are like milestone songs with deep pathos heartfully and soul stirringly rendered by Mohammed Rafi and Lata Mangeshkar.

Premchand's outlook was genuinely progressive and he advocated the rightful position of women the meaning of marriage and love, the nature of family relationships in the novel 'Gaban'. He appreciated the Europe's concept of female education. Through the character of Vakil sahib, one of the protagonists, he puts forth his view who suggests,

> "until the education of women is widespread, we'll never improve. You probably haven't gone to Europe. Oh! What a freedom, what wealth, what life what enthusiasm! In a word one knows its paradise! And the women are really goddesses! So cheerful, so independent! All this is the *prasad* of female education!" (Premchand 95)

The novel has a strong Indianness to it and reinforces the Indian values of renunciation, self-sacrifice and redemption. In the adaptation of the film from the novel, these values got reinforced strongly. The film 'Gaban' has a poetic visual style and its subject matter is a personal quest for spiritual reckoning in a materialistic world on the eve of independence. The search for narratives is in reclaiming the ethos of genuine richness of the Indian culture through the subversive reading of the narrative of the text. It places emphasis on high cultural forms for a more personally satisfying compromise than an expression of materialist social aspiration. Both the novel and the film, simultaneously, draw equipoise in gender relations, family values from the traditional side, in a way that is perceived to be subversive. While, being under the influence of western values, many a youth like Ramnath flounder in confusion, vice and immorality. Jalpa finds a voice of her own as a woman representation of gender in the identity between tradition and modernity.

The film shows the complex negotiation of identity required by female protagonists be it Jalpa or Devidin's wife Jaggo. Whereas Jalpa is from the relatively high status Kayasth community, Jaggo is from the very low status of Khatik community. In the systems, honour of male depends on the virtue of the female relatives even though they are generally undervalued and unrewarded. Both Jalpa and Jaggo function as carriers symbolically through their work in the home and the family. Gender differences and specifically the power differential forces between men and women may be seen as socially constructed, "but nonetheless they are deeply embedded and embodied practices." (Thomas Lyn 21).

Jalpa's subjectivity and consciousness relativizes her sense of herself and she effectively handles the situation when Ramnath goes missing. It's as if she sees subjectivity as a process, "open to change which it is not to deny the importance of particular forms of individual subjective investment which are necessary for our participation in social processes and practices." (Weedon Feminist 102). However rather than being liberated by the awareness of the construction of her subjectivity in discourse of the film and the novel, Jalpa is aware that she needs to retain the traditional notion of her identity. Her going back to the family along with Ramnath reinforces the social status quo and she succeeds in making it appear natural. She thus reinforces the myth that gender identity is the expression of an inner core of difference. She is aware that the site of domestic is the place in which tradition is instituted and has been recognised.

In the cultural ideology, whether within the household or outside, female's activities move along a limited range of possibilities. Indianness thus gets evoked in the sphere of domestic to which Jalpa has to return. In reality, according to Butler, gender and biological sex are cultural constructions, although identities are, in fact, fluid and unstable. "Gender performance is thus a strategy of survival within the compulsory system". (Butler Gender 139). It conveys that it's important to recognize the nature and limitations of the essentialist foundations of cultural forms of ideology. In powerful and established social convention, cultural practices of power are embedded in gender relationships, which require transformation for change to be realized, whereas binaries of gender identity are maintained by repeated performances of their respective roles. By moving back into the domestic sphere of the private space, she confirms the acceptance of hegemonic structures.

Her transgressive performance, for which, she gets valorized by her in-laws, surrogate parents-in-law Devidin and Jaggo and even her husband Ramnath, is limited. The claim for such a subversive role had a potential of transgression of gender identities only till she redeems her husband. She is back to the institution of the family, having done her task. There is no reason for her to stay on in the social space of public sphere where resistance to gender norms can be exposed. Her performance as the redeemer and saviour of her husband does subvert the strong forces of compulsory systems. It is ground breaking; nonetheless, that having performed in the public, she realizes that her identity there could be a problematic discourse of individualism, almost inaccessible in those times and even largely irrelevant.

Respectability would come to women who sought to avoid drawing negative attention unto them. The women's ontological security is found precisely in not being an individual, in the gesture of fitting in. Notions of self-image and personal space were not permitted as the intimate mode of self-expression. However, the representation of Jalpa in the cinema in sixties as the woman of the thirties when the novel was written seemed to construct a feminist social identity, which was politically aware and intellectual. Such specific instances of social interactions indicate the limitations of generalizations about masculinity and femininity of Ramnath's moral weakness and his flight from home; to bring about his redemption and their reunion expresses her identity and voice. She adopts a powerful position both within the social context and within freedom movement in stopping her husband Ramnath to become a willing tool as a fake witness of the Calcutta police.

Her strong character holds sway and brings about real progress, maturity and understanding in their relationship with her sanguine vision. Her moving back to the private space of domestic sphere is based on the codes of realism, which are crucial in everyday life. The notion of moving back to the private space seems consistent with the view of ideological role though it reflects a social change too. Feminism has been a tangible influence in the reflection of changes with reference to the position of women and in gender relations.

The relationship of tradition and modernity in the novel is identifiable with the corrupt India surging towards progress. Both the novel and the film combine tradition and modernity and add a hint of subversiveness to fundamentally held conservative structures. Radical tendencies are curtailed, perhaps, for the sake of the broader audience and readers so that the identification of viewers with a certain mindset, trapped in cultural values as an ideology, are maintained.

TRAIN TO PAKISTAN

The spirit of nationalism led to the independence of the country on 15th August, 1947. But, unfortunately, the greatest movement in the history of nation also led to the division of the country. Hindus, Sikhs and Muslims had been a part of the British Raj as its subjects or subordinates. Hence, the birth of the new nation Pakistan, which was created out of the body of India by its severance, was felt as great recoil of Indian history and culture. Sadly, the partition of India and Independence arrived together, like the one, at the price of the other. The Great Divide as it can be called, "was the simultaneous breach between Britain and her Indian Empire and between India and Pakistan". (Hodson ix). Hence, when a separate sovereign state was carved out on religious lines; it was an irony, as all Hindus, Muslims, Sikhs had struggled equally against the tyranny of the slavery against the British rule, until 1947. They remained inter-mingled because of a common civilization and outlook on life with each other. However, those who had intermingled with each other, were up-rooted and torn apart from each other. Historical circumstances, which had led to new geographical locations, also lead to the commonly viewed culture preserved over the years to the frightening alternative of discovering the face of the 'other'.

There was a prevalence of mass psychoses and it seemed hopeless to fight against it for most of the people then. The severance of the umbilical chord was thus not threatening in its construction, leading to the dark side of the birth of a nation. The demonic dimensions that the 'others' on both the sides acquired, leading to destructive fragments, was opposed to reason and culture. For a nation to be split into two nation states by a religious conflict was not a new phenomenon to happen in the contemporary world. Communalism, both in its Hindu and Muslim garb was, "really a product of British rule; the new rulers with their colonial outlook, sowed the seed slowly and gradually". (Zakaria xiv). There had been a strain in attitudes of both Hindu and Muslims, which did give the communal division a peculiar political importance. However, most Hindu political leaders and writers and many Muslims who were nationalists, first and foremost, blamed the system of communal electorates used by the British which was responsible for perpetuating and exacerbating inter-community conflict in the political growth of a national spirit, that which was characterized by social or economic beliefs rather than religion. In fact, "they charged the British, the system with all its consequences which lead up to partition in pursuit of 'divide' and 'rule'." (Hodson 15). A country, which was in the throes of freedom struggle and had a healthy outlook for national independence, was however partitioned. At Jinnah's Presidential address at the Muslim League's session at Lahore in March 1940, the idea of Muslim separatism floating in the Indian political atmosphere was given a concrete shape. It, "is a landmark in the history of Muslim Nationalism in India, for it made an irrefutable case for a separate Muslim Nationhood". (Aziz 128).

All this nationalism led to border setting, both geographically and politically. The idea of partition caused one of the great human tragedies in Indian history. The awakening and realization on the eve of partition was painful for many in Pakistan, as well as India. While, most of India and Pakistan celebrated Independence Day with peaceable rejoicing, in Punjab both east and west, the partition of the country in 1947 was the worst genocide act of the 20th century. The participation of Punjab came at a colossal human cost. There was rampant violence and terror. Unforeseen migrations of Muslims to Pakistan and of Sikhs and Hindus to India in and around Punjab took place. There was an exodus of refugees on both the sides of the border moving in trains and convoys leading to chaos and disorder. During the mayhem, the loss of lives enroute, slaughter, rape and destruction on account of rising communalism, marred the very spirit of independence. Communal bitterness was at a peak and the masses were egged on and inflamed by resolute men and strong groups of well-armed men determined to fight. Inert and resentful, most of the refugees seemed unable to help themselves. The political partition of India caused one of the greatest human convulsions of history. Never before had so many people exchanged homes and countries so quickly. Punjab was the key to the issue of partition. Every argument for dividing India was an argument for dividing the Punjab and every argument for keeping the Punjab united was an argument for retaining the unity of India.

The history of partition, which on account of the political developments that followed in the bifurcation of the country into two, had aspects of 'human dimension' to it, more than the implications of the demographic shift. The feeling of the loss and sharing, friendship and enmity, grief and joy, was a painful regret and left nostalgia for loss of home, country and friends. It was strongly felt on both the sides with an equally strong dimension. Identities suddenly got redefined and ordinary people who went with their day-to-day, mundane, peaceful living had to confront the reality of partition in the country. Thousands of women were raped and abducted and became the worst victims by the perpetuators of violence, irrespective of caste, creed, class they belonged to. Any recollection of partition is a painful reminder of the mad frenzy and its horrific repercussions. "Love, friendship and camaraderie were all got forgotten in the atmosphere of hatred and mayhem. For a generation, which grew up in the 1930s, and 40s the great schism of 1947 has remained a traumatic experience. Crossing the border becomes a metaphor for recalling this period in time, in writing theatre and film." (Sen Geeti 7).

One gets to know about partition through literary fiction, memoirs, and personal testimonies or through memories individual and collective. According to Urvashi Butalia, "partition lives on in family histories particularly in north India where tales of horror and brutality, the friendship and sharing are told and retold between communities, families and individuals." (Butalia 268). Any recollection of partition is a painful reminder. However, any such writing on partition has a timelessness relevance to it. Khushwant Singh's 'Train to Pakistan', written in 1953, is not only a novel of classic fiction, but a piece of nostalgia rooted in a reflection upon tragic reality. It not only speaks of a historical past, which encompasses the reality of the partition, it also portrays collective memories about the homogeneity vis-à-vis divisive factionalism of community in the face of disaster.

Khushwant Singh's own family, which belonged to Hadali was uprooted from its ancestral home and experienced at close quarters the terrible tragedy that overcome the north western past of the Indian subcontinent in 1947. Khushwant Singh was a practicing lawyer in Lahore. However after the partition of India he gave up his legal profession. In fact Mr. Jinnah had sent a word to his father that he should persuade him to stay in Lahore and he could consider him to be a judge in the High Court. Khushwant Singh however refused to succumb to the temptation as he puts it in his autobiography 'Truth, Love and a little Malice', published in 2002. After he returned from London he wrote 'Short History of the Sikhs' and then decided to start working on a novel. Khushwant Singh, with his varied experiences and a keen sense of observation could not have missed the experiences of the days of the Raj and its after-math. The theme that he had on his mind was the partition of India and the horrible massacre that accompanied it. However, he was not sure that how he should go about with it. He talks about it this in his autobiography and said the same to me in an interview with him at his residence, Sujan Singh Park. "I considered several plots and thought of many characters. I was obsessed with the idea that every individual had the trinity of Hindu Gods in him, Brahma (the creator), Vishnu (the preserver) and Shiva (the destroyer)". (Khushwant Singh in an interview with me on 26.3.2003 at New Delhi).

The Hindu religion has come to celebrate a position of special significance through the mythological stories existing in the *Puranas* and evolved out of the concepts embodied in the Vedas. The stories about them have found their place in the epics of secular literature. The evolution of the Hindu Trinity has to be traced only through the *Puranas*. The 18 *puranas* stand devoted in equal numbers to each of the members of the Trinity, which raise them to the supreme status of God. The rationalists among the Hindus have agreed to bring a sense of order in this confusion by blending the separate and independent 'Gods' into a Trinity by allotting different functions to each of them. According to their philosophy, Brahma is the 'creative power', Vishnu is the 'sustaining power', Shiva is the 'destroying power' and together they are even called *Trimurti*. This *Trimurti* is considered a composite image of each other. "The deities in Hinduism are but aspects of one but a deity may assume seemingly opposite qualities power of dissolution". (Dhani 38).

The Puranas say that these three powers are in fact three different aspects of the same supreme soul or Paramatma and that Isvara (the Lord). Paramesvara (the supreme Lord). Brahma (the soul of Brahmanda or Universe) and Para-tattva (the ultimate reality) etc are names. The three names have come down through history and tradition at the time the religious philosophy was being given a shape. The stories of Hindu mythology are embedded in the Indian national psyche. The mythological stories represent the mixture of fact and fiction, which is always true of all literature. Most of the Sanskrit mythological stories are available in verse or poetic form. Therefore while the theme of a particular story would be based on some actual happening, its narration would unsuspectingly and unavoidably and sometimes purposely, include poetic imagination. When such stories become popular and commonly acceptable as containing eternal truth, later day scholars utilized this fact to incorporate them in their fiction. The deities behave as much as men do in stories that is, because it is men who have written about them. The language used is the language of myth.

The stories about the deities although are not to be taken literally, yet, many people do believe them, as myths allows them to give definitions to the qualities he/she feels within and to conceptualise that which is beyond their conception. "Myths are logical; they are emotional. Myths persist, though often in a diluted form". (Chatterji Shoma The Distorted 29). However, the myths do help us to understand the ultimate mystery of the universe for which there are no words or pictures. The masculine deities have a feminine consort or partner. *Brahama's* consort is *Saraswati*, the goddess of wisdom and his vehicle is a goose. He himself is also called the god of wisdom and has a spiritual nature and has a sacrificial spoon in one hand and Vedas in one of his four hands. Vishnu is the preserver of the moral order. His chief function as preserver of the universe and order makes him the upholder of the drama. His consort is *Lakshmi*, goddess of good fortune. He may be seen on a lotus or riding on his vehicle *Garuda*, a half man half bird. *Shiva* the lord of destruction is usually represented as an ascetic light in colour, except for a blue throat, often with four arms and a third eye. His vehicle is *Nandi*, the bull, a symbol of fertility and his consort *Shakti* is represented in various aspects. Two different aspects of *Shakti* are most often characterized, one of the benign loving mother and wife. As wife she is represented by aspect of feminine power and characterized, as *Shiva's* consort *Sati* (and later in the next birth) as *Parvati*. Secondly the angry avenging one, when provoked she becomes destructor (so that there may be creation aspect). This is characterized as *Durga* and *Kali*.

However, Khushwant Singh employs the three masculine triads of trinity in characterization of his novel, *'Train to Pakistan'*. When asked by me in the interview with him about the female counterparts be said "well you can't fit too many characters in a novel". (Interview with Khushwant Singh on 26.3.2003). He said that he had used the philosophy of Trinity to evolve and build up his story. He felt that though one does start with a certain game plan at the onset in building up characters, but after sometime the characters get out of hand and take over the story and lead a life of their own. According to Khushwant Singh, in every person, one or the other aspects of the trinity predominate. In fact, his main protagonists are based on such a cultural ideology. He felt that Brahma aspect could best be portrayed by a peasant farmer called Juggut Singh, Vishnu by an upholder of the law by a magistrate represented by Hukum Chand and Shiva through a communist who wanted to destroy evil to build a better world, represented by Iqbal. However according to him "Iqbal could be Iqbal Singh, Iqbal Chand, Iqbal Mohammed. Iqbal was one of the few names common to the three communities, the Sikhs, the Hindus and the Muslims".[5] (Singh K. Train 35). In the story he is a social worker and feels that "with this partition there is so much bloodshed going on that someone must do something to stop it". (37).

Khushwant Singh worked on the draft of the novel in the peace of the Italian lakes. He discovered a small lake high up on the mountains called Lago Eilo on the Italian Swiss border. He spent a month there most of the day working on the novel and spent his evenings rowing and swimming. After a productive month he came back to London and then to India where he completed the draft of his novel in Bhopal. During the afternoons he went to railway station and acquainted himself with the way trains were directed to different platforms as a railway station is the central point to of his novel.

Khushwant Singh said in his interview, "I always wrote the way I saw things. There were no morals, neither is there any sermonising nor any such social message. Characters in my novel are characters that were taken up and built on people I came across personally though much to their annoyance. Hence, most of them were true characters in real life and some built up imaginatively". (Singh, K. Truth 198). During partition ordinary peace loving people faced horror and violence and were in turn forced to confront the violence within them too. Victims became aggressors, aggressors turned into victims and people began to partition their minds too against people from other religion. His novel *'Train to Pakistan'* deals directly with the rampant violence, riots and death, which preceded the partition and following it in the Indian subcontinent. In 1947, the country was divided and a ghost train becomes a symbol of the last link between the country divided into two, India and Pakistan. He evokes a fine portrayal of the partition as a result of which peace and harmony is disrupted along with brotherhood in a mixed Sikh-Muslim village called Mano-Majra. He also builds up literary characters, which personify the trinity of Brahma, Vishnu and Shiva. Passionate and romantic love between a Sikh boy Juggat Singh nicknamed Jugga and a Muslim girl Nooran gets woven as one of the strands in the narrative, motivating a dacoit like Jugga towards supreme sacrifice for his love.

The novel 'Train to Pakistan' is just not a piece of classic fiction skilfully drafted. According to Arthur Lall former ambassador and permanent representative from India to the United Nations, it has significant value as, "a social document that portrays vividly many facets of the great upheaval that accompanied the creation of Pakistan. The novel is laden with a deep ironic pathos, though there seems to be a fair abundance of a conscious mixture of contrived realism and deliberate melodrama". (Singh K. Train Preface). When Khushwant Singh had finished the draft of his novel, he gave it to Tatty Bell, the American wife of Walter Bell of the British High Commission who typed it for him. After she had finished the job, she told him bluntly that it was no good and that nobody was going to publish it. Khushwant Singh was crestfallen and downcast and he wanted to tear it up but he did not. He, infact, sent it to Grove Press as an entry for the best work of fiction from India and won the first prize of a thousand dollars and a contract to have it published. The novel was finally published as 'Train to Pakistan'.

Khushwant Singh received a proposal by the Ismail Merchant–Ivory James duo to make a film on his novel 'Train to Pakistan'. They even asked Zafar Hai to direct it and a well-known Urdu writer was commissioned to write the dialogues. Shashi Kapoor was to play the main lead and Shabana Azmi whom Khushwant Singh regards as one of the finest actress on the Hindi screen, was to play the heroine. However after six months of discussions the project was dropped. Earlier a Japanese producer had offered to adapt it for the celluloid in Japanese. However, as Khushwant Singh could not speak Japanese and the producer could not speak English, the project fell apart as their interpreter could not be much of a bridge between the two. Pamela Rooks at long last made the novel into a film. She made the film on a shoestring budget but did a splendid job of it. Khushwant Singh considers the film on the novel 'Train to Pakistan' as one of the important landmarks in his life. The film was however ready for its August release and premiered for the nation's Independence Day celebration shown on TV on 15th August, 1997 i.e. after 50 years of Independence. It was also shown for a few months in cinemas all over the country. According to Sartre one "cannot write without a public and without a certain myth of literature which depends to a very great extent upon the demand." (50-51). However, in a society like ours,

> "where we are conscious of separation in time (through our historical sense) as well as in space, literature is assigned the task of creating and sustaining communicable symbolic characters that must become part of the experience of every individual who is to take part in this society." (Dalziel 5).

The intellectual life of a nation, period or person manifests itself in language. However where a novel can sell 20,000 volumes and make substantial profit, the film adapted from it must reach millions. Even though, the film 'Train to Pakistan' may not have reached millions but Pamela Rooks picturised the film beautifully with the spirit of novel intact.

Partition was the dark side of Independence and hundreds of thousands of people died as a result of it. In India there is no institutional memory of partition. The state has not perhaps found it be fitting to construct any memorials to mark any particular places, as has been done say in the case of the holocaust memorials or memorials for Vietnam war. A visual representation of the partition, despite the rich archive of photographs that must exist in many newspapers and magazines, remains limited. Krishna Sobti, an eminent writer and recipient of *Sahitya Akademi* Award in 1980, who wrote 'Zindaginama' also voiced a similar opinion. "The idea that the people across the border are a part of us can never be erased from our memories". (Sobti 55). 'Train to Pakistan' looks back to the social milieu, "which reveals that Sikhs, Hindus and Muslims made the traditional fabric structures of the Punjabi society in the pre-partition India. Culture, language and customs contributed to the larger Punjab identity though at a certain level religion divided them into communal groupings–almost separate identities". (Prempati 111).

Mano Majra, the village represents an identity like that of the nation, India. The essence of belongingness to the village cutting across religious lines also operates at the immediate level, which subsumed even the separate religious identities. The novel had a stark realistic fidelity and a gripping narrative. It remains one of the finest realistic novels of Post-World War II Indo-Anglian fiction. The art of realistic portrayal shown by Khushwant Singh, while transposing the actual into symbolic image has been very effectively used in its adaptation on the celluloid by Pamela Rooks. 'Train to Pakistan' by Khushwant Singh though a piece of fiction, is filmed by Pamela Rooks as a partition memorabilia in that sense.

In the early 1960s, what might be called the 'classical' period of cinema there developed 'cinema veritè' genre. This genre was like a kind of agreement among filmmakers in America on what a documentary was and how was one to be made. What is projected on the screen in *cinema veritè* classic was to be a recording of something that really happened. "The ambition of *cinema veritè* in contrast to the older kind of documentary, was to capture the spontaneity of the human subject by recording people's behaviour and interactions in their natural setting". (Rotham 189).

'Train to Pakistan' was originally published under the name of the village Mano Majra that is a world into itself. The story is set in this village, which portrays the rich rural hinterland of Punjab. It is the arrival of the trainload of dead bodies, that sets the ball of murders rolling, fuelled and refuelled by the antics on either side. The novel 'Train to Pakistan' is not only a classic and a great piece of literature but is also an honest piece of historical fiction. According to Bhabha, "the process of evaluation in universalist and nationalist theories, which are overwhelmingly representationlist, becomes a process of establishing a mimetic adequacy. The text is not seen as productive of meaning but essentially reflective or expressive." (quoted in Ashcroft *et al.* 188). Khushwant Singh located the novel in Mano Majra, which was supposed to be one of the little villages and remained oases of peace like the scattered villages lost in the remote reaches of the frontier after creation of the new state of Pakistan was formally announced. Ten millions of people, Muslims and Hindus and Sikhs were in flight and almost a million of them were dead with almost all of northern India in arms, in terror, or in hiding.

The village of Mano Majra has only three buildings, one of them, the local *Gurdawara*, the other a Mosque. The third was the home of the moneylender Lala Ram Lal whose family was the only Hindu family in the village. However, there are about 70 families in Mano Majra with Sikh and Muslims about equal in number. The Sikhs are landlords and the Muslims their tenants, who share the tilling of land with their owners. There is a three foot slab of sandstone in the village that stands upright under a *keekar* tree besides the pond. "It is the local deity, *the doe* to which all the villagers Hindu, Sikh Muslim or pseudo Christians pray secretly whenever they are in special need of blessing." (Singh, K. Train 10). However, Mano Majra has a significant aspect to it, its railway station around which the story gets centred. Though it is a small railway station there is constant activity around it though not many trains stop at Mano Majra. Express trains do not stop there at all and of the slow passenger trains, only two stop there, one coming from Delhi to Lahore in the mornings and other from Lahore to Delhi in the evenings.

In the summer of 1947 when the partition of Pakistan from India has just taken place an uneasy peace reigns over hitherto riot free village of Mano Majra. However one day the "ghost train" arrives, a silent incredible funeral train loaded with bodies of thousand of refugees changing the very extrude of the Mano Majra fabric texture of a village. Migrations get provoked amongst the local Muslims as a consequence of it. The Muslim brethren who have until now been as much a part of the Mano Majra village alongwith Sikhs, feel alienated. Pamela Rooks, daughter of a Punjabi Hindu Sikh couple displays, "remarkable objectivity with regard to the Muslims of Punjab, who despite being natives of that region for centuries, were uprooted at one fell swoop by Partition of India to which they were not party". (Thorval 198). When a filmmaker uses cinema to express aspect of his or her culture or even to express a highly individualistic worldview, film, like literature or music becomes a tool for personal expression. On a shoestring budget Pamela Rooks went on to make a compelling and compendious work to express and speak in the collective consciousness of the battered partition psyche. She uses the *cinema verite* to present the novel. Khushwant Singh himself had called his novel actually a piece of documentation of partition.

Though, Khushwant Singh himself is a Sikh but he is not given to the rituals of the religion yet employs the mythic trinity of the Indian, rather Hindu cultural ideology in his novel since he felt that it was necessary to project the Indianness in the novel. He offers insight into the question of human values, community and solidarity; Pamela Rooks establishes and highlights it on the celluloid representation. Through a northern Indian ambience she enables to explain as to where and why identities are problematic and where and why they are empowering.

Juggat Singh called Jugga, the main protagonist is portrayed in the mythic cultural ideology of *Brahma*. A Jat Sikh and son of a dacoit is in love with Nooran, the pretty Muslim damsel, daughter of the blind Iman Baksh, the Mullah. When the story in the novel unfolds, he is shown having a licentious affair with Nooran who nags him. "You are just a peasant, always wanting to sow your seed even if the world were going to hell you want to do that even when guns are being fired in the village". (24) Meanwhile, Mali another dacoit and his companions loot and kill Ram Lal the only Hindu and moneylender of the village. However the local magistrate Hukum Chand orders the arrest of Jugga as a suspect in the crime against Ram Lal's murder.

In fact, the film opens as a flashback with Hukum Chand the local magistrate unravelling the facts of the real incidents that took place in that eventful summer of 1947. He is a personification of *Vishnu* 'the preserver' of the moral order. "His chief function as preserver of the universe and cosmic order makes him the upholder of dharma". (Donald and Johnson 49). He appears as a representative of the typical Indian bureaucracy. He is, however, an evolving character as he is sober inspite of having hedonistic taste. He is yet spontaneous and tender hearted. In the interview with me, Khushwant Singh said that those were the days when it was not easy to have an affair with another's sister or wife, hence one had to look out for unknown young fresh females from the flesh market i.e. the *mandi*.

Pamela Rooks highlights the effect of the nubile dancer prostitute Hansa has on Hukam Chand through the film songs sung by her popular in those days of yore. She evokes the ambience through the raw appeal of the young sixteen-year-old girl Hasina (played by Divya Datta with aplomb). Though Khushwant Singh commented that he did not think it necessary to have the female counterpart to the male mythic trinity yet both Hasina and Nooran could be *Lakshmi*, the giver of fortune and *Saraswati* the goddess of wisdom respectively. However, both *Lakshmi and Saraswati* are virgin goddesses. There are cogent reasons for it as both of them are not supposed to be virgins since one realizes it as the plot unravels. Moreover, with control of sexuality being intertwined with patriotism by leaders like Mahatma Gandhi during the freedom movement, it was only *Kali/Durga* the triune goddess who was considered as a mother in all her aspects. By substituting woman for nation, the political struggle for achieving power became mystified into spiritual struggle. "She was no longer merely the bearer of tradition but woman becomes tradition itself". (Zuthshi 101). However, it is always believed that it is the wife who maintains traditions despite all her shortcomings. Moreover, Nooran and Hasina are Muslims involved with Jat Sikh and a Hindu respectively. Now that the country is being partitioned on religious lines, it does really matter to what community one belongs. Being Muslims both the girls have been perhaps erased from being the counterpart of mythic cultural ideology of the trinity.

The triad of the mythic male trinity gets completed with the arrival of Iqbal a young communist activist in the village, who forms one of the strands in the sub plot of the story. The name "Iqbal" has a metonymic kind of anti position. This can be further reinforced by the meaning of the name Iqbal which means 'He who Accepts' and was in the original sense, the word of God as revealed to the prophet. Iqbal, the third main protagonist is also a mythical representative of Shiva. He believes that he has to do his duty for India as befits a good citizen. Since '*Train to Pakistan*' is a profoundly moving tragic story of the sad times of partition, all the three male protagonists are like the doomed heroes. They are all mystical archetypes of the '*triad*' in the Indian cultural ideology and in the novel. They seem to be out of touch with the modern age's skepticism and banality. "The Australian critic H.M. Williams discovers in the novel what he calls 'doomed heroes'. Perhaps Hukum Chand, Juggat Singh and Iqbal are the 'heroes' of this category being a mystic archetype totally out of touch with the modern age's skepticism and banalities, an age for whom the natural heroes are not kings but pop-singers and footballers." (Prempati 112).

In the modern era, trains had become new rivers, a link with the other side, connecting people. The train in motion was shown in one of the earliest pioneering films and was shot by *Freres Lumiere in the film L' Arrivee d'un train en gare de la Ciotat*. The train in question, incidentally, was coming from Marseilles. Several decades later, Orson Welles excitedly defined cinema as "the biggest electric train set any boy ever had !". (Adair 9). Trains, on account of motion attributed to them like cinema, were a favourite with filmmakers for filming. The train which carries passengers from Lahore to Delhi and vice versa, acquires a great significance in the novel and brings about symbolically kind of dynamism in a static, dull, drab village of Mano Majra. After dark, when the countryside is steeped in silence, the whistling and puffing of engines, the banging of buffers and clanking of iron couplings can be heard through the night. All this has made Mano Majra very conscious of trains, which is beautifully evoked and enhanced cinematically in the film. "Before day break, when the mail train rushes through on its way to Lahore and as it approaches the bridge, the driver invariably blows two long blasts of the whistle. In an instant, all Mano Majra comes awake". (24). All the activities of the people of Mano Majra centered on the arrival and departure of trains metaphorically acting like a clock chiding time. It had been always been so until the summer of 1947 till a ghost train arrives laden with dead bodies. Ironically in '*Train to Pakistan*', the train also becomes a summon for death along with a symbol of transition to a new promised land called Pakistan.

Earlier, too, Hukum Chand had been prophetically wary of the idea of trains with corpses, passing through Mano Majra. When the sub-inspector narrates to him the horror tales of mobs looting, raping and murdering in the market places at Sheikhupura and Gujranwala he gets apprehensive and is emphatic about the idea that law and order must be maintained. However, once the ghost train arrives, Hukum Chand along with the sub-inspector is at his tether's edge and with his sanguine device, plans to pacify the chaos which otherwise could envision communal disharmony. Iqbal, the communist who is actually a Sikh, is arrested. He is declared to be one of the members of the Muslim League masquerading under a false label. Mali, a local hoodlum and his companions who are the actual culprits and murderers of Ram Lal are on a looting rampage. Juggut Singh who has been earlier arrested on suspicion of murdering Ram Lal is held behind the bars still.

A clever game plan is hatched out by Hukum Chand to lead Muslims across the border for a safe passage to Pakistan. They are sent to the refugee camps at Chandernagore for their safety. From there on they would be sent to Pakistan by train. In the novel Khushwant Singh beautifully evokes the pathos of partition between the Sikh and Muslim villagers who fall into each others arms and weep like children at the very thought of separating from each other. When Nooran's father Imam Baksh breaks the news to Nooran sleeping in her bed oblivious of the happenings, she's shocked and refuses to go to Pakistan. She is with the child of Jugga. She walks in the rain towards Jugga's house with the intention to meet him. Rain has been falling incessantly. Rain otherwise is symbolic of regeneration and arouses in her a feeling of renewed union with him. She hopes that perhaps Jugga had been released from the jail like Mali. Though, she knew that it was not true yet the hope persisted and moreover it gave her something to do. However, neither Jugga nor his mother is at home. She waits for Jugga's mother hoping that Jugga might walk in. She is, in fact, in no mood to face Jugga's mother alone but does not want to go home too. When Jugga's mother arrives probably after visiting her Muslim friends, she is shocked to see her sitting in the dark at such a late hour. Nooran addresses her as '*Beybey*' and asks her about Jugga. The mother is however annoyed with Nooran and accuses her of being a tart. She refuses to soften towards her even when she tells about her leaving for Pakistan .

Nooran however musters up courage and tells her that she could not leave for Pakistan since Jugga had promised to marry her. The idea of marriage between her son a peasant, Jat Sikh and Muslim weaver's daughter sends the mother into frenzy. She in fact calls her a bitch and tells her to get out of the house and leave her Jugga alone by going away to Pakistan. Nooran goes down on her knees and clasps her legs and tells her that she was with Jugga's child. After hearing that, she softens towards her yet commands her to stop whining. She tells her that she could not keep Nooran there with her as that would spell trouble for her. She however assures her that Jugga would fetch her once he was back home to be his wife. A vague hope gets filled in Nooran's very being and she felt as "if she belonged to the house and the house to her, the charpoy she sat on, the buffalo, Jugga's mother all were hers". (152) Pamela Rooks portrays this scene between the two ladies with great sensitivity. There is a shift in Jugga's mother's attitude on learning that Nooran is with Jugga's child. Even though Rooks sees the images of women in film as the vehicle of male fantasies and the scapegoat of men's fears, she also sees the film as a complex text which may contain competing even subversive voices.

Sharon Smith in her article, 'The Image of women in film: Some Suggestions for Future Research' is concerned to expose the false and suppressive limited range of images of women offered by films. In her account, she says, "films both reflect social structures and changes them according to the fantasies and fears of their male creators". (Smith Sharon 15). Khushwant Singh, infact, presented things as he saw and felt and wrote without being moralistic. He mentions the rape of Sundari, the daughter of Hukum Chand's orderly with piercing subtleness. Married to one Mansa Ram she had red lacquer bangles and henna on her palms as symbolic of marital status. Her marriage with Mansa Ram was not yet consummated and she was told not to take any of the laquer bangles off as it brings bad luck by her girl friends. However when she's on her way by bus to Gujranwala with her husband the bus is stopped on the way. She's raped by the mob and all her bangles are smashed in the process. Khushwant Singh without being sarcastically barby as a matter of fact says that should have brought her a lot of good look. Pamela Rooks does not highlight any such rape scenes or looting episodes but its only through snatches of conversation and mutilated bodies shown either in the train or in the river that such gory incidents get conveyed. As Urvashi Butalia puts in 'The other side of silence',

> "for women who had been through rape and abduction the reluctance to speak was of another order altogether... speaking about them making them public not only meant opening up old wounds was another trauma". (Butalia 360).

It was Pamela's feminine sensitivity, too, as a director, which keeps her away from showing such gory incidents on the celluloid. In fact, she uses the renderings of Amrita Pritam's Panjabi poetry as an enhancing device for highlighting this progression from fiction on to celluloid. Madan Bala Sidhu, the singer along with accompanists conveys the pathos of suffering of rape and destitution of thousands of women during partition. The soulful song beseeches Waris Shah to create a verse upon the sad plight of women raped, separated from their families. The seventeenth century unpartitioned Punjab produced a great poet called Waris Shah who wrote the legendary love lore 'Heer Ranjha'. He had lamented in his lyrical poetry on the separation of Heer from Ranjha when the former is forcibly married off to the one chosen by her parents the first time. Amrita Pritam expressed the pain of partition of India in her poetry as a rejoinder to Waris Shah's Heer. Her poem in Punjabi *"Aaj Akhaan Waris Shah Noon Ke tun Qabran Wichon Bol, Ik Roi Si Dhi PunjabDi, Tu Likh Likh Maare Vaen. Aaj Lakhaan Dhiyan Rondian Tu Kabran Wichon Bol"*. translated (I beseech Waris Shah to speak from his grave, one daughter of Punjab i.e. Heer had cried, you wrote great heart rendering verse. Today lakhs and lakhs daughters of Punjab are crying, I beseech you to write about it from your grave). This poem stirred thousands of Punjabis to the depth of their souls. In fact Pamela Rooks opens the frame of the film with lyrical music of Heer when somebody is being hanged and a young boy very innocently looks on. This loss of innocence gets passed on to the look of experience and knowledge of Hukum Chand, who narrates the story from his vision and point of view in the film. Pamela Rooks uses the male's eye to see the film, perhaps, since the author of the book is also a male.

The novel, though, talks about partition and its gory details, it also expresses the fantasies and subconscious needs of men portrayed in the form of a trinity triad of the mythic Hindu ideology. The role of women Nooran and Hasina revolves around their physical attraction and mating games they play with the male characters Jugga and Hukum Chand. Iqbal, who is supposed to portray the role of Shiva, is not shown involved with any woman as Khushwant Singh himself said he was apprehensive of handling too many characters. Iqbal is rather shown to be apprehensive of places teeming with life. For instance, during the time when he first reaches Bombay, he felt that the population of India which went up by six every minute was a mockery to the planning in industry and agricultural. However, the cultural ideology of trinity embedded in his psyche makes him say. "But how could you in the land of *kama sutra*, the home of phallic worship and the son cult?" (58). However, he believes in equations in gender relations, like which is symbolized by Shiva-Parvati, the ideal couple in mythical matrimonial relationship. When Juggat Singh and Iqbal are thrown in the same prison by sub inspector as suspects for the murder of Ram Lal, they get friendly. Jugga who is supposed to be exceedingly passionate and full of virility, extorts him to explain his escapades with mem-sahibs who according to him are *houris* (beauties) from paradise whom Iqbal must have met when he was in London. He nonchalantly remarks that there is no difference between women. When Juggat Singh exaggerates and brags about his sexual prowess, Iqbal talks about equations in gender relations like the dual male-female energy called *Shiva Shakti. Shakti* is supposed to be female counterpart of Shiva. However, the concept that male and female are both part of the whole is so fundamental that Shiva-Shakti is often represented as one person half female, half male. Iqbal tells Jugga, "when you get married and you find your wife a match for you, you will be beholding your ears and saying 'toba' 'toba.'" (127). Pamela Rooks portrays many such scenic episodes centering around the lives of Jugga, Hukum Chand and Iqbal in keeping with the storyline and its spirit.

Khushwant Singh beautifully brings out the sensitive natures of both Jugga and Hukum Chand for their ladylove Nooran and Hasina respectively. Pamela Rooks also evokes their sensitivities on the celluloid though there are no love duets, sung by Nooran and Jugga in the typical Indian film style. Rather, there are only a couple of scenes between them showing them in sexual intimacy. With a very realistic approach, Pamela Rooks shows the denial of the reality of myth in operation "within a sexist ideology and a male dominated cinema, woman is represented as what she represents for man". (Johnston 33). However, even if Nooran is shown to be an equal partner in their intimacy, she's rendered powerless once she's with the child and Jugga is locked up away in the prison. On account of partition and their need for safety, when the Muslims of Mano Majra are told to proceed to the refugee camp and finally leave India on the train for Pakistan, Nooran otherwise a self-willed woman, wants to stay back in Mano Majra to be with Jugga. Similarly, Hasina, the young Muslim singer prostitute brought to entertain Hukum Chand in the guesthouse, gets attached to Hukum Chand and wants to stay back with him as his mistress. She is also sent by him to the refugee camp and put on the train to Pakistan. Both are doubly marginalized on account of their femaleness and as the 'other' now on religious lines.

According to Gayatri Spivak,

"the ideological construction of gender keeps the male dominant. If, in the context of colonial production, the subaltern has no history and cannot speak, the subaltern as female is even more deeply in shadow". (Spivak Can 287).

Hence, both Nooran and Hasina face displacements on account of partition. In such a case according to Teresa de Laurteis, "this is not merely reconfiguration of boundaries but a qualitative shift in political and historical consciousness". (Lauretis Displacing 138). The displacements for both are personal and conceptual and hence painful. Both of them are motherless, helpless, rudderless and hence vulnerable. Nooran has a father who is blind and loving and caring like a mother but asserts his patriarchy in decisions like one about going to Pakistan. Nooran is expected like any woman to obey her man. Though Nooran is going to be a mother herself and Hasina lends her bosom for Hukum Chand to rest his woes on and provides solace and protection symbolic of motherhood. Hukum Chand himself snuggles up against her bosom like a child and falls asleep after he had been through ordeal of viewing a trainload of dead bodies on the ghost train. However, in his endeavour to get the Muslims out of Mano Majra and near by areas, he dispassionately lets Hasina go. He faces life as it was and did not feel the need to recast him or rebel against it. Though he declares to Hasina that, "he was ready to lay down his life for her." (124). Yet symbolic of the Vishnu of trinity who believed in restoring the chaos and moral order, he believed that "an individual's conscious efforts should be directed to immediate ends like saving life when endangered, preserving the social structure and honouring its conventions". (118). He packs her off to Chander

Nagger refugee camp and onwards on the train to Pakistan. Rooks poignantly captures the sensitive bond between the two. Hukum Chand admonishes her caringly that she might marry a refugee and be his wife once she is in Pakistan.

In the meanwhile, Hukum Chand learns that Mali and other dacoits were out to create communal disharmony. The simple Sikh villagers of Mano Majra were being provoked regarding their masculine virility and questioned whether they were potent or impotent. They instigate them by informing them about the trainloads of dead Sikhs and Hindus, about rape of Sikh and Hindu women folk. Meet Singh, the Granthi, along with the *lambardar* of the village and other sensible Sikhs tries to pacify them. Meet Singh in a subdued manner reasons out,

> "What bravery is there in killing unarmed innocent people? As for women, you know that the last Guru, Gobind Singh made it a part of a baptismal oath that no Sikh was to touch the person of a Muslim woman". (172).

His pleadings, however, go unheeded and they go on a looting rampage. Even the blind Imam Baksh, Nooran's father is not spared and very symbolically his forehead is marked with religious mark that is scratched by a dagger by one of the hoodlums. Luckily, Nooran is away to meet Jugga's mother and hence escapes the ordeal of being raped. Meanwhile a plan is thatched to kill the Muslims on their way to Pakistan by train. Meet Singh cautions them that there would be Mano Majra Muslims too on it. He is however mocked at. A group of 'real men' which includes Mali and his friends gear up for the 'mission' the plan was to be executed at sunset when it was dark. For that a rope was stretched across the first span of bridge, which the train was to cross. The rope was to be a foot above the height of the funnel of the engine and when the train was to pass, it would sweep all the people sitting on the roof of the train, which will account for the loss of at least four to five hundred lives.

In the meanwhile Hukum Chand is a shaken and tired man after disposing the carnage of trainloads of dead bodies, which had arrived from Pakistan. Though he's been playing the art of diplomacy in daily administration, the sub-inspector instigates him emotionally, now. Hukum Chand releases Jugga and Iqbal. The sub-inspector informs them that they would find great changes in Mano Majra as all Muslim population of there had left for refugee camps to leave India that night by a train to Pakistan. At the same time they are informed that Malli would have finished all of them had they not left Mano Majra in time. However, he tells them about Mali and his gang going on a looting rampage of the Muslim homes in the village. Jugga along with Iqbal and Bhola the driver go through a long uneventful journey towards Manomajra. Whereas Iqbal and Bhola are occupied with the idea of their safety, Jugga's immediate concern was the fate of Nooran. At the back of his mind persisted a feeling that Nooran would be in Mano Majra still since no one would have wanted her father Imam Baksh to leave. He feels that Nooran would be hiding somewhere in the fields or would have gone to his mother. He hopes that his mother had not turned her out. If she had done so, he would let her have it. He would walk out and never come back. She would spend the rest of her days, regretting having done it. This is what he actually does later. The altercation between the son and mother leads to Jugga's moving away from the house. He goes to the Gurdawara and requests Meet Singh the 'bhai' to read the Guru's word, *'Vak'* from the Guru Granth Sahib. When Meet Singh tells him that Guru Granth Sahib had been laid to rest for the night, he beseeches him still to read a few lines. Meet Singh rather chides him for not coming to the Gurdawara earlier, yet he reads him a piece of the morning prayer and shuts the prayer book and puts it to Jugga's forehead. He then begins to mumble the epilogue to the morning prayer and explains him the meaning that the Guru's word means that, "if you are going to do something good, the Guru will help you, if you are going to do something bad the Guru will stand in your way". (198).

Jugga sets on a mission to save the Muslims on train to Pakistan since he wants to save his lady love Nooran who has boarded the train along with other Muslims. Even Hasina, the danseuse prostitute is on the train. It is Jugga who musters up the guts to take up such a brave venture. The *mise en scene* of Jugga's bravado has been filmed with great tautness and suspense. Pamela Rooks beautifully portrays the acknowledgement of Hukum Chand's salutations to Jugga's bravery in the film. When Jugga is on his way to 'save Nooran mission', Hukum Chand declares that people like him would do everything to live, but there are people like Jugga who sacrifice their lives, don't do anything to live or survive and because of this history remembers them. He holds Jugga in great awe for the brave deed he does.

Pamela Rooks picturises the scene with heart rendering poignancy. The train is chugging away in the clear of light with the black smoke emanating out of it. She uses the train as a metaphor and the speed of the train creates a fast pace rhythm of momento which seems threateningly menacing. The coal is being fed to keep the chugging train get going. The black smoke rises up in the sky forming black clouds which seem to engulf the very train and the refugees in it. With bated breath Jugga waits to view the arrival of the train. Pamela Rooks manipulates the look of the viewers in synchronization with Jugga's anticipation. However, near the bridge there is very little moon light leading to obfuscation of vision. Men who had spread themselves on either side of the railway line for the sabotage could hardly recognize even each other as a result. Hence they just talk loudly, though one of them commands silence as they would be able to hear the train coming. Hence they begin to talk in whispers and take their positions ten yards away from the track. However they do see a man run up to the line and put his ear on the rail. It is Jugga, the fact of which is unknown to them. Thinking that there is someone amongst them up there, the leader fiercely asks him to get back as the noise of train approaching in vicinity is heard. Meanwhile they shift to the rope as a shaft of steel. "If the train was fast it might cut many people in two like a knife slicing cucumbers". (p. 206). Khushwant Singh vividly draws an imagery of such a spine chilling scene which Pamela Rooks aptly picturises. The viewers shudder at the death waiting in wings for the passengers on the train. While the men are looking at the lights of the train and awaiting the impending disaster, Jugga climbs up on the steel span unnoticed until he gets to the top where the rope was tied. In fact they think that he was one of them testing the knot. As the train gets closer the engine acquires the demonic form with sparks flying from its funnel. The whole train could be seen clearly against the moonlight. From the coal tender to the tail end, there was a solid crust of human beings on the roof. In fact Pamela Rooks shows the innocent passengers sitting in the train oblivious of the fate that awaits them. Nooran is shown sitting pensive, tears flowing down her eyes with no hope for future in her eyes. She's unaware of the fact that Jugga is lurking around somewhere close by to save her life. Jugga with single minded passion is stretched on the rope and whips out a small kirpan (small dagger worn by the devout Sikhs along with comb, kanga, underwear (Kutcha), unshorn hair (Kesh) and kara, i.e. iron bangle around the writst). He slashes at the rope with the kirpan and hacks the rope vigorously and simultaneously. Meanwhile the would be sabotagers realize that there is something amiss and their leader fires at Jugga. His body slides off the rope yet he clings onto it with his hands and chin. He catches the rope under his left armpit and hacks at the rope with his right hand. The rope meanwhile gets cut into shreds and he cuts the thin, long strands with his teeth. He is attacked by a volley of shots and finally collapses as a result alongwith the rope which is snapped at the center. He falls down and very dramatically the train goes over him and moves onto Pakistan. Jugga's supreme sacrifice goes unnoticed as Nooran is simply unaware of it. It's only through the flash back device used by Pamela Rooks in the film does one get to know that Hukum Chand is aware of it.

The morning prayer (*Japji Sahib*) of the Guru Granth Sahib, which Jugga had listened to before going on his mission to save Nooran and the passengers of train to Pakistan, is symbolic in the context of Jugga's supreme sacrifice. Meet Singh, the Bhai shuts the prayer book and puts Guru Granth Sahib on his forehead blessing him with the Guru's words.

> "By thought and deed he judged forsooth, for God is True and dispenth truth. There the elect his court adorn, and God himself their action honors, there are sorted deeds that were done and bore fruit". (199).

Jugga, symbolic of 'Brahma' the creator gets himself destroyed by destroying evil (symbolic of Shiva in the Trinity) only to recreate. The cutting of the rope and its snapping off, is symbolic of the cutting of the umbilical chord, which he snaps off to create and bring forth the baby in

Nooran's womb. The baby yet to be born of Nooran's womb will be symbolic of the new creation.

The epilogue of the Morning Prayer says: "Air, Water and Earth of these we are made. Air like the Guru's word gives the breath of life. To the babe born of the great mother earth sired by the water" (198). Pamela Rooks and a right ambience have beautifully captured the ethos of the prayer and sanctity of it is maintained. Though Khushwant Singh in his autobiography goes on to say that he is not a religious man and is not given to rituals however by using the words of Guru Granth Sahib, he infuses a spiritual aspect to the novel along with the three male characters built on the mythic trinity of Indian cultural ideology. In fact Khushwant Singh exhibits a genuine faith in humanism through the deeds of the three male protagonists even if he sets them up in accordance with the mythical triad of the Hindu gods.

Brahma is the Lord of Creation. He is also the God of Wisdom and is shown carrying the Vedas in one of his four hands, which symbolize wisdom, and learning through Brahma. He is sometimes shown carrying a water flower, which symbolizes prosperity and may also have a string of pearls or a sacrificial spoon in one hand symbolizing his spiritual nature. The fourth hand is usually raised in a gesture of promise of fulfilment. Jugga, a dacoit as a peasant basically represents procreation. His name, too, has a symbolic significance in that sense. Jugga, the dacoit who thrives on his basic instincts enters realms of spirituality and finally he gets enlightened and awakened to the call of true love. Jugga, the name when translated in English means 'The awoken one'. Similarly the name Hukam Chand means 'order' when translated. Hukam Chand is represented as *Vishnu*, the preserver of the moral order and as the local magistrate. According to mythology, he is an object of loving devotion rather than awe or fear. His chief function as preserver of the universe and cosmic order makes him the upholder of dharma. *Vishnu* is considered to have his life divided and imprisoned by time. He lives in history and man's life in this world. He has more to do with man's social and political realities and the working out of a moral balance on earth. Vishnu's history is closely linked with *Sansara, Karma and Dharma*. According to the Indian culture ideology, history is a constant battle between two forces, which over the long cycle of the existence of the universe, will balance out. However at certain points in history, the balances get pushed out of harmony and the forces of evil gain an upper hand. Partition was one of those tumultuous times.

According to the nature of *karma*, good forces and evil forces are both present on earth. Hukam Chand personifying *Vishnu* tries to set right the balance though not to destroy evil but as Vishnu actively intervenes on behalf of law, he intervenes as a magistrate. He believes that opposition must exist if there is to be a game, like wise evil must exist for good to operate. Hukum Chand like any *Vishnu* avatar acts to redress the balance of good and evil. In releasing both Jugga and Iqbal from the jail he manipulatively puts them on a specific mission to actively strike the balance of good and evil. Iqbal is a mild fellow compared to Shiva. Shiva's role in the trinity is that of destroyer. However, the act of destruction is closely related to creation. Tradition holds that Shiva is greater than Brahma and many myths tell of the feud between them and of Shiva's ultimate victory. Shiva's rivalry with *Vishnu*, on the hand has not resulted in victory for either of god and gods in Hinduism. However, in the novel and the film Hukum Chand as *Vishnu* restores the order through the help of Shiva and Brahma i.e. Iqbal and Jugga respectively.

Both the novel and film metaphorically show the life of game through the co-ordination of all the three deities guiding towards a goal, an understanding that the undifferentiated essence is not only mystical but beyond one's ability to measure. The Indian idea of existence of both opposites where every quality has its anti-thesis, male has female, up has down, light has dark and good has evil, is reinforced. The triad of Brahma, Vishnu and Shiva point to such a truth, the movement and ebbing and flowing of the universe. In the novel as well as in the film, using the Shiva's representation through the sign of male phallic *'lingam'*, is not emphasized. Rather Khushwant Singh represents Iqbal as Shiva of the triad who is suspected to be a Muslim by the name of Mohammed Iqbal and a member of Muslim League by the police. Iqbal, in fact, is a circumcised Shiva's sign, of the male phallic *'lingam'* which is Shiva's most familiar representation and is a symbol of his creative powers too. This is the form to which the devotee of Shiva offers his/her worship as is universally considered as a symbol of fertility. There are two shots of the naked male bottom of Iqbal enacted by Rajat Kapoor in the film when he is asked to strip by the police who wants to check whether he is a Hindu or a Muslim. This is a scene which had great difficulty to get passed through the censor as his posterior is shown naked. He is made to strip to find out whether or not he was circumcised. It is however confirmed that he was but he clarifies it by telling them about a surgery he had undergone in England. Iqbal however protests and feels deeply humiliated. The posterior is shown in the cinematic representation hence one can feel his humiliation which is evoked in the scene. In fact Pamela Rooks objected to the censor cut demanded for this particular scene. She felt it was an unnecessary demand on the part of the censors and that most certainly the purpose was not to titillate or expose. She could see no logic in their stand. She felt then that if she was to agree to all the deletions and cuts most of which according to her were ridiculous and arbitrary, she would have to shorten the film by as much as 20 to 30 minutes. To chop merely a line or two here and there, could also have led to re-editing of the sequence so as to maintain a flow of narrative very essential for any cinematic representation. In the novel, however, he does not possess the qualities of Shiva and is the weakest link in the structure of *'Train to Pakistan'*. "The religious ambivalence implied in his name is only an aspect of the base of the basic rootlessness of Iqbal's personality". (Shahane 74). In the film the mythical connotation to Shiva in the cultural ideology is alluded in a subverted manner. In the novel, it has a great significance and is an aspect to the question whether he is a Muslim, Hindu or a Sikh, which can be confronted and derived from his physical examination. When a separate sovereign state was carved out on religious lines, it led to the truncated bifurcation of India. It was ironical that to establish identities as Hindus, Muslims, Sikhs who had together equally struggled against the British rule until 1947, such devious devices had to be used.

According to the cultural ideology, energy cannot be released without the combination of male female powers and that no system can be all male. The man needs a woman and vice-versa to be complete. The dreams of man need the female touch for their actualization. For Jugga to actualize his dream, he has to save Nooran and let the child in her womb survive and be born. Nooran whose name denotes 'light' of the world, has to keep on shining symbolically in this world and prevail even if she has to cross the boundary and move to the 'other side'. She carries the light within her, which has to be carried and brought forth and Jugga with his supreme sacrifice endeavours to release it.

The name of the other female protagonist 'Hasina' means the beautiful one. She is like goddess Saraswati who reminds us that life without music, poetry and art would be barren and empty. Hasina in the process of earning some wealth for her *nani*, is like *Lakshmi* too for her. She utilizes her talent of singing and dancing to entertain Hukum Chand as a source of livelihood. However, her vulnerability and natural innocence makes her more Haseen i.e. more beautiful. Even the crude, treacherous Hukum Chand pensively reflects that she is of his daughter's age had she been alive and even mutters it as he holds her in an amorous hug. In fact, the whole plan to save the life of refugees is thatched by Hukum Chand in a manipulative manner. However, even though, it sounds devious, it gives meaning to his character in the novel and the film, in its adaptation too. It's like a perpetual new beginning in any human being's life, which he/she makes when one realizes that serving the others and sacrificing for the other is a great service. In it is the essence .of life in a moral manner. In the case of Jugga, the simple uncalculating love of a man for a woman asserts itself and averts the catastrophe of the danger to his Muslim beloved Nooran. Jugga, a burly hoodlum, redeems himself by saving the lives of thousands of Muslims leaving on the train to Pakistan.

In a stirring climax, Pamela Rooks cinematically evokes a search for the most deeply hidden human values. Jugga eventually finds his path to the divine. Amidst the universal madness and communal frenzy, a sense of humanity pervades through him irrespective of his caste and religion and nationality. People, on both the sides of border have passed through a collective catastrophe, unconsciously rooted mistrust of reality, an illusionary and equivocal evasion. However, to promote it, aesthetically meaningful cinema is a vehicle when it adapts good genuine literature. It helps to affirm trust in things, affects people and evokes the basic goodness in the human spirit. Such an endeavour requires a true and real interest in what has been happening, along with a search for the deeply embedded human values in it. It has been the essence of any culture and more so of the peace loving Indians.

When a question is raised like what can the filmmaker, who essays to adapt novels to the screen, make of the tradition? He/she is then supposed to make a serious adjustment to the set of different and often conflicting conventions, which have historically distinguished literature from the cinema and made each a separate institution. "Films are capable of proceeding on two levels as Elizabethan tragedy: poetry and psychology for the gentleman's gallery action and blood for the hit." (Bluestone 4). In an understanding of the shaping power of viewers and of its thematic convention, the story enables cinema's ability to handle time and space. Any comparative analysis of a novel and film reverts finally to the way in which consciousness absorbs the signs of both language and photographed image. Pamela Rooks manages to evoke through conceptual imaging, as in Jugga's action, a difference between the images of things, feelings, the conceptual images evoked by the verbal stimuli of the 'words' of the morning prayer uttered by Meet Singh. They can be distinguished as evoked by the non-verbal action of Jugga through his behaviour. For, the moment when thought is externalized, it is no longer thought. The film, by arranging external signs for our visual perception leads us to infer thought. Though it cannot show us his thoughts yet we perceive his thoughts and feelings through his action. The fact that, "a film is not thought, it is perceived, proves true here". (Bluestone 48)

According to Kum Kum Sangari and Uma Chakravati, since the historical periodisation of ancient, medieval and modern times, a standard pre-occupation has been reflected.

> "It has constituted a patriarchal and communal ideological unity that overrides historical evidence, deriving from the orientalist thesis of an unchanging India. This ideological unity linked the stereotypes of the exemplary ancient Hindu woman and the demonized Muslim male during the colonial and nationalist periods. Though, the ideological assumptions of periodization have been amply and repeatedly critiqued by historians and feminists yet it has not been dismantled". (Sangari and Chakravarti xii).

Khushwant Singh, in presenting the three male protagonists of the Indian cultural ideology and while basing them on the pattern of mythic Indian trinity of Brahma, Vishnu and Shiva, inextricably links their lives along with the two Muslim female protagonists in the novel. He thus dismantles such a periodisation and that too when the country was passing through the momentous period of partition in the history of India. "The relationship between 'woman'—a cultural and ideological composite as the 'other' is constructed through a diverse standard representation". (Uberoi 324).

In depicting the relations of power and struggle by focusing on the three male protagonists by Khushwant Singh, it becomes a male conspiracy by him. Pamela Rooks, however, in her cinematic representation, strikes a balance of power within which the analysis of culture ideology can be situated. According to Chandra Mohanty,

"the average third world woman leads an essentially truncated life based on her feminine gender and her being third world (read ignorant, poor, uneducated, tradition-bound domestic family oriented, victimized etc)". (Mohanty 95).

Here, both Nooran and Hasina are trapped in such a system and the independence of the country leading to the partition and birth of nation to which they are going to belong, has no liberalizing factor for both of them. For both of them independence and the birth of a new nation of Pakistan to which eventually they are going to belong to, which the train to Pakistan is going to take them, have no hope of liberating them and let them have control over their lives. The universal images of the third world woman as the construct of veiled chaste virgin etc, images, constructed seem to persist for them. John Berger observed that while, "a man's presence suggests what he can do woman's presence suggests what can be done to her". (Berger 75).

One still does not know whether there is hope for Nooran and Hasina. Nooran perhaps is right in telling Jugga's mother, "Beybey, I have Jugga's child inside me. If I go to Pakistan they will kill it when they know it has a Sikh father". (152). As for Hasina, who wants to stay back with Hukum Chand, he dissuades her from doing this since she is a Muslim. However, she persists and says, "Singers are neither Hindu nor Muslim in that way. All communities come to hear me." (122). She talks about the *hijras* (hermaphrodites) who are not Hindus or Muslims or Sikhs too and neither males nor females. Inspite of the philosophy mouthed by her, she has to leave. Hukum Chand shows her the rosy picture of being a young refugee's wife, which is better than being an old magistrate's mistress.

The search for a national identity extended to such genres such as history and anthropology, all of which focus on the significant events and figures, "from the past and were a combination of fact, myth, legend and folklore" (Chakravarty 310). As a reflection of the way India envisioned itself, films constructed a self-image for the nation by borrowing from different indigenous sources, and often this was based on a classification of the past. It is the past of India's independence in 1947, which led to the sad chapter of partition of India, which gets reflected in novel of Khushwant Singh's 'Train to Pakistan' and the film Pamela Rooks adapted from the novel for the celluloid.

The film has been acclaimed from both classical and mass appeal point of view. It is the tragic story of partition of love between a Sikh boy and a Muslim girl. By all accounts it is doomed becaus∩ of the difference in religion and now a different nationality because of bifurcation of India into

India and Pakistan on account of partition. At the time of partition the milieu was teeming with unrest amongst the population of Hindu, Sikhs and Muslims. Both Jugga and Nooran belong to two different religions who are predominantly young and good looking with youthful zest for life. Pamela Rooks brings Nooran's entrance in the film with a whiff of freshness by showing the vibrantly youthful love scenes between her and Jugga. Inevitably the sparks were going to fly irrespective of caste or religion on the eve of partition melee with a bout of passion bustling in them. Pamela Rooks achieves a transparency to match the superlative clarity in her direction. The rural setting evokes a feeling of earthiness and endless trials the villagers undergo on account of partition which becomes the vehicle of forced migration of their Muslim brothers. The setting of the village Mano Majra and the narrative with two strands of sub plots poignatitly blends in it. "The costumes designed for the characters highlight the bygone pre-independence era". (Patel and Dwyer 4). The bright blue *sharara* of Hasina and casual bright yellow and green Kurta and Salwar worn by Nooran is drawn from the real world they seem to inhabit and shows the life styles of the two female protagonists. The mise en scene in the Gurudwara when there is an inflow of refugees from Pakistan alongwith dead corpses found sailing in the river, adds to it a level of trauma of human endurance. The Shabad (hymn) sung by the devotees along with the Bhai Sahib (p. 168) *Awal Allah Noor Upaye Kudret Ke Sab Bande : Ek noor sai sab jag upgaya : Kaun bhale kaun mandey* ; translated—"It was Allah first and then his light ; All human beings are part of his creation; With that one light the entire world came into being; Is there any among them who is good and any who is evil?" This hymn raises the very morale of the villagers and helps them to transcend the suffering that has been meted on them on account of displacement due to partitition. It displays their pathetic yet courageous strength with moral resolve of humanism to protect their fellow villagers irrespective of their religion. Every strand of action and account is visible and audible without being unduly highlighted in the film. Pamela Rooks never allows the chill in atmosphere to mask the romantic hearts of two.

The film 'Train to Pakistan' yields to a glimpse of the dark and silent period in which women suffered the most in a rhetorical way, though it is put a little melodramatically. Yet, it tugs at the inner chord of the heart of a post partition generation too. To look back into the history and study the cultural idea, points not just to the question of language, but the whole ethos of that captured by the film in such a rich tone. Nooran and Hasina may not be the embodiment of the values and codes of behaviour derived from mythology, cult worship, social traditions and customs which form the very basis of traditional Indian society but are living images of real life. There is a vulnerability about both of them that is not only touching, but also full of humaneness, which transcends any Indian mythic cultural ideology. Nooran is a steadfast woman, true and sincere to Jugga and wishes to marry him. Hasina, young and innocent, gets so emotionally involved with Hukum Chand that she is ready to stay back in India with him and is even ready to be his mistress. Inspite of the exploitation of her physical body, her innate innocence reflects in her acts. Nobody could crush the purity of Hasina's soul.

Nooran's impending motherhood evokes the ethos of the Yashoda and the infant Krishna. During the period of nationalism the nation was conceived as the mother because she gives birth to us all. In fact, she is like the Indian Madonna, the mother earthly and divine, sensuous and pure. "The apparently secular images of Indian women spontaneously call forth the conceptual distinction and oppositions that re-emerge in analysis of the Hindu Pantheon". (Uberoi Feminine 324). However, the female sexuality depicted transparently, here, contrasts the non-sensuality of the faithful wife/devoted mother with the negative and dangerous and sensuality of the vamp/temptress. When Jugga's mother accuses Nooran of making her son a *'Budmash'* i.e. an evil character and tells her to go to Pakistan, "Leave my Jugga alone", (152) she does not speak in a woman's voice. She is herself a captive of society's dominant patriarchal ideologies and is alienated even from her ownself as a gendered subject. Such women are very often the most immediate and conspicuous oppressors of their own sex. Jugga's mother's callous indifferent attitude towards Nooran however gets softened once she hears that she is with Jugga's child. Even when she tells her to leave for Pakistan, she promises that Jugga would fetch her back once he comes back from the jail to be his wife.

The tragedy of partition has never been the subject, which has been much of a favourite with the Indian filmmakers.

> "Presumably, they did not want to dig up past wounds and create further embarrassment to a society which had come to terms with an unfortunate episode in our history. It not only divided the nation, but also its film industry. The film community was all along working harmoniously as a unified happy joint family. The best example is the Prabhat 'partners, Govind Damle and Sheikh Fatehlal which got disrupted after partition." (Nair 9).

It was like a break up of the joint family as a unit, which was a part of nation. Iqbal Masud, a critic believes that, "partition was an irreversible cultural mistake-the real disaster of partition was cultural not political or humanitarian as has been made out". (Masud Memories 34). He poignantly points to the sensitive couplet of Faiz Ahmed Faiz, the famous Urdu poet who had this to say about the partition of 1947, "Ke Interzar tha jiska yeh woh shehar to nahin" translated "This is not the dawn which we had anticipated".

The debate of the film's representation on partition is still a keen one and raises important questions regarding the role of cinema as the site where ideological battles of representation may be fought. Perspectives on gender relations in the backdrop of partition, leading to communal disharmony and the atrocities on women, their suffering, pangs of separation from the motherland, uprooted-ness from homeland, need to be interrogated. There has been a great need to look into it. The idea is not how true to the source the film has been, but to examine it for its narrative complicity with the prevalent cultural ideology of those dark days in the history of India. The articulation of cultural nationalist ideology revolves around the beliefs concerning the distinctiveness, integrity, uniqueness and superiority of one's culture and such a culture is supposed to be a proper determinate and legitimate repository of the collective consciousness. Pamela Rooks, in the cinematic adaptation of the novel *'Train to Pakistan'* returns to India's past, half a century later after independence and subsequent partition. She seeks to pinpoint the historical moment when new meaning was given to the cultural ideology in the insensitive exploitation of men and especially women, the ideal vessel to carry out the theories of state and ruthless exploitation manipulation of the innocent refugees.

To fulfil the grand vision of independence and a truncated country, sadly, the callous discard of the 'other' on religious lines was regarded fair and life or love held no meaning for the other. Such a culture needs to be named and identified and its contours delineated and lineage traced, its rise and fall in history must be noted and the potential threats to it also need to be identified. "Cultural nationalistic articulation is a process that sets forth the nation as an ideological cultural construct". (Aloysius 132). The complex process of selection, rejection, modification and codification does not take place in a vacuum. The partition of India is a historical event and the most massive experience of any kind, "it became an encounter between man and reality, a collision between a political agenda and a long tradition of pluralism," according to Krishna Sobti. (Sen, Geeti 54).

The film as a means of expression celebrates the validation in its attitude, which, however, remains highly discussable. On account of the foul words used in the film by Jugga and other dacoits in it too, the release of the film was delayed because of the censor board clearance. However, Pamela Rooks elevated the film to a subtle sublime level with the use of poignant poetry of Amrita Pritam on partition, along with the imagery of visuals and the craft of editing. The long track shots, chiaroscuro lighting and the juxtaposition of extreme long shots evoke richness of her repertoire. What makes the film unique is the double image altering between close ups of main protagonists and the long shots of refugees in the train, moving on tracks surreptitiously. The screenplay and direction, along with a well-written script enhance the novel on the celluloid. The setting of the mud houses, showing the villagers as they used to live in the pre-partition days, lends a great deal of authenticity, along with nuances of set designing employed therein.

It is a perfect and lucidly narrated tale, thanks to the convincing acting of all the actors of the films who played their roles. A special mention should be made of Nirmal Pandey who enacted the role of Jugga with élan along with Mohan Agashe as the magistrate, Hukum Chand, Rajit Kapoor as Iqbal, M.S. Sathyu as the blind Imam and father of Nooran and Bhai Meet

Singh's role played by Singh. Smriti Mishra as Nooran and Divya Dutta as Hasina, the young innocent prostitute, have enacted their roles beautifully and with great sensitivity. Rivers, borders, forests and memory intermingle with the span of their journey to Pakistan. The two refugee girls, though not a counterpart of mythic goddesses to the trinity are yet raised to higher planes. They transform themselves, so they evoke the primal theme of identity, homelessness and journey. According to Ania Loomba, "attention is now being focused on the role of the women of colonized nations and their relation to their position of contradiction within this order." (quoted in Doraiswamy 170). There is a depth of characterization and a breaking away from the stereotypes of the female characterization in the book that is highlighted in the film.

The most effective articulation of the Indian cultural ideology may not be a point to reckon with in such a film like *'Train to Pakistan'*, but the actions and behaviour of the characters drawn in the novel from the Indian trinity, effectively articulate such an ideology. The nationalist cultural ideology of the film arises from its female characters, too, and interpersonal gender relations "which lend voice to small scale motivations of romantic desire are quite indifferent to the larger designs of patriotic duty and national interests." (Niranjana 15). Pamela Rooks doesn't think of herself only as a woman director. She transcends gender boundaries; as she prefigures the theme and stylistics that becomes a part and parcel of Indianness in the film and goes on to show the working of the human mind in the face of distress.

The film opens, with one of the male protagonists, Hukum Chand narrating the story and the male point of view of the film does make it an overwhelming male film. Even the novelist S. Khushwant Singh agrees that he had the male trinity of gods in his mind while writing the novel. However given the nature of the nationalist formulation, with partition as the main theme of both the novel and the film, women were presented with problems of victimization that need be to the dealt with. Conceived in a pervasive 'powerlessness' wherein the males take decision, "since the ideology of gender makes of woman's life script a non-story, a silent space, a gap in patriarchal culture, the ideal woman is self-truncated effacing rather than self promoting." (Probyn 130). The larger narrative of gender cancels the stories of the lives of Nooran and Hasina. Their being the 'others', belonging to a different nation at the time of partition on account of their religion, they represent "opposing poles of the myths of feminity sexuality as grace and innocence". (Johnston 38).

The central articulation in their existence as performers for the pleasure of men they are involved with, contradicts between their desire to please their males counterparts and to be self-willed women. Both the men, Jugga and Hukum Chand redeem themselves with their sense of propriety to save their lives. True to the cultural ideology of the trinity as *Brahma and Vishnu*, both Jugga and Hukum Chand help in the procreation and restoration of order in their lives. It is as Gayatri Spivak puts, "thinking of the ethical relation as an embrace, an act of love in which each learns from the other, is not at all the same thing as wanting to speak for the opposed community". (Landry and Maclean 5). Both Jugga and Hukum Chand may not be speaking for the opposed community as the 'others' from themselves, unlike Iqbal who represents Shiva. He had basically come down to Mano Majra to establish communal harmony. However, in transcending harsh fact of communal conflict and strife at the time of partition in saving the lives of Nooran and Hasina both Jugga and Hukum Chand contribute to the construction of a saner vision of social order. It is this phenomena that is a pointer to the novel's and film's broader "ideological agenda" a term borrowed from Madhava Prasad (5). Both Khushwant Singh as the writer and Pamela Rooks as the director of the film respectively focus on the redemptive vision and role of both Jugga and Hukum Chand. It is a triumph of love, humanism, and faith in the innate goodness of man in a moment of challenging crisis. It underlines the central aspect of the novel and is evoked and enhanced beautifully on the celluloid visually.

J.N. Dixit, a former foreign secretary in an article 'Zero credibility' says,

"Nehru said 50 years ago in the Lok Sabha that the partition lesson, which India should always remember is, that the communal and caste antagonisms within Indian society pose a far more dangerous threat to India's independence and security than any external threat". (Dixit 8).

Memory and myth play a definite role in the understanding of phase of any contemporary life. According to Sukriti Paul Kumar, "Massive literature on the partition depicting communal carnage, atrocities and salvaging humanity by portraying the moments of compassion amidst the deluge of violence has been churned out". (Paul 85). However, the weave of common culture was so strong and dense and its ideology so deep rooted that it still lingers not as a memory but for many as a source of inner strength. While, the political dividing line after partition had to be functionally realized, many aspects of the cultural baggage could not remain undivided. For a culture to acquire its own identifiable shape and colour, it has to remain in the womb of history over a period where it is protected, fed and cherished. Cultural memories, with a nostalgia of the past relationships helped the villagers to confront reality of those gruesome times, of human survival of the other and the predicament they were faced with on account of communal disharmony.

The stark reality and harsh truth had to be confronted not with callousness but with the realization that both the segments of population had been an integral part of a common cultural heritage and this was a poignant realization Mano Majra Hindus and Sikhs had not lost sight of. They reached out to their Muslim brethren helping them to cross the borders. The scenes of shared sentiments connect them together. The pathos on their separation while getting onto the trucks to reach the safe refugee camps to be taken to by a train to Pakistan is portrayed with a heart rendering sensitivity. Not only the novel but also the film adapted on the celluloid, portrays a reservoir of authentic human experience, salvaging humanity from inhuman practices perpetuated at time of partition in the name of the religion.

Shyam Benegal believes, "political cinema will only emerge when there is a need for such a cinema" (Datta, Sangeeta 1). The cinematic representation of '*Train to Pakistan*' after fifty years of Independence by Pamela Rooks and its all India telecast on 15th August, 1997 at 9.00 pm may not have evoked the idea of political cinema. Yet, it did lead many a post partition generation to understand the pangs of separation and the ramifications of the geographical and political bifurcation of the nation[6]. Today, in 2004-2005, we have the World Punjabi Conferences all over Punjab and Lahore. Delegates from both the sides shed tears and get nostalgic when they visit their hometowns on either side. The memories of their homeland still haunt them, lead to an emotional upheaval and a surge of overflowing emotions that are inexplicable.

The role of women against the backdrop of the freedom struggle, evolving nationalistic ideology and partition has been looked into in this chapter. The patriarchal, hierarchical, insensitive gender organization of the family, relationships of power, the peculiarities of Indian modernity within which the traditions that impede self-expression survive, are recaptured in various reinvented forms. All these get reflected in the films adapted from the novels set during that period in this chapter. The most potent visual manifestation of this period in the cultural domain came through the so-called 'empire cinema'. "Empire cinema is a term now accepted for both the British as well as Hollywood cinema made mainly during the 1930s and 1940s which projected a certain vision of the empire in relation to its subjects". (Chowdhry 1). However, it was a cinema, which emerged as a most influential propaganda vehicle and showed a viewpoint and the acceptance of certain ideological concerns and images, in keeping with the imperial vision. It emphasized unique imperial status, cultural and racial superiority and patriotic pride, not only of the British but also of the entire white western world. In India, some filmmakers who had been deeply stirred by the nationalistic feelings projected what can be called genuine patriotic feelings through the Indian cinema. "They were influenced either by personal contact with senior political figures of the time, or were inspired by major milestone events of the national freedom struggle." (Kaul 59). However, the films based on literary texts discussed in this chapter are not essentially patriotic films; rather they reflect pre-independence period and the immediate aftermath of the tragic period of partition after independence. Colonial or modernist reform projects or nationalist responses to them are reconstructed in the novels and films adapted from it in the related areas of social subjectivities and cultural production, gender identities and social organization of families, and households in this section. Colonialism is said to have introduced major renovations, if not an absolute break with the past. The nationalist resolution of the 'women's question' and the older traditional mores in the name of cultural ideology were pitted against social reforms. The women's question, "was a central issue in the most controversial debates over social reform in the early and mid-nineteenth century Bengal-the period of its so called Renaissance". (Chatterjee 116).

The Indian process of self-definition had its counterpart in the western definition of Indian identity. Orientalism or Indology was the discourse, which offered this definition in the field of literature, and was not an isolated development. It was an integral part of global programme of literature ordering congeniality to western imperialism. Indology was a method of cultural study of a nation that was condemned to a perpetual decline and logistic vulgansater. The rise of Indology was concomitant with the rise in Europe of acute awareness of history as the past. Indology therefore, could not perceive Indian culture as a dynamic force. The leaders of the Indian Renaissance tried to counter the Indological unwillingness to permit Indian culture a complete status, but their way to do so was to emphasize the presence of all European virtues in Indian society and culture. The attempt of self-definition and establishing a native identity was catching up with the west for vying with it in claims of conceptualization.

The nineteenth century discourses of reform often saw education for women as a mean of exercising agency. Education held out possibilities for women for chiselling out a new female identity for them. The women's struggle to free them incorporates the history of torment, of torture and loss. The price exercised by patriarchal society is often a terrible one as seen in 'Ghaire Bhaire' and 'Train to Pakistan'. This world of loss could not have been captured by Jalpa in 'Gaban', which locates her within certain social conventions. Jalpa struggles, accepts a few traditions and rejects and question others. It is the female subjectivity which manifests itself as a process that questions stereotypical representations and problematic in gender relations, with the limited choices available to women. Jalpa develops and evolves within the cultural ideology an inversion of gender relations within the ferment of social change. Jalpa's character in the film 'Gaban' is a positive one, like the role models of women in the cultural ideology that they need to identify with. For Premchand, she is a strong woman character who does not get led or taken over and reconciles as someone who understands gender politics. She does not put the pleasure of stability and of the domestic ritual to stake as Bimal unwittingly does in 'Ghaire Bhaire' and has to pay a price of being reduced to widowhood. Premchand was sensitive to women's oppression and supported abolition of child marriage, widow remarriage, female education and property rights for women. "Yet, in his fiction he upheld a separate sphere for women and saw westernisation as disruptive of tradition. The independent woman was frowned upon as immoral'. (Krishnaraj 26). The same idea gets reflected in the film also.

The conceptulization of Indianhood as a spirit was one of the major issues in the Indian nationalist thought by the turn of the century. The nation as a mother was constructed, "by turning her into a principal Hindu

Goddess." (Zuthsi 95). This was most completely articulated in the novel 'Anandmath' by Bankim Chander Chatterjee. The powerful mother image can be that of mother goddess (Durga/Kali) as an important figure in the pantheon at once nurturant and destructive. This imagery, "leads to the secular domain where even the theme of patriotism is involved as the earthly mother/ the mother goddess/the mother land/Bharat Mata all coalesce". (Uberoi Feminine 332). Nooran's impending motherhood in 'Train to Pakistan' is symbolic in that sense. However, the contours of the nationalist history made it clear that the history of the mother was represented as the nation, which only her true children can inherit. It was believed that, "this certainly does not include the worthless heathen as they are to stay on the other side of the border". (Zutshi 94). Nooran is hence rendered powerless and rudderless and has to migrate to Pakistan. As it is, partition had led to the objectification of women, where they had become objects or things to be appropriated with. According to Krishna Sobti,

"When families of migrants meet they don't talk about the partition because it is a painful subject. It troubles everyone, especially the women. The fate of women during the partition was a great burden on the minds of families who migrated on both sides and who had to pay very heavily as they were the victims of mob violence". (58).

Within the ambit of direct human experience, especially of the unfortunate women who suffered, whether they were wives, sisters, daughters, there were some families, which surrounded such women with deep silences. Partition produced a range of questions concerning the status of the category 'woman'. These were those times in women's collective experience when discussions about them had become almost a forbidden subject. Real lives of women and men's ideal of women intersect at various points during the freedom struggle movement. Women were caught up between two worlds, firstly of the social world that they had known and the new one that was emerging. Spivak, particularly in her accounts of the double subjection of colonized women and her discussion of the silencing of the muted native subject, in the form of the 'subaltern' woman says, "There is no space from where the subaltern (sexed) subject can speak". (Spivak Can 122).

The realm of female education was opened up on account of the nineteenth century reform movement and it even enlarged the space for women's activities. The concept of spheres, the public open to men and the private being women's domain, has been a major orienting principle of women's history in the determination of gender relations. "Increasing historians found that notion of women's sphere had permeated the language and its usage was wide spread in the nineteenth century". (Sonali and Wadhwa 37). Yet; conceptually and in practical feasibility equipoise in gender relations could not be achieved and gruesome atrocities meted upon women during the period of partition in 1947, played havoc with their well-being and happiness. Bengal's first partition in 1905 reinforced both the *swadeshi* movement and Muslim separatism as shown in '*Ghaire Bhaire*'. The fate of women during the partition in 1947 was a great burden on the minds of all those who migrated, as it yielded a glimpse of the dark and the silent void beyond. It shows the tenuous conflict between tradition and modernity, between decorum and freedom and between constriction and emancipation that marks the woman's transition from the realm of the private space to that of public domain. Gender relations evolve under the duress of the problematics of a dominant cultural ideology, which had a potent influence on the minds of male characters who would not allow the women to transgress.

Notes and References

1. All subsequent citations are followed by page numbers in parentheses from the text: Tagore, Rabindernath. *The Home and the World*. New Delhi: Penguin Books, 1999. are followed by page numbers in parentheses.
2. Satyajit Ray takes subjective shots of Bimal, the female protagonist to implicate the spectator into the narrative so that he or she identifies with her point of view.
3. All subsequent citations are followed by page numbers in parentheses from the text: Premchand, *Gaban*. Trans. Chistopher R. King. New Delhi: Oxford University Press, 2000 are followed by page numbers in parentheses.
4. Middle of the road Cinema, "was distinguished by its narrative of upper caste middle class life with ordinary-looking deglamourized stars. It consolidated it self by elaborating a negative identity based on its difference from the mainstream cinema". (Prasad 127)
5. All subsequent citations are followed by page numbers in parentheses from the text: Singh, Khushwant. *Train to Pakistan*. New Delhi : Ravi Dayal Publishers, 1988.
6. Partition in 1947 has left its imprints on the formation of two countries, India and Pakistan. There has been a history of wars between the two nations and of terrorism and counter-terrorism. Yet, after years of Independence and partition there is a revival of hope of good relations between the two countries.

5

Conclusion

Films can be interpreted as personal dreams of the filmmakers and the collective dreams of their audiences. This fusion is however made possible by the shared structures of a common ideology and one of the main functions of the films is to entertain. Films are not taken seriously or thought about much. It is generally said, "its only entertainment, for filmmakers as well as for the audience, full awareness stops at the level of plot, action and character in which subversive implications can be disguised and presented as a kind of partial sleep of consciousness". (Wood Robin 189). Adapting and basing a movie on a well-known novel has its perils too. A well-established means of considering the relationship between writing and cinema is through direct comparison of written texts and their filmed adaptations. According to Stuart Laing, such a study, "of a novel and a film version would have value in its identification of the specific properties of each text in being a case study of an adaptation task in its illumination of the intrinsic technical possibilities and limitations of novel and film as specific art forms". (Laing 134).

Despite a built-in audience of readers, there is always a risk that fans will dislike the way the characters they have imagined, are portrayed. But if successful, the film portrayal of literary character can make the nuances of a character even more compelling and of enduring interest. If a filmmaker is adapting a novel or a short story that is both widely read and intensely loved, the filmmaker has a certain responsibility then. "Films are faced with the task of presenting not only a narrative that is logically connected, but one that contains a maximum of emotion and stimulating power." (Eisenstein 14). Hence, the filmmaker's version has to be more effective than the novel and that's a tall order to be met by the filmmakers. The cinematic embodiment of characters sometimes proves controversial too. People who have read the novel or short story love to interrogate every incarnation of a book on the film. Sometimes casting choices are made that the authors did not envision but then realize, have enhanced their work on celluloid. Yet, there are directors who choose their own approaches to adapting books on the screen. Some may keep the novel as an ever-present guide on set while others don't refer to the book during its cinematic adaptation. However every director brings his/her own sense and sensibility to the film he/she makes. According to Rahul Bose,

> "For a filmmaker, it becomes imperative to decide on what to keep and what to throw away. Within two hours, he or she has to keep the soul of the novel alive and tell the story in a hypnotic fashion. At the same time, cinematic licences and directorial flourishes should be encouraged." (quoted in Modi 37).

The screenplay can change dramatically when the director lends his/her personality and stamp to it. He/she understands that cinema is a visual art and a great masterpiece can be transformed and highlighted on the celluloid. A piece of good literary writing has affinity with good cinema, but one should realize the difference in the two mediums for a good cinematic representation. The director's job is the toughest in film making in comparison to experts in the audio-visual medium. The role of the screenplay writer in adapting novel is also not an easy one though. There have been many screenplays adapted all over the world from novels, but not many have been successful commercially. As there is more escapist cinema in India, the screenplay writer adapts the materials given to him from a novel and play accordingly, to create escapist cinema. Hence, the original creative work of well-known writers suffers when transcribed to cinema. A good script basically leads to a good film.

Cinema is primarily a story telling medium. It is a script of the film that determines how the story unfolds cinematically. The scene wise form of conveying the story is unique to cinema and is called a script. "The screen writer is often referred to as a technician–the equivalent to the draftsman in architecture". (Dancyger and Rush 3). A feature film tells a story, which a scriptwriter 'creates' out of disjointed ideas, and situations he is told to put into the script by the director. The scriptwriter's job is to use the words and put on paper what the director has imagined and visualized in the course of the script sessions. The scriptwriter then creates a cohesive narrative. Conflict is central to all story telling and without it the story is flat and tends to become a mundane series of events. "Cinematic representation through visualisation of screenplay leads to atmosphere. Film dialogue should be believable since dialogue is a metaphor for a state of mind". (Dancyger and Rush 10). Whether cinema goes on to subvert the piece of ideology that inheres in fiction or relies on it in the matter of portrayal of cultural content, is a discerning matter. The writer, who fully understands the way of words, can beautifully etch and delineate the ideals of heroism, justice and moral achievement. However, in no way can the role of the director be minimized. He is clearly the most important person on the set, since his influence touches every phase of production. The film director reveals his talent through his ability to elicit and judge the talent of the others. His inspiration is embodied in his capacity to inspire his associates, calling into play their mechanic or professional expertise. For, film may be a decidedly mechanical art, much more than painting or music or literature, yet it distinctly contributes to artistic execution. In a more exacting sense, tools of the filmmaker prompt and shape his creative achievement.

The old tendency to dismiss cinema as an escapist media, always defined escape as merely negative, not perceiving as a kind of recourse to illusions that help to weather the reality. Dreams are also reprieves from the unresolved tensions of our lives into fantasies. Yet, the fantasies need not be totally meaningless. They can at times represent attempts to resolve those tensions in more radical ways than our consciousness can countenance. The nostalgia and fascination associated with old classic movies adapted from fiction, is present in profusion even today. Classics are adapted because they have an evergreen quality. Through adaptation, filmmakers just cast them into another mould and keep them alive. Undoubtedly, the script, music, acting, director and behind the scene happenings and anecdotes have contributed immensely to the making of these classics. However, neither texts nor readers exist in a vacuum and the same goes for the films and viewers, once the novel is adapted on celluloid. Both are shaped by and participate in a social, political and material context of the total culture.

Culture shapes the beliefs and practices as if they were part of nature. What is intriguing is the possibility that, "culture even shapes how biological scientists describe what they discover about the natural world". (Martin 179). It is within the systems of this wider culture that analysis can be located. Prominent in this wider context is ideology. Narrow usage equates ideology with specific principles or propaganda and specifically with some false consciousness. Ideology acts or functions in such a way that it transforms the individuals into subjects. Interestingly what really takes place in ideology seems to be taking place outside it. According to Louis Althusser,

"that is why those who are in ideology believe themselves by definition outside ideology. One of the effects of ideology is the practical degeneration of the ideological character of ideology by ideology: ideology never says, 'I am ideological.' It is necessary to be outside ideology in scientific knowledge to be able to say: I am in ideology as a quite exceptional case or in the general case. I was in ideology. As is well known, the accusation of being in ideology only applies to others, never to oneself." (Althusser Ideology 112).

When one thinks of the, "advantages and strengths of cultural forms, of which cinema still forms a linchpin be it in America, India or anywhere

in the world, culture ideology leads onto and produces endless conformity."
(Branton 63). Such a regular flow of ideology involves advantages at certain
symbolic, signifying levels. It leads to the bank of imagery, which includes
song, music, and also at the same time to the saturation of such imagery.
This in turn allows a much less mystifying view of creative talent, which can
then be "glimpsed not as innate but as having the capacity to be largely
learned within such systems." (Branton 64).

Gender has been acknowledged as a fundamental determinant of social
existence, along with equally important perception of gender as a cultural
construct rather than a biological construct. This has paved the way for the
radical complex work of dismantling the hidden edifice of ideology
operating within literary texts and films adapted through gender lens within
the constitution of culture. The cultural environment gets linked to the
construction of gender relations as the product of the cultural forces
prevailing.

Nonetheless women's culture forms a collective experience within the
cultural whole that binds women to each other over time and
anthropological critics. Critics like Gerda Lerner have argued that,

> "it is important to understand that 'women's' culture is not and should
> not be seen as subculture. It is hardly possible for the majority to live
> in a subculture. Women live their social existence within the general
> culture and whenever they are confined to patriarchal restraint or
> segregation into separateness (which always has subordination as its
> purpose) they transform this restraint into complementarily asserting
> the importance of woman's function and redefine it, thus women live
> a duality as members of general culture and as partaker of women's
> culture". (54)

However, when historical aspects are looked at, considering the
feminist consciousness as an essential aspect and with a focus on woman
centered inquiry, considering the possibility of the existence of a female
culture within the general culture shared by men and women, then, the
central question it would raise is "what would history be like if it were seen
through the eyes of women and ordered by values they define". (52).
Gender relations are identified in terms of dominance, deference,
antagonism and solidarity that are constantly at work.

The gender arrangements of a society involve social structure e.g. in
religious, political conversational practices, all of which place men in
authority over women. It can be very clearly underlined as a patriarchal
structure of gender relations. This leads to a socio cultural structure, which
conditions practice and gets established as an ideology. As a result, the
structure of gender relations has no existence outside the practices through
which people and groups conduct those relations. For instance, women
entering the public domain have an uphill battle to have their authority
recognized through the struggle for credibility. Their authority has been

undermined as a flagrant contradiction with the ideas of a patriarchal society, culture and ideology. In the case of films taken up in this book, strong case of seeing gender relations as internally complex and involving multiple structures as reflected in films adapted from Indian literary texts, is being made. Power as a dimension of the inequality of gender relations was central to the women's liberations and women's oppression. It involves not one aspect but various structures such as eco- production, socialization and sexuality. This power operates oppression through the institutions of family and state and becomes an important part of the structure of ideology as culture; (*parampara*) (*sabhayata*) cultural heritage gets conceptualized. However total domination is not possible as there is always resentment and even resistance against it. Inspite of conditioning subjugation, discursive power also gets contested or transformed and challenged.

The consciousness of gender runs through literary texts and inevitably even in the films which get adapted on the celluloid. From them encodes our cultural existence. Literature also offers a varied field for theoretical and critical study not simply because it singles out an exemplary body of texts. "It is a space of contention: already determined by ideology, yet offering, through the very act of writing, the possibility of a break, even an escape, from complete ideological control." (Chaudhuri and Mukherji 2). This dissertation has considered the relationship between reading and viewing and has been concerned with the fact that how at times writing literally appears on the cinema screen, by extending the meaning and signification[1] imparted therein evocatively through cinematic devices. Through the cinematic representation of select Indian films adapted from Indian literature, an endeavour has been made to extend the understanding of the issue of gender relations in films viz. the cultural ideology reflected therein. Such a study looks into how the film adaptation narrowed, sharpened or altered the core meanings of the novel. The novels or short stories on which the films have been adapted are both seen as separate works each with its own integrity. However, there is no such attempt being made in this study for a comparison between the literary texts and films adapted from them. Both chapters third and fourth deal with the set of narratives through the cinematic representation of literary texts depicting how the two narratives contribute to and gain meaning from each other's cultural themes in the Indian cultural ideology.

Constructions of gender differ according to the placing of femininity and masculinity within a nation's cultural traditions. When one thinks about cinema and its cultural traditions wherever they may be located on, one should be mindful of the fact that belief in western domination in terms of cultural hegemony is often a little closer to fiction than fact. Indian popular cinema, especially Hindi popular cinema, has its own filmmaking practices, which have little to do with Hollywood production styles; nonetheless it is a cinema of entertainment or instruction. In a way, it represents an imagined mythical India, for instance in epic melodramas, of self-sacrificing females especially symbols as mothers and heroic men as swashbuckling heroes.

Yet Indian cinema has produced another cinema that resists the popular film form. This cinema is called the so-called new Indian cinema, whose beginnings in 1969 were interestingly funded by the state to propagate good cinema. The new cinema films in a way targeted the nation's mainstream or so called popular cinema. There was a need felt in the 1960s to project images of the indigenous realities, which was done in a variety of ways. It mainly depended on the filmmaker's vision. New cinematic codes and conventions were developed. There was a great desire to address the problems of oppressed, marginalized classes. The issues of class, race, culture, religion, gender and national integrity were looked into.

Indian cinema tends to influence the socialization process and reinforces gender relations and "it has a much wider catchment area than any written literature cutting across class and caste boundaries" (Jain and Rai Films 119). Ever since the pioneer of the Indian cinema, Dada Phalke got inspired and the first film 'Raja Harishchandra' got released, the woman as a sensuous object was shown. For instance, the bathtub sequence where Harishchandra comes to call his wife Taramati, who is in the tub with her fully drenched attendants (a couple of whom are playfully trying to stop the sprouting fountains in the middle). "Only a fertile mind as that of Phalke could have incorporated a sensuous scene in what is primarily a religious subject". (Vasudev 52). Surprisingly all the females supposed to be in their wet *sarees* and blouses are in fact males in the garb, but one keeps wondering at the extent of eroticism, which is being provoked. It was not just an accident that the first Indian film happened to be a mythological subject. Phalke himself came from an orthodox Hindu household, a family of priests with strong religious roots. So, when it became possible to tell stories with technical finesse, the Indian film pioneer turned to his own ancient epics and *puranas* for source and the movie was a great success. This kind of source showed not only how strongly the filmmakers' mind is steeped in their mythology, but also the extent to which the source material of epics gets perpetuated in movies after movies.

On the other hand, the women's groups, who were trying to grapple with the value and meaning of a female image, struggling for different ways to negotiate the same, were articulating new definitions of gender and sexuality. The mainstream filmmaker, however, very cleverly and fruitfully, used different archetypes of mythical goddesses to model many of their women characters. These mythical goddesses Sita, Radha, Durga, Kali, Shakti and even the poet singer Meera, go to form a composite archetype in the Indian culture. In fact, the innumerable myths can be interpreted numerously. Myth occupies a particular space in our culture, mediating between the sacred and the profane and between the individual and the social. Myths are public dreams, the product of an oral culture nursing itself.[2] They are basically associated with ritual, as the beliefs based on action both define and co-relate the transcendental and luminal space to the mundane existence.

Studying the myths of various cultures leads to a better understanding of their social and religious underpinnings. By turning the myths inwards, inviting them into our lives and learning their language of imagery and symbolism, we learn more about ourselves. In almost every culture, the metaphor of descent serves as a powerful, sacred source. The knowledge gained through mythic imagery carried into everyday world, equips to deal with issues and conflicts with wisdom, clarity and understanding.

"In the case of literary texts, which get translated from one language into another at a minimum, the domain involves philosophy and interpretation hermeneutics and literary exegesis, art and aesthetics, rhetoric and cultural anthropology." (Cohen 128). While reading the film adapted from literary texts translated or original, the question of faithfulness occurs. Language is also a chief concern when adaptation is considered as it reflects the culture, ethos and aspirations of a people. Often, the novel and film may be in two different languages. According to Chander Prakash Dwivedi who adapted *Pinjar* in Hindi from Amrita Pritam's novel in Punjabi by the same name,

> "every language has its own nuances, idioms and cultural specificities. A film has to reach audiences in North India, South India and the overseas market. So, one has to write the dialogues accordingly. At the same time if one makes it too simplistic, the flavour of the language may be lost." (quoted in Modi 38).

Yet it cannot be a pertinent factor, since the original can never be replicated. The filmmakers confront with various challenges to literally do so as they have their own reading and interpretation while shifting and transforming the renowned text into a set of transpositions on the celluloid. They all put their own stamp of creativity and select from the immense material offered by the respective literary text as they transform it on the celluloid.

> "An original text offers a point of departure for a possible world with a generally definable cognitive scheme to which a new version offers a set of variations and transformations" (Bignell 129)

Where as in addition, the cognitive schema also provides the aesthetics which one may applaud or decry. However, it is the effective cognitive schema which enables the viewers to take notice of the highlighted aspects transformed on the celluloid and wonder at and marvel as he/she does it through cinematic language and other aesthetic devices such as lighting effects, *mise en scene*, music, acting of actors etc.

The writer uses words; the filmmaker uses pictures. Words are arbitrary signs or symbols, which are meaningless in themselves signifying only by conventional agreement. Pictures, in contrast, are generally thought of as natural signs or 'icons', which represent things on the basis of some sort of inherent resemblance to them.

"On another level, literature and film can both be seen as containing symbolic and iconic signs; while the relationship between iconic signs and what they represent is a much more intricate one. The most basic difference between images and words as signifiers is in the highly encoded nature of the other." (Boyumm 7).

The distinction between image and word is that visual imagery tends to the iconic; the words tend to be a good deal harder to come by than likeness. They both mean and involve perception and cognition and also involve what is known as the process of 'decoding'. More than merely perceiving a cinematic image, one has to link that perception to prior perceptions, previously gained knowledge and experience. Some degree of cultural training has to go into one's ability to see a film. In case of adaptation, one cannot rule out the possibility of a disagreement between the author of the novel and the scriptwriter of the film. The subject matter chooses its own medium. Some stories are better told in the written form and others are suited for the screen. Cinema basically captures movement. Therefore, stories that are dictated by a lot of externals can be adapted into films. However, since film is capable of replicating the world with such fidelity, the process of perceiving an object on screen is no different from perceiving it in actuality. Almost everyone agrees that adaptations are a difficult task-right from deciding which novel to adapt, getting the right milieu, to casting the right people and trying to be truthful to the original. To make a great film out of a great book one can never mimic. The novel and the film are separate but sometimes authors and filmmaker may have great collaborations.

However, cinema is the only medium through which we can directly deal with the problematic and paradoxes of a given society and bring about a change. In fact, its strangehold on the attitudes, mental make-up and certain perceptions, which colour the very fabric of our society informing our collective psyche, is enormous. The crucial question is... "How the 'who' (of culture) and 'what' (of politics) relate to each other. How to characterize the resulting imbrications? Are there any pre-requisites of citizenship-economic, cultural or gender? However, the cinematic institution in India has a great deal to say about all this. Between the agencies of 'release' and 'reception', the cinema is always situated literally, in the present tense."(Dhareshwar 318). According to an Indian film theorist Ravi Vasudevan, it can be "put more simply, as any film editor would testify, the basic shot before it is edited *prima facie*, consists of both its immediate textual 'subject-matter' and a kind of excess spill over that can potentially take the meaning of its subject matter into a number of directions". (Vasudevan Making 268).

Indeed, the representation of women in Indian films is a fascinating area of study and has been explored by a number of writers. It does illuminate dominant forms of patriarchal ideology in gender relations and shows women subjugated as either the nurturing mother, the chaste wife, the vamp or the educated modern woman. Cinema not only reflects cultures but it also affects and shapes cultures. There are Indian films that have promoted modernization, westernisation, urbanization, new ways of life, a sense of Pan-Indianism secularisation and the emancipation of women, too. "Indian film studies began to acquire an identity as a separate discipline identity in the eighties." (Prasad viii). Feminists from Simone De Beauvoir onwards, had seen cinema as a key carrier of contemporary cultural myths. It is through these myths found in religious traditions, languages, tales, songs and movies, that material existences are viewed and lived. And though the representation of the world, which like the world itself, is often considered to be the work of men, they describe it from their own point of view, which they confuse with the absolute truth, and women, too, inevitably see themselves through these representations.

The translations of text from their original language e.g. Hindi, Urdu and Bengali which have been taken up for the cinematic representation of films as a study, do have certain limitations on account of translations which may have suffered intrinsically. Firstly, one has to be aware of the fact that a study, which involves film adaptations of literary texts for celluloid, can be fraught with problems. There is always a possibility of film adaptations narrowing, sharpening or altering the core meanings of the novel, play or short story taken up for film adaptation. There can be an emphasis laid on the importance of seeing the novel or short story and film as separate works of entity, justifiably each having its own integrity and hence be judged without necessary reference to the other. Academic critics may wish to emphasize the specificity and separateness of individual filmic or literary texts, the way in which such narratives and stories circulate in contemporary culture. Yet it is often much less pure and is unaffected by concern for textual integrity.

According to Laing, "as with fairy tale, myth or romance, the existence of different forms of the same story (novel, film, play radio adaptation, etc) creates a more generalized, somewhat imprecise, cultural object, the meaning and significance of which derives from the interaction and overlapping of meanings of the multiple versions, as well as from its place among more general cultural themes and symbolic forms." (Laing 134). Like words in literature, images in film are capable of carrying both denotations and connotations that not only signify entities other than them in the literal sense but also have feelings surrounding them—even if inherent potential, literary and cinematic languages are markedly different in their emotional and intellectual charge. Films naturally address the feelings more immediately, directly, and powerfully than it does in language. The sights and sounds, which are part of the inherent film's mixed language, allow the filmmaker perfectly capable of underplaying and even totally undercutting it. Literary texts are all works of art, which means,

> "they carry emotional import and that their formal texture is central to their effect. However whatever the differences in their ultimate capacities, the language of film and the language of literature share the same crucial ability: to address both intellect and emotions, to make us feel and make us think, and sometimes to do both at once." (Boyum 18).

Reading gender through and across literary texts and at the same time its adaptation in cinema, is a complex process, which can be fraught with "ambiguous status of all representation. It is liable to be based on pre-determined concepts and social roles set by the cultural ideology." (Chaudhuri and Mukherji 3). Language and gender oriented research has associated women with questions in negative ways, many a times. Research, which looks at gender differences in personal narratives, has found that "woman's stories are more often about experiences that are embarrassing or frightening than about personal skill or success." (Johnstone Barbara 66).

The study of the Indian cinema cannot only be helpful in understanding India as a country, but is also instrumental in deepening and broadening one's understanding of the world. India has a deep, rich and diverse cultural tradition that has evolved over 5000 years. India is pluralist and diverse in a way that few countries are. It is not easy to think of another country that has many flourishing languages and literatures. India is the largest film-producing country in the world, as it produces over 900 films annually. Cinema rather opens a most useful window onto a culture. Its study brings us intimacy and immediacy, unavailable from most other media of communication.

Culture has many definitions and "it is a whole way of life" and has "the webs of significance that human beings spin around themselves." (Gokulsing and Dissanayake 7). By studying culture, one acquires a deeper understanding of the customs, behaviour patterns, values, arts and crafts and the practices of everyday life of the people inhabiting that culture. Likewise, deeper, insight into the complex processes of modernization, colonialism, nationalism and freedom for women can be acquired through Indian films. In all the six films, all the different characters relate to the personal and collective gender experiences. All the cultural myths from the Indian epics and sociological histories get woven as a mosaic at different spans of time in the Indian society. The literary texts encompass several spaces through their narrative discourses, especially domestic and emotional spaces.

Each of these films analysed in this book problematises both culture and gender relations, which entraps the woman more than her male counterpart in Indian cultural ideology. "The move from the early agendas of feminism to a place in the sun as a human being still remains an incomplete narrative in itself. The women's cause is constantly under pressure to retreat, to alter and to succumb." (Jain, Jasbir, Gender xxi). The cultural ideology affects the gender relations as it tilts the equipoise and equations in relationship. As it is, the Indian cultural ideology has undoubtedly more or less intrinsically a patriarchal ideology; as a result, many a lived culture gets explained accordingly in its terms. Such a cultural inheritance vis-à-vis the Indian cultural ideology is justified by the socio cultural circumstances, portrayed in literature and cinema both. The focus has been on the need to explore the nature of the narrative, both in the literary texts and in the films adapted from it on the celluloid. Each literary text through the film narrative reflects aesthetically the theme and stylistics in an enriched way in the different genres, be it in the new cinema, popular cinema or middle of the road cinema. It still incorporates all the ingredients of the written narrative whether it is dramatic, poetic or replete with myths or fables in the epical or oral literatures of Indian cultural ideology.

When one talks about gender, the word as a category evokes-a wider significance than feminism. Both men and women have their own manner of conceptualising, analysing and communicating on account of different societal conditioning perhaps. According to Jasbir Jain, their social locations roles, inherited strengths and constraints have been different. Hence "the manner in which history constructed them or cultures negotiated through them was different". (Jain, Jasbir, Gender x). As a result, the nature of narration at one level gets negotiated accordingly.

Story telling plays a central role in perpetuating and so does interface between different segments and generations of society, since "narrative is a central function of language and is an immensely flexible technology or life strategy, which if used with skill and resourcefulness presents the most fascinating of all serials." (Coates 112). Role of oral speech in constructing women as gendered beings, offers a wide range of ways of being, but all these ways of being are gendered. In such a bifurcated world one still inhabits male visibility and female invisibility and is the best place, so far in which it is to be found in the realms of the arts. "Literature extended to include other forms of textualties than fiction, drama and poetry, including letters, memories, autobiographies and biographies, offers the richest find so far". (Bannerji 188).

Cinema is an advanced narrative art of story telling. It has an advantage over the traditional literary forms of *nautanki*, theatre and other oral narratives, on account of its rich array of visual and verbal presentation in India. The conventional devices of costume, spectacles, music, dance, lighting, imagery are all-inclusive in it. Films reach a wider audience than literature as they move across the barrier of caste, class, gender, literacy, religion and even language. Films may be primarily a non-verbal experience, but narrative is based on the cultural experience of society. The imagery used in literature may be symbolic but can be realistic too. Films not only reflect reality but also construct reality. Their reach and impact makes it imperative to work through rhetoric and melodrama of the medium to unearth the subtleties and antiquities, which lie within the literary text. Films are also the most effective way of making a statement on life.

The novel in India was a genre developed directly out of an imported plural heritage. The economic and the social determinants interacted to make the shaping of this literary form, a tangled and complex process in our different languages. Each of the Indian language represents the culture and development of the thought process of India in its manifold forms. What makes Indian literature specifically rich is, "distinct stamp of a mind that feels that Indian literature in the singular does exist and it can be codified because of a continuous dialogue between forces of radical changes and of synthesis" (Panja 3). As to what makes Indian literature specifically Indian, is the voice of dissent, ultimately incorporated into the longer aesthetic pattern, which is both invigorating, harmonious and pleasing to the eye. In Indian films based on literary texts, film technique borrows from this contribution of literary aesthetics, when one wonders what could be the advantages and disadvantages of a cinematic adaptation that foreground the time of a writer and what his/her life stood for. Certain novels and stories offer a good example of cinematic licence, by virtue of which the filmmaker takes to relive his vision on films. Indian cinema's range like Indian literature, "covers many styles, themes, approaches, specific treatments and languages." (Vasudev 136). Inspite of the complexity and difference between the two mediums, the cinematic presentation offers a better representation of the perspectives of narration in fiction.

There is a belief that films made by women filmmakers lead one to believe that the feminine aesthetic sensibility is concentric towards social concerns and women's issue, but this is tantamount to taking a rather myopic view of things. Silvia Bovenschen has posed the question in 1976, whether there is a feminine aesthetic and she herself gave an answer to it. "'Yes' and 'no': certainly there is, if one is talking about aesthetic awareness and mode of sensory perception. Certainly not, if one is talking about an unusual variant of artistic production or about the painstakingly constructed theory of art." (quoted in De Lauretis Aesthetic 27). In the early 1970s, Anglo-American film theory accounted that feminist film culture is of two types of film work that seemed to be at odds with each other. One was for the purpose of political activism in the sense that it was a consciousness raising drive for self-expression or the search for the positive 'images' of women. The other was, rigorous formal work on the medium, which would understand cinematic apparatus as a social technology. This would be of a great help in order to analyse and disengage the ideological codes embedded in representation.

Laura Mulvey was responsible for heralding such two successive movements of feminist film culture, which led women filmmakers and critics to the use of and interest in the aesthetic principles and terms of reference provided by avant-grade tradition.[3] Later on, it was amalgamated with the debates on language and imaging that were going on, the outside of the aesthetics of cinema, in semiotics and psychoanalysis. However, it is necessary to look into the matter whether feminine sensibility differs from male sensibility? Does the feminine aesthetic sense, in terms of cinematic image while reconstructing reality, is different when made by men? Not really, if one were to go by the telling works of women, who have shattered the myth of cinema being a male created field through their strong efforts at creating their *oeuvres*. The idea is that a film may address the spectator, irrespective of the filmmakers' gender. Claire Johnston in her article, 'Women's Cinema as Counter Cinema', suggests a viable alternative to the rigid hierarchical structures of male dominated cinema. "Voluntarism and utopianism must be avoided if any revolutionary strategy is to emerge... we can best interrogate and demystify the workings of ideology from insights... that a conception of counter cinema... will come". (Johnston 40).

Mira Nair, an Indian born filmmaker of the *'Salaam Bombay,' 'Mississipi Masala'* and *'Monsoon Wedding'* fame has forged a new hybrid aesthetic in her filmmaking style, as she seeks to challenge and rupture the borders of identities based on class, race, gender and location. She says that,

> "certainly cultural and historical determiners must be kept in mind when making or talking about films on the culturally invisible; the culturally silenced and politically oppressed subalterns of the world; but cultural historical knowledge must not be repositioned as a new frontier border or silencing mechanism itself." (Foster 265).

At times, writers and filmmakers are unwittingly involved in a ceaseless struggle to define gender. As Chris Weedon puts it, "The nature of femininity and the masculinity is one of the key sites of discursive struggle for the individual." (Weedon Feminist Practice 23). A continuity of older social and cultural forms and norms pertaining to man-woman gender relations are a discernible matter. A century and a half ago, "there was no theory of gender in the modern sense. Theories emerged as products', secular, rationalist and skeptical culture which took its modern shape so far as human sciences are concerned in the second half of the nineteenth century." (Connell 116). The ideas, produced by intellectuals of great imperial powers in Europe and North America, rapidly circulated in other parts of the world from Chile to Japan. These theories came into existence by the gradual transformation of the older discourses of gender, which were religious, non-rational and moralistic. The separate spheres of men and women were powerfully emphasized in the mid-Victorian bourgeois culture.

Reflections of the imperialistic culture of the kind are shown in *'Ghaire Bhaire'* (The Home and the world). In the milieu of evolutionary thought symbolized by Darwinism, it influenced gender issues. Women were then viewed as an important social base for a utopian society. It was to be only if women remained in their proper sphere as comforters and nurturers of women. 'Women question' was placed on the agenda by an emerging movement of women and subjugation of women was unavoidable for middle class intellectuals trying to formulate theories of social progress in social science. Along with the suffrage movement, the social scientists made emancipation of women a test of progress achieved by any society. Gender relations were focused by many European intellectuals mainly on personal interaction at the most easily grasped level of analysis. "To the Victorian intelligentsia, the main determinant of gender patterns was the dynamic of progress loosely linked with biology in evolutionary speculation but to all intents and-an autonomous social progress." (Connell 114). It was progress supposed to be in moral, economic and political arena that was thought to be breaking the bonds of ancient custom and lifting gender relations onto a higher and more rational place.

In traditional societies, especially in India, women have been constrained by social constructs and the ethos of cultural ideology. As a result, in the patriarchal set up, women have been governed by their positions relating to the outside world through their men, be it a father, husband, lover or even a son. Indian nationalism, however, proved to be a dynamic force of gigantic magnitude influencing Indian life in various ways. The essence of social regeneration was felt to uplift women.

> "In fact the new woman typology (*nabina*) and the older, pre-colonial one (*Prachina*) were pitted against each other by the male intellectuals of the time respectively signifying households where women were in the inner quarters or present outside of them". (Bannerji 189).

It was thought that what was good for the family or the nation was good for women themselves. It was a stage of transition period leading to a transitory change and in many a male mind, then, apprehensions and doubts about it might have still persisted. There was perhaps this dilemma and apprehension that Tagore might have had while writing 'Ghaire Bhaire' whether 'outside world' 'Bhaire', was feasible for the women who had been cocooned by the 'Ghaire'. The question of gender when examined in depth encompasses mutual recognition and a high level of shared understanding. Jalpa, in 'Gaban' may not be considered a feminist as she is depicted as being a part of conservative or more accurately liberal culture, where the representation of strong women characters is permissible but where the familial status quo remains unquestioned. Jalpa's inheritance from her mother is not of the *chandrahaar*, neither of any property nor the physical ownership since only the patriarch can provide a patrimony. In fact, the legacy of mothers to their daughters was an ambiguous and elusive one since there were no property rights for women. Hence, mothers were, "not in a position to give as much of the world, which also lay beyond their reach." (Banerji 186). All the films taken up from the literary texts for the study show how women grapple to cope with the subordinate positions thrust on them as a result of such cultural ideology. Even if the female protagonist realises that, "she is not expected to speak the same language as man's; women's desire has doubtlessly been submerged by the logic," of the culture ideology. (Irigaray This Sex 25).

Important ideological changes were taking place in India in the nineteenth century. It led to the question of education of women into citizenship and identity in the twentieth century, which was fascinatingly broached by Rabindra Nath Tagore in 'Ghaire Bhaire' (The Home and The World, 1916). Premchand, in 'Gaban' threw light on the complexities in the cultural fabric of traditional set up, which is basically grounded in the patriarchal order, where gendered subordination is imaged in domestic middle class. "The respectability of woman from the emerging middle classes was being defined in counterpoint to the 'crude and licentious' behaviour of lower class women. Decent middle class women were warned against unseemly interaction with lower class women and against the corrupting influence of the wandering women singers and dancers." (Tharu and Lalita 9). All the three female protagonists Hirabai, Umrao Jaan and Sanichari in 'Teesri Kasam', 'Umrao Jaan', and 'Rudali' are marginalized not only by their gender but also by their caste and class too. All three Hirabai, Umrao and Sanichari in the respective films have male counterparts in the films who are reconciled to conformity and convention in their life style; yet, all the three female protagonists in the respective films metamorphise through self discovery. They do not seek their sustenance through plenitude and fulfilment from the 'other' and do not feel that they are annihilated by the trials and tribulations of fate and circumstances. What happened to Hindu, Sikh and Muslim women during the bloody days of partition, speaks of the most shameful and barbaric moments of human history in the Indian subcontinent. They were molested, raped, and abducted by human beasts as has been told in the blood chilling account of the partition by writers like Khushwant Singh, Bhisham Sahni, Amrita Pritam etc. Most women, even when they were recovered, ended their lives or were killed by the parents and husbands to save their honour, which underlines the sense of honour of the male patriarchy.

There may be a belief that films cannot do the languages job more effectively, but words are equally powerless to emulate the cinematic effects of a film. "However both two art forms-verbal and visual are not merely parallel but reciprocate and interdependent." (Jain and Rai 9). Some films are held to be influential, historical or even just spectacularly typical. The films based on fiction have an evocative and potent impact in the visual pleasure with regard to the use of aesthetics employed by the filmmaker. The *auteur* of the cinema i.e. the director according to the '*auteur* theory' characterizes his/her work by distinctive thematic concerns and visual style.

A strategic projection of ideas employed in the cinematic representation of literary texts by the directors portrays their personal creative expression. Gender relation is an issue, which affects the human relations and the very fabric of the society all over the world. A tilt here or there upsets the values of society, leading to an imbalance with the pros and cons all out of balance. According to Gayatri Spivak, "literature is a vehicle of cultural self-representation, the Indian cultural identity projected by the Indo-Indian fiction, however, can give a little more than a hint of the seriousness of the contemporaneity of the many 'Indias' fragmentarily represented in the many Indian literatures." (Spivak How to 127).

However, Indian films adapted from the literary texts be it in English, Hindi, Bangla etc. are all representative of the Indian cultural ethos.

In all the six films, imbalance in the equation of gender relations in the literary texts and films adapted from it still reflect the imprints, "of a monolithic unchanging patriarchy, which would seem to have no connections with other hegemonies say of class or race and an equally fixed and resilient female self." (Tharu and Lalita 29.). It has the cultural context as a mindset, which traps and proves to be a hindrance to transcend and completely transform from the constrictions of such an ideology, which is basically patriarchal as an inheritance. Such a familiar ideology also constitutes male subjectivities, as it is along with female subjectivities.

The film hoardings that are used to advertise films, which are composed as a collage of scenes from the film, are actually a process of choosing a set of stills from the film, which serve as metonyms to the storyline. However, the juxtaposition of reselection is done to find an intuitive match between an audience expectation and the cinematic offering. The hoardings provide a visible space that has a masculine structure and the female whether a heroine or a vamp, is constructed through a desire for her screen body, which promises delights that may only be imagined. This is in keeping with Laura Mulvey's terse description of women in Hollywood cinema and the same is, applicable to the Indian cinema.

"Women displayed as sexual object is the leitmotif of the erotic spectacle: from pin ups to striptease where she holds the look, place to signify male desire," according to Mulvey (quoted in Tharu Looking at 75). Susie Tharu believes that, "this is particularly apt for the woman imaged on the hoarding too." (Tharu Looking at 75).

In all the six films 'Teesri Kasam', 'Umrao Jaan', 'Rudali', 'Ghaire Bhaire', 'Gaban' and 'Train to Pakistan', one sees the past haunting the present. The interrogation of the present by the past, or perhaps the under scoring of the present by an eruption of the past in its midst, is part of continuing concerns. The recognition of the stream of history flowing from the past through the present into the future permeates into these films. The patriarchal ideology shows its imprints and the view of the past, personal and collective perpetuation of patriarchal ideology continues and one gets a glimpse of the social past in the present in which broader social past takes shape in the life of all female protagonists. It is represented by the family and the social whole, and by the repercussions of the incidents, which occur in their lives. All of these helped them to gain a deeper understanding of their personal and social selves. All these individuals represent in themselves certain predicaments, social situations of the family and society at large that they are part of the social positions in gender relations and are the mirror images of each other. The precarious balance in gender relations gets reflected in them.

We have no doubt come a long way from the Indian family, which was based on an extended or joint family system, which originated in Vedic lives. It was not only patriarchal, where the oldest male member was the absolute head, but members were also related by an interlocking pattern of mutual dependence where individuality was subordinate to collective solidarity. The joint family is a microcosm of the professionally pluralistic nature of Indian culture in all its manifestations. The emotionally constrained interpersonal relationships, which are still found today in the typical rural joint family, have had decisive consequences for every aspect of life in India. Women were rigidly confined in the courtyard or the four walls. Life revolved around the common hearth and the children, with a status subservient to that of men.

No doubt, India is yet new to the ideology of personal freedom, even after 59 years of independence from the British yolk. Both Indian men and women have functioned according to rigid hierarchies and have learned to curb their freedom, condition themselves to suppress their needs, silence their senses and sublimate their desires. They thrive on a philosophy of self-denial, self-effacement and subservience. The temptation to follow the path blazed by the western feminism may be irresistible but, "one hopes for a revival of sensitivity to the uniqueness of the Indian situation and the capacity to respond to this uniqueness by forging new ways of self affirmation" (Chitnis 95). Meaningful Indian cinema, reflecting practical issues and the Indian ethos and conviction, would pave the path for the same. Films open various vistas on to a wider cultural context and by watching them and exploring them, one can attain a deeper understanding of the Indian culture better.

Culture has great power and its pursuit concerns and encompasses almost all the aspects of society which it encompasses through literature, social habits and customs, journals, magazines, films, radio and television. Culture heightens the skills of an individual and society in totality, in all walks of life. It is through the viewing of culture that one gets an insight to the customs and habits and a whole way of life. India is a country of motifs and symbols. Indian legends may seem to be ancient, yet the myths embedded in it are so great that they are capable of countless interpretations. In India, mythology often influences our social life and the renewal in material consciousness in keeping with the times, can find inspiration in mythological tales. The mythological tales can be made to acquire a new meaning and a newer perspective under the searching light of an appropriate treatment of the same. The epics and legends are otherwise deeply embedded in the minds of even the sophisticated audience. Being a part of our cultural heritage, the myths get embedded in them. They have become so deep rooted in the collective Indian consciousness that even today, they have not been able to elude the Indian collective psyche and tradition as such lives on. We cannot grasp the infinitude of such beliefs. However, we can question and adapt without fear, because such concepts are culturally rooted in the Indian soil.

In the initial phase, Indian cinema was dominated by the mythological film, which used Hindu myths as their major resource. They went on to become the major resource and also the cultural context not only in Hindi cinema, which was considered Indian cinema, but also in regional cinema like Marathi, Telegu, Tamil, Bengali etc. However, soon the other genres developed such as the social, historical, devotional, stunt and action oriented films. It was as a need to maintain, as there were indigenous identities against the fascination for western cultural behaviours. Even though, it was felt that social films would displace the mythological and irrational culture for a modern social grounding of film narratives, the storylines were still along the themes of moral affirmation. Melodramatic mode of representation became popular in the process.

> "In fact, the recent analyses of the popular cinemas in the non-western world have indicated that the melodramatic mode has, with various indigenous modifications been a characteristic form of narrative and dramaturgy in societies undergoing the transition to modernity." (Vasudevan The Politics 134).

There are filmmakers who still draw attention to caste and gender inequalities-those basic unavoidable realities of Indian life that are brushed off or perhaps airbrushed out of the rosy images conjured up by most of our filmmakers for the benefit of a global market. There is a great need to focus on filmmakers who raised their voices from the margins and articulated concerns of gender, caste and class of the marginalized sections and about the national identity.

Good literature of a nation carries a saga and tales in which lie deep human concerns of life including those in the periphery. In each of the film selected, lie deeply humanist narratives, which the study of gender encompasses, as they are problems of humanity, at large, both for males and females. In the aesthetics of cinematic rendition, while adapting the novel or short story, each filmmaker has gone beyond his/her specific settings evolving credibility of narrative. The *oeuvres* of the filmmakers also reflect their narrative experiments and social messages conveyed by the writers in their literary works. With their sensibility and ideology they have portrayed to manage and reach out to their viewers. All the filmmakers reflect their own sensibilities and purpose to tell stories, reflecting society, gender relations while adapting the literary texts for cinematic representation.

Whereas most of the films selected in this dissertation just do not degenerate into sheer entertainment, however, they are all aesthetically, pleasing and profound. Quite a few of them belong to the genre of the new cinema, alternate cinema or parallel cinema. According to the critic, Chidananda Das Gupta, "the new cinema in India is a creation of the intellectual elite that is keenly aware of the human condition in India."(Das Gupta The New 23).

Whereas, popular cinema has been degraded by many a critic like Ashish Nandy in his article 'The Slum's Eye View of National Politics' (Nandy 1-17) which reinforces the oppositional discourse of high art and mass culture. Wilson Minzer, a western critic said about Hollywood cinema, "that it was a trip through a sewer in a glass-bottomed boat." (3). Film after film, filmmakers in their sheer attempt to hit at the box-office, have indulged in devices of escapist cinema with an eye on the commercial circuit. However, changing social values, marked with a shift in ideology away from the reformist zeal, have characterized Indian cinema of the 1930s and early 1940s with films like '*Achut Kanya*', '*Mukti*', '*Duniya Na Mane*' etc. Bombay Talkies, Prabhat and New Theatres and filmmakers like V. Shantaram, Mehboob Khan, Bimal Roy and Guru Dutt have explored the ideology of gender relations, highlighting womanhood and created strong individual female characters in their films. Some filmmakers of parallel cinema or new cinema brought a freshness and excitement of perspective to the immediate post colonial context of the 1950s as they were different in their approaches, techniques, aims and intentions. Satyajit Ray perhaps can be called a pioneer of this school. There were many later in the 50s and 60s like Mrinal Sen, Ritwik Ghatak and Mani Kaul with their differing ideologies, views and structures. Basu Bhattacharya, Basu Chatterjee, Hrishikesh Mukherjee, and many others followed suit, each with his/her own cinematic device. Shyam Benegal, Govind Nihalani, Muzaffar Ali, Kalpan Lajmi, Pamela Rooks etc are a few of them to name.

Desire for a woman's freedom and her struggle in patriarchal households with traditional norms, may perhaps never be completely realized in real life nor in reel life on celluloid. The same gets represented on celluloid, sometimes highlighted or even exaggerated but always as an issue, which needs to be looked and re-looked again and again. Today, Indian cinema, especially Hindi cinema coined as Bollywood may be considered to have arrived. It has become a brand name and a consumerist oriented, marketable product. It has become the stuff of cultural studies courses at Stanford and London. Though, many recognize that it is a process, which has been a strange journey–an odyssey from contempt to adulation. Yet, people still have recognized it as a framework of analysis, a critical view of society that challenges and matches critical social theory in India. According to Shiv Visvanathan,

"it is time we recognize Aparna Sen, Govind Nihalani, Shyam Benegal, Yash Johar as social theorists who are at par with our social scientists like Ashish Nandy, T.N. Madan or Rajni Kothari in their understanding of the critical changes and tensions that India is undergoing". (Visvanathan 6)

A study of the kind, which entails an attempt in understanding of Indian cinema, with reference to cultural ideology vis-à-vis gender relations can lead to understanding culture in a broader perspective. At the same time, it retrieves the feminine from its stereotypical archetypal association with inferiority. Indian cinema has been more forward looking at a time social science was trying to be progressive. Even when Indian cinema was considered crude and illiterate, it had in fact a greater cultural confidence and could capture the area of feminism. Ironically, social sciences in being objective, missed crucial social cultural facts, whereas Indian films in enacting fantasies, captured fragments of reality.

Even though, Indian cinema has been churning out stereotype images of gender relations and even showing mother-in-law or a sister-in-law as a bully, who were all inadvertently perpetrating patriarchy in a way, yet Indian cinema always struggled to describe evil. Tradition and change feature constantly hand in hand in films. The encounters of the kind, both with film and literature as comparative genres might trigger something new. Social movements during the Renaissance, the Independence movement, the understanding of partition and post independent movements have given both literature and films adapted from such texts, a new vitality, at all times. Cinematic devices used internationally by the masters of world cinema as by the likes of Eisenstein, Antononioni or Luc de Godard have also been employed by them in realistic and art cinema. Whether it is a commercial film or not, good cinema exists and falls in-between realistic films with commercial background or commercial films done realistically. Traditional societies do not take kindly to change, since, for nearly 3000 years, traditionalism has had a firm hold on the Indian mind, which continues today.

Indian cinema has been accused of simply having not mastered the 'classic' story telling idiom, even if in some way it fashions it on the Hollywood mode of story telling. The mainstream Indian cinema has been often remarked to depend upon ingredients of the '*masala*' such as a number of songs and dances, fight sequences, comic routines with the plot providing the barest outline for all that goes on in the film. According to Kaviraj,

> "the telling of a story brings into immediate play some strong conventions invoking a narrative community. Ordinarily these are coincident in terms of their frontiers with social commitments of some form. To some extent all such communities form the stable to the emergent, use narrative as a technique of staying together, redrawing their boundaries or reinforcing them". (23).

In fact, there is a need to look into the representation of the equality and disparity of gender equations that Indian cinema refracts undoubtedly. India has a long tradition of five thousand years of history, tradition and cultural context, which has a strong bearing on Indian cinema. Mainstream symbols and aesthetics may be used in cinematic representation to both reveal and mock dominant culture in the name of traditions. Gender should not be the significant aspect to differentiate the sexes and hegemonies. Our ability to think about sexual difference is limited by a cultural system that originates against sexual difference in a hierarchy. Gender should not be perceived and conceptualised with a tinted cultural lens. Awareness of biases in gender relations and their presentation in the Indian cinema, can lead to a critical examination and better understanding and a more satisfying level of holistic approach of society with the focus on gender relations impinging on women's lives.

In defining culture, the gender roles, activities and behaviours are prescribed through epics, ancient stories, myths and legends. Women protagonists are definitely locked in the trappings of cultural ideology, which they find difficult to shackle off as they are considered appropriate for women and are generated out as a cultural norm for their lives. Patriarchy operates through gendered structures and positions men and women accordingly in a kind of hierarchy of superior and inferior position. A woman still gives meaning to her life and defines her existence in relation to another. When it comes to the tears and turmoil, the agony and heartache caused by traditional expectations and straitjacketing, there is a silence of complicity. In fact, women are culturally accustomed to speaking and employing suitable rhetoric. Gender relations are a way to focus on the existence of a female culture within the general culture shared by men and women. The exercise to understand cinematic representation adapted from purposeful good literature retains all its drive. All the texts and films unfold stories not as masterly strokes of the writer's pen, but in the films adapted, as a painful representation of women's sufferings at the hands of patriarchs. The cinematic devices employed in films complement the subtlety of presentations, linked by a common thread of pain and servitude, which women in all the films have to undergo. There are no solutions and suggestions put across, yet they all attempt to sensitively portray many an anguished women in the lives of protagonists both males and females on account of a set cultural ideology they all have to adhere to, which is subtly understood by them all.

This book is an attempt in reflective film criticism with an attempt to study serious social studies through a study of gender relations in a select study of Indian films adapted from literary texts. The societal set up with reference to cultural ideology is an important component of the Indian life in the private and public sphere. Films are components of the important aspect of our popular culture. All communities, irrespective of their caste, creed, and gender find meaning in the narratives,

"Indian films not only set the literary agenda in many forms. Film narratives also establish social and intellectual priorities. Indian cinema has been just that Indian in a true multicultural sense." (Sardar Zia Uddin 21).

The dialogue between the film theory and the social analysis of cultural ideology is in conformity with the concerns of this book in looking at gender relations in films adapted from literary texts, which reflect as well as shape public life in Indian society. Whereas, popular culture is not just a reservoir of mass culture, but, rather,

> "an arena of the interaction and contestation among indigenous traditions of folk culture, the popular culture of middle classes and the massified sensitivities of South Asians more comfortable with mass culture, as it has emerged from the society 150 years long confrontation and dialogue with the West." (Nandy The Secret ix).

Gender issues arose within such a frame as a dimension or problem of the movement between progression and regression. "The idea of theory of gender as an intellectual undertaking in its own right was alien to this whole way of thought." (Connell 119). Along with the convection of gender with the science of progress, there was a thought laid to decoding or deconstruction of gender accomplished by the new depth of psychology. "However, it is impossible to escape from the spirit of female power." (Walter 216). Notion of independence can be ingrained in both the sexes as to an aspect to be looked upon as a heterosexual norm. Gender inequality as a part of modern India in the twenty-first century is being looked at from different dimensions with, "the metrosexual man, the baby cuddling as the corporate honcho. It is the form of male adaptation to the inevitable evolution in women's roles." (Rajan 12). The new Indian woman is evolving 'contrarian' as the contrasexual woman, even though the tide of change is in urban India, "the metrosexual male gets into a feminine mode and the female has her aggressive, macho moment and bends the rules." (Walia 4).

Cinema is, in a way, a mirror of the Indian society and its value systems. Cinema as a unique medium has amalgamated all the arts and fused them to offer a wide-ranging experience of audio-visual dreams. One of the most significant phenomena of our times has been the development of cinema from a turn-of the century mechanical toy into the twentieth century's and now twenty-first century's most potent and versatile art form. Cinema is a powerful medium of expression. Today cinema commands the respect accorded to any other form of creative expression. According to Satyajit Ray, "in the immense complexity of its creative process, it combines in various measures the functions of poetry, music, painting, drama, architecture and a host of other arts, major and minor." (Ray, Satyajit 19).

Most films reflect the existing societal attitudes of prejudice. Literature, too, does the same and also gives an open space to imagination. Film is an open-ended media and filmmakers in cinema give it a setting right in front. All the films discussed are multi-layered and probe deep into bigoted perceptions about women generated by the traditional standards of mythological religion, folklore, history, conventions, rituals, and aesthetics of *rasa* theory.

"What ever the future of the films, Indian films appear to be perhaps the most powerful cultural product based on non-Western aesthetic principles presently alive, and it is very much alive at that." (Pfleiderer and Lutze 14).

NOTES AND REFERENCES

1. The order of signification occurs when the surface literal meaning operating as connotative agent meets the values and discourses of the culture. The order of signification reflects subjective responses, which can only be motivated by the fact that they are shared by the community of a particular culture, "a sharing that refers to intersubjectivity. This intersubjectivity is culturally determined." (Friske and Hartley 46). Thus on the one hand our individual response is affected or influenced by the culture in which we find ourselves and, on the other, that response signifies our appertaining to that culture.

2. Myth is the way in which we are enabled to understand the culture in which we find ourselves, as myths provide cultural meanings. The traces of the cultural connections between, "signification and legitimation: the way that beliefs, practices and institutions legitimate the dominant social order or status quo-the existing relations of domination and subordination are found in the representation of sectional interests as universal ones." (Bhatia 53).

3. "The first blow against the monolithic accumulation of traditional film conventions (already undertaken by radical film-makers) is to free the look of the camera into its materiality in time and space and the look of the audience into dialectics and passionate detachment". (Laura Mulvey 69). She however, feels that there is no doubt that this destroys the satisfaction, pleasure and privilege which highlights the way the film generally has depended on voyeuristic active/passive mechanisms. Women, whose image has continually been stolen and used for this end, cannot view the decline of traditional form with anything much more than sentimental regret.

Interviews

RENDEZVOUS WITH SWATILEKHA CHATTERJEE

Rendezvous with Swatilekha Chatterjee, the Bimla of 'Ghaire Bhaire' on 17.10.2005 at Himachal Bhawan in Chandigarh was like a dream come-true. It was like meeting a creation of Satyajit Ray. It had been a great desire of mine to see him in person, to have a rendezvous with him to discuss Nikhil, Bimla and Sandip's relationship and the complexity of gender relations in 'Ghaire Bhaire'. That I was sadly aware could never take place in reality.

Meeting Swatilekha was like quenching queries to so many questions gnawing at my mind which I might have put to Ray while trying to understand Bimla's position. I set off asking Swatilekha how did Ray look

An Interview being conducted by the author Indubala Singh with Swatilekha Chatterjee.

at Bimla and why and how was she selected for the role. What made Nikhil so obsessed with the idea that his wife should step out of the inner *Ghaire*, which almost drove his innocent wife Bimla into the trap of the evil, treacherous, flirtatious friend Sandip whom he had known as a lady killer in his hey days. Was his male ego being pampered in the process to put the gullible Bimla on this hazardous acid test to prove her *kasauti* Sita style. No doubt Nikhil himself had been the Rama kind of a *purush*, but there was no Swaroopnakha to instigate him even though one can put *Bari Rani* in that scale, yet there was no such provocation on her part too.

Swatilekha who was 63 years old when I met her in Oct. 2005, was incidentally, a more beautiful woman than she was as the young Bimla, on the screen. She had perhaps got etched markedly in looks with age. She looked more pure and ethereal sans make up but for a bindi and dash of kajal in her creamish white sari. She looked more vulnerable and really the pristine pure one in contrast to what Bimla was on screen. No doubt she had acquired the depth and wisdom and pragmatism of having experienced life and blossomed into a wise thoughtful woman, though not outgoing still. Yet she seemed to have a mind of her own and was very much aware and absolutely conscious of what she genuinely wanted to do in her professional and personal life too.

She said that she was selected for the role of Bimla when she was spotted on the stage doing a small inconsequential role in a Greek play adapted in Bengali, which Ray had gone to watch in a theatre in Calcutta. After that he sent a word to one of his close assistants that he had found his Bimla in Swatilekha. He was told to meet her and talk to her about the role of Bimla. On hearing that, so awed was Swatilekha with the idea to be in Ray's film that she just could not deny it even though she had not read the script. It had been a dream of her to act in his film though she had not acted in films before, nor was she ever interested in acting in films. After her selection Ray did not talk much to her about her role too, but gave her, her lines for dialogue delivery. He had in fact been impressed highly by the way she had delivered her dialogues on the stage in a Greek get-up though she had few lines in the play. Her dusky complexion and her intelligent intentlook was one of the reasons he found her befitting for the role. He gauged that she was an intuitive actress, yet a very intelligent one who did not need many takes. She had just to be told the scene and she could face the camera with great ease. She had been initially instructed by Satyajit Ray how to face the camera and precautions to be taken while facing it, as to how to be in the frame at the proper angle. Swatilekha grasped it all immediately hence she and Ray never had long discussions even though it was one of those difficult roles. As regards the famous kissing scene between her and Victor Banerjee she said she took it in her stride as any other shot, but it was Victor's wife who was very much conscious about it and was present on the sets that day who perhaps felt uneasy about it. In fact Rudra Sengupta, Swatilekha's husband, who happens to be actor and director of the famous Nandikar group, was not present on the sets and took it as a matter of fact as a scene to be shot as part of the film. Rather he used to keep good, nourishing food cooked by himself ready for Swati every evening when she got back home after the shoot and while eating both discussed as to what happened on the sets and what work did she do during the day.

On my asking her was she not smitten by Ray during the shooting she said she was so awed and so very much taken up by his bearing, his looks, his style, his attitude, his directoral skills that she obediently acted out what was required of her to do, without giving much of thought. Though at times she was apprehensive about Bimla's complex relationship both with Sandip and Nikhil and as to why was Bimla treated as a pawn by both of them. However since she was so much of a docile thing then, hence she felt she could not muster up enough courage to bring herself up to question him so bluntly. Surprisingly Victor was made to use glycerine in a scene when he was supposed to shed tears, but Swatilekha was not as she could flow with the scene, a fact about which Ray was confident. In fact she even sang the Bengali and English song in her own voice in the film 'Ghaire Bhaire'. Though Swatilekha, a postgraduate in English spent her childhood in Allahabad, she was trained in Rabindra Sangeet in childhood by her mother who like any true Bengali was obsessed with it which proved to be a boon and asset for the film. On being questioned did she not fall in love with Satyajit Ray eventually, she said nobody could help falling in love with the man and so even did Rudra too. He was impressed by Ray's working and thoughtful unobtrusive style.

However, Swatilekha never had any personal contact with Satyajit Ray after the film was completed and even did not go to meet him or approach him for a role in any of his films later. Though Ray would tell Rudra on phone at times and on their occasional meetings as to why Swatilekha would never come and meet him. Swatilekha confessed that she did not feel the need to do so as she was really happy and satisfied having done the role of Bimla in 'Ghaire Bhaire' to the best of her truest ability.

A TELEPHONIC TALK WITH HRISHIKESH MUKHERJEE REGARDING THE MAKING OF 'GABAN'

Hrishikesh Mukherjee, recipient of the prestigious Dada Saheb Phalke award, had not been keeping good health for quite some time when I spoke to him. Yet he was kind enough to talk to me on the telephone when I told him that I was working for my dissertation on adaptation of 'Gaban' for celluloid. Inspite of his ill health he showed great enthusiasm and felt very pleased about the fact that somebody would think of 'Gaban' for a study which had been made in 60s, in 2004. Though he was rather apprehensive initially about the fact that one would be interested in a film like 'Gaban' which ran into trouble during its making as the original director Krishan Chopra had passed away, after which Hrishikesh Mukherjee took reins. He however felt that it was the true novelisation of Premchand's 'Gaban' which was so culturally rooted and had essence of the spirit of non-cooperation movement of 1930s. The film, he felt, uncovered the face of the vast Indian middle class with its virtues and foibles like his other films 'Anari', 'Abhiman', 'Anuradha', etc. which made them universally appealing on the celluloid. As a film maker he had his own subtle style at portraying things as they were, which played a significant role in evoking modern times and crafted heartfelt narratives, driven as much by the need to entertain, yet entertain by an unwavering commitment to artistic integrity. He identified more with reality and added his own unique middle-of-the-road touch to his *oeuvres*. He said he had tried to do his best, while doing the patchwork direction for the film as he was not there at the incept of the making of the film, but the film 'Gaban' still carried his sensibility and signatures. He was one of those rare masters who summed it up all effortlessly with his rare simplicity, though he was aware that it is not easy to discard flourishes and yet be elegant.

He felt greatly contented on the completion of the film, as he felt it was a classic story which deserved to be adapted for celluloid.

AN INTERVIEW AT THE NAWAB JAFAR MIR ABDULLAH'S RESIDENCE IN LUCKNOW

A trip to Lucknow in September 2004 was necessary to understand the making of 'Umrao Jaan' and also to get a feel of the making of the film 'Umrao Jaan' in the local milieu outside the studios. Visiting the Chowk in old Lucknow, eating kababs at the Tunda Kabab Dhaba and talking to an old pavement hawker in the vicinity of the area was like going back in time. In soft hushed tones the old Lucknawi kurta seller shared those times of Lucknawi ada of dancing girls who would not even give a dekho to his types. They just hung around at the bottom of footsteps of their kothas true to their status, to hear melodious singing of courtesans. A contrast to it was the information shared by Nawab Jafar Mir Abdullah last of the descendants of Nawab Asaf ud Daula on my meeting with him on 23rd September, 2004 in Lucknow at his residence. Not only he and his '*marhoom abba*', i.e. late father and other have-beens of nawab lineage were a part of the scenario during the making of 'Umrao Jaan' but they even led credence to the mise en scene in the filmmaking of 'Umrao Jaan'. The artifacts and pieces de la resistance used were from their households. So forthcoming were they in their helpful attitude towards Muzaffar Ali, the director of the film besides the other Lucknawis during the making of film 'Umrao Jaan' that it seemed according to Nawab Sahib that the whole of Lucknow thought that it was their film. The song "*in aankhon ki masti ke*" was picturised in Lucknow in its palatial *Baradari* (a room with 12 doors) with

The author Indubala Singh and her husband Dicky S.P. Singh at the residence of
Nawab Jafar Mir Abdullah at Lucknow.

great authenticity. His own father and uncles including he himself, had lent
an aura of genuineness by being the *shorha* (gathering) of the Mehfil. The
song in the Baradari thus had the cream de la crème of Lucknavi nawabi
then, still living as part of the *shorha* (gathering) in the mehfil to lend a
flavour of genuine authentic ambience. Nawab Sahib related an interesting

episode of an old nawab in his 80s then with Rekha who was enacting the role of Umrao Jaan. She had unwittingly asked him after the shooting of the dance of the song *'in aankhon ki masti'* as to how did he find the dance sequence. He very coolly commented, "you are okay but your Nani Amma used to dance better", which left Rekha stunned and tight lipped. So taken up were the old Nawabs with the authenticity of sets and ambience of the making of 'Umrao Jaan' by Muzaffar Ali that they were transformed to an era when they were a part of such mehfils. They almost thought that they were living up those cherished glorious times of singing and dancing of courtesan era which were banned officially in the 50's by the Indian Government.

A DISCUSSION WITH NASEER-UD-DIN SHAH ABOUT HIS ROLE IN 'UMRAO JAAN'

The author Indubala Singh and her husband Dicky S.P. Singh with Naseer-ud-din Shah and Ratna Pathak Shah at Chandigarh.

I was lucky to have a meeting with Naseer-ud-din Shah on his visit to Chandigarh when he staged 'Ismat Aappa Ke Naam' in Tagore Theatre in 2003. He was kind enough to take some time away inspite of a hectic schedule for which I was highly obliged. In fact I was frank enough to tell him that Farookh Shaikh stood out of all the three male characters in the film 'Umrao Jaan', though it may have been on account of a romantic lead and the length of his role. Naseer-ud-din accepted it graciously and conceded the fact. In fact he was frank enough to say he was a little casual in his attitude during its making and that he perhaps could not realize the importance of his role then and if he were to do it all over again he would have a completely different approach. For that, first of all he would try to learn to dance kathak and perform some of its steps in the film as an add on to his role, since he understood the nuances requisite for the role much later for which he had certain regrets. However he felt that 'Umrao Jaan' was a good film and Rekha lived up her role to the hilt and performed as Umrao Jaan with great aplomb.

INTERVIEW WITH S. KHUSHWANT SINGH

On 26.03.2003 I called up S. Khushwant Singh, the writer and told him that I was working for my research on the adaptation of his novel 'Train to Pakistan' by Pamela Rooks for the celluloid. I sought an appointment to meet him and discuss certain aspects of the novel. Luckily for me he was most forthcoming and asked me to make it to his Sujan Singh Park residence at sharp 7.00 p.m. that very day. With trepidation and anxiety I reached the place at 6.45 p.m., but I was undoubtedly impressed and amazed too by the genuineness of his behaviour. He came across as a very sincere, honest, forthcoming human being, who perhaps I feel having led a fulfilling life was wanting to lead a more meaningful existence by wanting to share with others finer aspects of life. Long flowing curtains with Urdu or was it

The author Dr. Indubala Singh with S. Khushwant Singh.

Persian printed on them attracted me immediately. He grinned and said the curtains were a gift to him from friends from Pakistan. He felt that it was important for us to keep the common cultural heritage alive inspite of partition. He had been a witness to partition yet he did not let the bitterness of partition affect him. He did not speak at all in a bitter way but rather spoke with logic and passion. This brought me to the discussion of the novel and its adaptation for the film. He said that he was thoroughly satisfied with the making of the film.

Khushwant Singh said in his interview, "I always wrote the way I saw things. There were no morals neither is there any sermonizing nor any such social message. Characters in my novel are characters that were taken up and build on people I came across personally though much to their annoyance. Hence most of them were true characters in real life and some built up imaginatively". The characterization of Hukum Chand, the local magistrate in the novel has been fashioned by Khushwant Singh on one local magistrate he knew in his Lahore days, who had a roving eye for beautiful women.

In fact Khushwant Singh told me that he had received a proposal by Zafar Hai for adaptation of novel 'Train to Pakistan' somewhere in the 70s. Shashi Kapoor was to play the main lead role of Jagga and Shabana Azmi whom Khushwant Singh regards as the best actress on the Hindi screen, was to play the heroine i.e. Nooran and Zohra Sehgal was to play Shashi Kapoor's i.e. Jagga's mother in the film. However after six months of discussions the project was dropped. Earlier a Japanese producer had offered to adapt it for the celluloid in Japanese. However due to language problem as Khushwant Singh could not speak Japanese and the producer could not speak English, the project fell apart as their interpreter could not be much of a bridge between the two. The novel was at long last made into a film by Pamela Rooks. She made the film on a shoestring budget but he felt she did a splendid job of it. Khushwant Singh considers the film on the novel 'Train to Pakistan' as one of the important landmarks in his life. The film was however ready for its August release and premiered for the nation's Independence Day celebration shown on TV on 15th August, 1997 i.e. after 50 years of Independence. It was also shown for a few months in cinemas all over the country.

INTERVIEW WITH DR. YOGESH PARVEEN

Dr. Yogesh Parveen, a historian from Lucknow, was a coordinator in the making of the film *'Umrao Jaan'*. The film maker of *'Umrao Jaan'* Mazzaffar Ali consulted him during the making of the film for the sake of authenticity and historical perspective and crosschecked whether Umrao Jaan was a fictitious character of Rusva's novel. For that he narrated an

incident when they both went to the *kabvrastan* (cemetery) where Umrao was buried. There was an epitaph on which is inscribed, *"Umrao jisse farishtey farsh se arsh ki aur lene aaye"* translated as "Umrao for whom the angels descended from heaven to liberate her and fetch her from this earthly existence to the celestial heaven". Dr. Yogesh Parveen had in fact been present during the film making of *'Umrao Jaan'* in Lucknow most of the time as a resource person for many a historical fact.

Dr. Yogesh Parveen—a historian and co-ordinator during the making of the film 'Umrao Jaan" in Lucknow.

Glossary of Some Cinematic Terms Used

AUTEUR : An *auteur* is a director who transcends the script by imposing on it his or her own style and vision. An *auteur* film involves subjective and personalized film making, rather than a mechanical transposition of a script on the film.

CAHIERS DU CINEMA : In the 1950s, a seminal journal (still in existence) was headed by André Bazin, a film critic and was written by regular group of film critics Luc de Goddard, Truffant, Jean Renoir and many others known as Cahiers group. Through the Cahiers' discussions on the politique des *auteurs*, a polemical debate surrounding the concept of *auteur* developed.

CHIAROSCURO LIGHTING : It is a high contrast lighting created by lighting, setting and use of shadows, reflecting the inner turmoil mood and alienation signalling the distorted effects in the workings of the unconscious state.

CINEMATOGRAPHER: This person is responsible for the general composition of the scene (the *mise-en scene*, the lighting of the set or location the colour balance). He is responsible for the choice of camera, lenses, film stocks, quality of image and concerned with actual printing of film.

CINEMA VERITÉ : A kind of documentary technique, which attempts to catch reality on film and inform a sociological investigation that occurred in the 1960s in France and United States. It is now used to refer to any kind of documentary technique that gives a sense of exactitude more readily.

CONTINUITY EDITING: It is all about coherence and orientation. The way shots are edited together, controlled and regulated by a series of techniques that permit the spectator to fit them together like the pieces of a puzzle.

CUT: The splicing of two shots together. This cut is made by the film editor at the editing stage of a film to switch from one image to another.

DEEEP FOCUS PHOTOGRAPHY : It keeps several planes of the shot in focus at the same time (foreground middle-ground, background), allowing several actions to be filmed at the same time.

DIEGESIS: It refers to the narration, the content of the narrative, the intuitional world as described inside the story. It refers to all that is really going on on-screen. Characters' words and gestures, all action as enacted within the screen, constitute the diegesis.

DIEGETIC SOUND : It is sound that naturally occurs within the screen space.

DIRECTOR : The person responsible for putting a scenario or script onto film and supervises over the process of shooting.

DISCOURSE : Cinematic discourse differs from the novel or a play for it tells the story through image and sound.

DISSOLVE : It refers to a transition between two sequences.

EDITING : It refers to literally how shots are put together to make up a film. It consists of breaking down a scene into a multitude of shots. It allows the director to fully involve the spectator in the action at the expense of breaking the film's spatial and temporal unity. It brings about a synthetic unity and restores the film by means of technique like eyeline match, point of view cutting the match on action and directional continuity.

FADE IN : It is a term used when the image appears and brightens to full strength when the screen is black.

FADE OUT : A term used when the image gradually fades to black.

FADE: A transition between sequences or scenes associated with earlier cinema until the late 1940s.

FLASH BACK : A narrative device used in films (as in literature) to go back in time or to an earlier moment in a character's life and/or history, and to narrate that moment.

FOCUS : It is the sharpness of image or matter viewed with seriousness.

FORM/CONTENT : In film studies, form and content are seen as inextricably linked. The form of a film emerges out of the content and the content is created by the formal contents of the film.

FRAMING : The way in which subjects and objects are framed within a shot produces specific meanings.

IMAGE : It is the smallest unit of meaning in a filmic text in the sense that it is composed of a single shot.

LIGHTING : It involves technology. Earlier natural lighting was used, then three point lighting system through artificial mercury lamps came up then colour films worked with carbon arc lighting. Day for night and night-for-night shooting are elements of lighting practice.

LONG TAKE : A long take refers to a shot that is significantly longer than the norm. Any shot significantly longer than 9 second (60 seconds or more) is a long take.

MELODRAMA : It makes moral conflict its main theme, particularly the one's experienced by women in a patriarchal society. The plot consists of unexpected twists and sharp reversals in the storyline.

METONYMY : A mode of communicating meaning is characterized as a substitution of the name of an attribute for that of thing e.g. crown for king.

MISE-EN-SCENE : One of the most frequently used terms in film analysis derived from a French term, which literally translates as 'putting on stage' or staging. It means what appears in front of the camera – set design, lighting and character movement.

MISE-EN-SHOT : It literally means "putting into shots" or simply shooting (a film).

MONTAGE : It creates associations (symbolic meanings)˙ when two shots are created by a chain of associations. It confers metaphorical meanings onto filmed events.

NARRATIVE : The concept of 'narrative' refers to what happens or what is depicted in films (as well as novels) and 'narration' refers to how that narrative is presented, to the film spectator. So narrative refers to actions, events and characters.

NON-DIEGETIC SOUND : It refers to sound that clearly is not produced within the on-screen space e.g. voice over or added music.

POINT-OF-VIEW : They are usually marked to indicate that they represent the characters optical vantage point.

SEQUENCE : A sequence is normally composed of scenes, all relating to the same logical unit of meaning.

SET DESIGN : Art directors are people who design or select sets and décor of a film to create a background which the action of the film is to unfold.

SETTING : It is unfold part of the total concept of mise-en-scene. It is literally the location, where action takes place and it can be artificially constructed as in studio sets or naturally what is termed location shooting.

SHOT : It is considered in terms of camera distance with respect to the object within the shot. There are basically seven types of shots : extreme close-up, close-up, medium close-up, medium shot, medium long shot, long shot, extreme long shot or distance shot. It is a single piece of film, however long or short, without cuts, exposed continuously representing spatial and temporal continuity.

STEREOTYPE : Applied figuratively, it means at its simplest, a fixed and repeated characterization.

STILL : A single photograph or similar publicity photograph from a film.

SYMBOL : A sign that represents something by resemblance, association or convention.

WIPE : A transition between two shots whereby the earlier one appears to be pushed aside by the latter, creating the effect of wiping off a scene and replacing it with another.

ZOOM : A zoom shot is one that is taken with the use of variable focal length lens (known as a zoom lens). A zoom forward normally ends in a close-up, a zoom back in a general shot.

List of Works Cited and Consulted

Adair, Gilbert, ed. *Movies*. Harmondsworth, Middlesex : Penguin Books, 1999.

Agarwal, Bina. *Structure of Patriarchy*. New Delhi : Kali for Women, 1988.

Allen, M., Gertrude. *How to Write a Film Story*. London : George Unwin Brothers Ltd., 1926.

Allen, Richard and Murray Smith, eds. *Film Theory and Philosophy*. New York : Oxford University Press, 2000.

Aloyius, G. *Nationalism Without a Nation in India*. New Delhi : Oxford University Press, 1997.

Althusser, Louis. *Essays in Ideology*. London : Verso, 1984.

———, "Ideology and Ideological State Apparatuses". *Reading Popular Narrative a Source Book*. Ed. Bob Ashley. London and Washington : Leicester University Press, 1989. 120-128.

Anand, Raj, Mulk. "Tagore, Reconciler of East and West". *Rabindranath Tagore (Political Thinkers of Modern India)*. Ed. Verinder Grover, New Delhi : Deep and Deep Publications, 1994. 160-190.

Andrew, Dudley. *The Major Film Theories*. New York : Oxford University Press, 1976.

———, *Concepts in Film Theory*. Oxford : Oxford University Press, 1984.

Ashcroft, Bill, *et al.*, eds. *The Empire Writes Back Theory and Practice in Post Colonial Literatures*. New York and London: Routledge, 1989.

Ashely, Bob. *Reading Popular Narrative A Source Book*. London : Leicester University Press, 1989.

Asnani, M. Shyam. "The Art and Artifice of Khushwant Singh". *Critical Response to Indian English Fiction*. New Delhi : Mittal Publications, 1985. 94-107.

Aziz, K.K. *The Partition of India and Emergence of Partition*. New Delhi : Kanti Publications, 1990.

Bahadur, Satish. "The Context of Indian Film Culture." *New Indian Cinema*. Delhi : Directorate of Film Festivals, 1982 : 7-14.

Bannerji, Himani. "Re-generation : Mothers and Daughters in Bengal's Literary Space." *Literature and Gender Essays for Jasodhra Bagchi*. Eds. Supriya Chaudhuri and Sajni Mukherji. New Delhi : Orient Longman Ltd., 2002. 185-215.

Barnouw, Erik. *Documentary : A History of the Non-Fiction Film.* New York: Oxford University Press, 1974.

Barnouw, Erik and S. Krishnamurthy. *Indian Film.* New York : Oxford University Press, 1980.

Basham, A.L. "Religion : Cults Doctrines and Metaphysic : The Mother Goodess." *The Wonder that was India.* London : Chieseter Sidwick and Jackson Limited, 1967. 234-347.

Basu, Anandnath. "Female Instruction." Second Report on the State of Education in Bengal, 1836. Calcutta : 1941.

Bathla, Sonia. *Women Democracy and the Media.* Delhi : Hampton Press. London, 1998.

Bazin, Andre. *What is Cinema?* 2 Vols. Trans. and Ed. Hugh Gray. Berkeley : University of California Press, 1967.

Beauvoir, de Simone. *The Second Sex.* Trans. H.M. Parshley. Middlesex : Penguin, 1972.

————, *After the Second Sex Conversation with Simone De Beauvoir.* Ed. Alice Schwarzer. Trans. Marianne Howarth. New York : Pantheon, 1984.

Berger, John. *Ways of Seing.* Harmondsworth, London: Penguin Books, 1972.

Bharucha, Rustom. *The Politics of Cultural Practice, Thinking Through Theatre.* New Delhi : Oxford University Press, 2001.

Bhatia, Nandi. *Acts of Authority/Acts of Resistance Theater and Politics in Colonial and Post Colonial India.* New Delhi : Oxford University Press, 2004.

Bhatt, Mahesh. Interview on *Star News* at 8.50 a.m., 10.1.2002.

Bhatty, Nikhat. "Controversy of Censers and Sensibility". *The Sunday Times* 14-20 September, 1997 : 44-45.

Bhatty, Zarina. "Status of Muslim Women and Social Change." *Indian Women from Purdah to Modernity.* Ed. B.R. Nanda. New Delhi : Vikas, 1976.

Bignell, Jonathan. *Writing and Cinema.* Harlow : Pearson Education Limited, 1999.

Biswas, Moinak. "The Absolutist Gaze". *Ideology of the Hindi Film, A Historical Construction.* Ed. M. Madhava Prasad. Delhi : Oxford University Press, 1998. 52-87.

Bluestone, George. *Novels into Films.* Berkeley: University of California Press, 1957.

Bordwell, David and Thompson Kristin, eds. *Film Art : An Introduction.* USA : Addison-Wesley Publishing Company, 1979.

————, *Narration in the Fiction Film.* London : Methuen, 1985.

Boyum, Gould, Loy. "Film as Literature." *Double Exposure.* Calcutta : Seagull Books, 1989. 1-26.

Branton, Gill. *Cinema and Cultural Modernity.* Philadelphia : Open University Press, 2000.

Braudy, Leo and Marshall Cohen, eds. *Film Theory and Criticism.* New York : Oxford University Press, 1999.

Brooks, Ann. *Post Feminism : Feminism, Cultural Theory and Cultural Forms.* London : Routledge, 1997.

Brooks, Peter. *The Melodramatic Imagination*. New Haven, USA : Yale University Press, 1976.

Buckland, Warren. *Film Studies*. London : Hodder Headline Pic., 2003.

Burch, Noel. *Life to those Shadows*. London : British Film Institute, 1990.

Butalia, Urvashi. *The Other Side of Partition : Voices from Partition of India*. New Delhi : Penguin Books, 1998.

Butler, Judith. *Gender Trouble : Feminism and Subversion of Identity*. New York : Routledge, 1990.

———, *Bodies that Matter On the Discourse of 'Sex'*. New York : Routledge, 1993.

Chakrabarty, Dipesh. "The difference-deferral of a colonial modernity : public debates on domesticity in British Bengal." *History Workshop Journal* 36 (Autumn 1993) : 1-33.

Chakravarty, S. Sumita. *National Identity in Indian Popular Cinema 1947-87*. New Delhi : Oxford University Press, 1996.

Chandra, Moti. *The World of Courtesan*. New Delhi : Vikas Publishing House, 1973.

Chatterjee, Partha. *Omnibus Nationalist Thought and the Colonial World The Nation and Its Fragments A Possible India*. New Delhi : Oxford University Press, 1999.

Chatterji, Shoma. A. "The Distorted Mythological Symbol." *Subject Cinema, Object : Woman A Study of the Portrayal of Women in India*. Calcutta: Parmita Publication, 1998. 28-57.

———, "Sound Design." *Encyclopedia of Hindi Cinema*. Eds. Gulzar, Govind Nihalani and Saibal Chatterjee. New Delhi : Encyclopedia Britannica and Mumbai : Popular Parkashan Pvt. Ltd. India, 2003. 169-184.

Chaudhary, Nandita. *Listening to Culture Constructing Reality from Everyday Talk*. New Delhi : Sage Publications, 2004.

Chaudhuri, Amit. *The Picador Book of Modern Indian Literature*. London : Macmillan Publishers Ltd., 2001.

Chaudhuri, Supriya and Sajni Mukherji, eds. *Literature and Gender Essays for Jasodhara Bagchi*. New Delhi : Orient Longman, 2002.

Chitnis, Suma. "Feminism: Indian Ethos and Indian Convictions". *Women in Indian Society A Reader*. Ed. Rehana Ghadially. New Delhi : Sage Publications, 1988. 81-95.

Chopra, Yash. "Is the Bollowood Formula Dead, Waiting To Be Buried." *The Sunday Times of India*, December 22, 2002 : 8.

Chowdhry, Prem. *Colonial India and Making of Empire Cinema Image, Ideology and Identity*. New Delhi : Vistaar Publications, 2000.

Christian, Metz. *Film Language : A Semiotics of the Cinema*. Trans. Michael Taylor. New York : Oxford Univ. Press, 1979.

Citron, Michelle, *et. al.* "Women and Film : A Discussion of Feminist Aesthetics". *Feminist Film Theory A Reader*. Ed. Sue Thornham. Edinburgh : Edinburgh University Press, 1999. 115-121.

Cixous, Hélène. "Sorties." *Modern Criticism and Theory A Reader*. Eds. David Lodge with Nigel Wood Delhi : Pearson Education, 2003. 263-270.

Coates, Jennifer. *Woman Talk Conversation between Women Friends*. Oxford, UK : Blackwell Publishers Ltd., 1996.

Cohen, J-J. Alain. "Three Madame Bovarys : Renoir, Minnelli, Chabrol." *Writing and Cinema*. Ed. Jonathan Bignell. New York : Pearson Education Limited, 1999. 119-133.

Conell, R.W. "Gender Relations." *Gender*. Cambridge, UK : Polity Press, 2002. 53-70.

Cook, Pam. *The Cinema Book*. London : British Film Institute Publishing, 1985.

Cooper, Darius. *The Cinema of Satyajit Ray Between Tradition and Modernity*. USA : Cambridge University Press, 2000.

Cowie, Elizabeth. *Representing the Woman:Cinema and Psychoanalysis*. London : Macmillan Pvt. Ltd., 1997.

Culler, Jonathan. *On Deconstruction:Theory and Criticism after Structuralism*. London : Routledge and Kegan Paul Ltd., 1982; rpt.1987.

Curthoys, Jean. *Feminist Amnesia The Wake of Women's Liberation*. New York : Routledge, 1997.

Dalziel, Duncan, Hugh. *Language and Literature in Society*, Chicago : Oxford University Press, 1953.

Dancyger, Ken and Jeff Rush. *Alternative Script Writing*. New York : Focal Press Butterworth Hienemann, 2000.

Das Gupta, Chidananda. *Talking about Films*. New Delhi : Orient Longman, 1981.

———, "The New Cinema : A Wave or a Future?". *Indian Cinema Superbazar*. Eds. Aruna Vasudev and Philippe Lenglet. New Delhi : Vikas, 1983.

———, "Satyajit Ray and the Bengali Cinema". *Indian Cinema*. Ed. Manjulika Dubey. Directorate of Film Festival, New Delhi, 1993.

Das Gupta, Susmita. "Commercial Cinema and Sociology." *Encyclopaedia of Hindi Cinema*. Eds. Gulzar, Govind Nihalani and Saibal Chatterjee. New Delhi: Encyclopaedia Britannica and Mumbai : Popular Prakashan, 2003. 367-390.

Das, Sisir, Kumar. "The Idea of Indian Literature." *The Idea of an Indian Literature: A Book of Readings*. Ed. Sujit Mukherjee. Mysore : Central Institute of Indian Languages, 1981. 1-40.

Das, Veena. "Draupadi and the Breach of the Private and Public." Paper Presented at the Indo French Seminar on "Women:Myths and Rights." New Delhi : Nehru Memorial Museum and Library, Nov. 16-17, 1989.

Datta, Kalikinkar. *Renaissance, Nationalism and Social Changes in Modern India*. Calcutta : Bookland Pvt. Ltd., 1973.

Datta, Sangeeta. *Shyam Benegal*. New Delhi : Lotus Collections, Roli Books, 2003.

Davis, Kingsley. *Human Society*. Berkley : University California, 1963. Rpt. New Delhi : Surjet Publications, 1981.

De Lauretis, Teresa. *Alice Doesn't : Feminism, Semiotics Cinema*. Bloomington : Indiana University Press, 1984.

———, "Displacing Hegemonic Discourses : Reflections on Feminist Theory in the 1980s". *Inscriptions* 314, 1988 : 127-145.

De Lauretis, Teresa. "Aesthetic and Feminist Theory : Rethinking Women's Cinema". *Feminisms*. Eds. Sandra Kemp and Judith Squires. New York : Oxford University Press, 1997. 27-36.

De, Sushil, Kumar. "Rabindranath Tagore." *Indian Awakening and Bengal*. Calcutta : Nana Nivandha, 1952.

De, S.K. *Bengal Literature in the Nineteenth Century*. New Delhi : Macmillan India Ltd., 1954.

Desai, Neera, ed. "A Decade of Women's Movement in India : Collection of Papers Presented at a Seminar Organized by Research Centre for Women's Studies." S.N.D.T. University Bombay:Himalaya Publishing House, 1988.

Deutscher, Penelope. *Yielding Gender Feminism, Deconstruction and the History of Philosophy*. New York : Routledge, 1997.

———, "Le Doeuff, Kofman and Irigaray as theorists of Constitutive Instability." *Yielding Gender Feminism, Deconstruction and the History of Philosophy*. New York : Routledge, 1997. 59-85.

Devi, Mahasweta and Usha Ganguli. *Rudali From Fiction to Performance*. Trans. Anjum Katyal. Calcutta : Seagull Books, 1988.

Devy, G.N. *After Amnesia Tradition and Change in History Criticism*. New Delhi : Orient Longman, 1992.

Dhani, S.L. "The Hindu Trinity". *Politics of God Churning of the Ocean. (A Samundra Manthan) A Scientific Analysis*. Panchkula : DD. Books Divya Drishti Prakashan, 1984. 37-55.

Dhareshwar, Vivek. "Our Time History, Sovereignty and Politics." *Economic and Political Weekly* 30 (6) 11 February 1995.

Dissanayake, Wimal and M. Sahai. *Sholay : A Cultural Reading*. New Delhi : Oxford University Press, 1992.

Dissanayake, Wimal. "Issues in World Cinema." *World Cinema*. Eds. John Hill and Pamela Church Gibson. New York: Oxford University Press, 2000.143-150.

Dixit, J.N. "Zero Credibility." *The Hindustan Times*, 10 April 2002 : 8.

Dmytrik, Edward. *On Filmmaking*. London : Focal Press, 1986.

Doane, Ann, Mary. "Film and Masquerade : Theorising The Female Spectator." *Feminist Film Theory a Reader*. Ed. Sue Thornham. Edinburgh: Edinburgh University Press, 1999. 131-45.

Donald and Johnson, Jean. "The Major Triad." *God and Gods in Hinduism Other Important Avtars*. New Delhi : Arnold Heineman, 1972. 40-52.

Doraiswamy, Rashmi. "Tamas and the Call to Remember." *Partition Films South Asian Cinema*. Ed. Lalit Mohan Joshi. London : South Asian Cinema Foundation, 2004 : 82-91.

Dutt, Helena. Interview in Calcutta Sept. 25, 1975 quoted in "Women In The Nationalist Movement." *Women in Modern India* Ed. Geraldine Forbes. U.K. : Cambridge University Press, 1996. 121-188.

Dwyer, Rachel and Divia Patel. *Cinema India The Visual Culture of Hindi Film*. London : Reaktion Books Ltd., 2002.

Eco, Umberto. "Casblanca: Cult movies and intertextual Collage." *Modern Criticism and Theory A Reader*. Eds. David Lodge with Nigel Wood. New Delhi : Pearson Education Ltd., 1988. 394-402.

Eisenstein, M. Sergei. "Word and Image." *The Film Sense*. Trans. By Jay Keyda. London : Faber and Faber, 1986. 1-30.

Evans, Jessica and Stuart Hall. *Visual Culture : The Reader*. London : Sage Publications, 1999.

Felski, Rita. "The Dialectics of 'Feminism' and 'Aesthetics'." *Feminisms*. Eds. Sandra Kemp and Judith Squires. New York : Oxford University Press, 1997. 423-29.

Flax, Jane. "Postmodernism and Gender Relations in Feminist Theory". *Feminisms*. Eds. Sandra Kemp and Judith Squires. New York : Oxford University Press, 1997. 170-178.

Forbes, Geraldine. "Reform in the Nineteenth Century." *Women in Modern India*. U.K. : Cambridge University Press, 1996. 1-31.

Foster, Audrey, Gwendolyn. "Mira Nair". *Fifty Contemporary Filmmakers*. Ed. Yvonne Tasker. New York : Routledge, 2002. 263-271.

Friedan, Betty. *The Feminine Mystique*. New York : Penguin, 1965.

Friske, J. and J. Hartley. *Reading Television*. New York : Methuen, 1978.

Frye, Northrop. "Myth, Fiction and Displacement." *Twentieth Century Criticism The Major Statements*. Eds. William J. Handy and Max Westbrook. New York : The Free Press A Division of Macmillan Publishing, 1974. 156-169.

————, "The Archetypes of Literature." *Twentieth Century Criticism The Major Statements*. Eds. William J. Handy and Max Westbrook. New York : The Free Press A Division of Macmillan Publishing, 1974. 233-243.

Gallagher, Margaret. *Women and Media Decision Making the Invisible Barriers*. New York : Sterling UNESCO Publishers, 1987.

Gandhi, M.K. *Women and Social Justice*. Ed. Jaisree Raijee. Ahmedabad : Navjivan Publishing House, 1954. (Rpt. 1976).

Gandhy Imhalsy, Rashna. *The Psychology of Love Wisdom of Indian Mythology*. New Delhi : Namita Gokhale Editions, Roli Books, 2001.

Garga, B.D. *So Many Cinemas. The Motion Pictures in India*. Mumbai: Eminence Designs Pvt. Ltd., 1996.

Gargi, Balwant. *Theatre in India*. New York : Theatre Arts Books, 1962.

George, T.J.S. *The Life and Times of Nargis*. New Delhi : Harper Collins Publishers, 1994.

Ghadially, Rehana, ed. *Women in Indian Society A Reader*. New Delhi : Sage Publications, 1998.

Gledhill, Christine. *Home Is Where the Heart Is : Studies in Melodrama and the Woman's Film*. London: British Film Institute,1987.

————, "Pleasurable Negotiations." *Feminist Film Theory*. Ed. Sue Thornham. Edinburgh : Edingburgh University Press, 1999. 166-179.

Gokulsing, K. Moti and Wimal Dissanayake. *Indian Popular Cinema-A Narrative Cultural Change*. New Delhi : Orient Longman Ltd., 1998.

Grant, Barry, Keith. *Film Genre Reader*. Austin : University of Texas Press, 1986.

Greer, Germaine. *The Female Eunuch*. London : Paladin Grafton-Collins, 1971.

———, *The Whole Woman*. New York : Doubleday : A Division of Transworld Publishers Limited, 1999.

Grossberg, Lawrence, Paula Treichler, and Cary Nelson. *Cultural Studies*. New York : Cambridge University Press, 1992.

Grosz, Elizabeth. *Space, Time, and Perversion*. New York : Routledge, 1995.

Grove, Elliot. *Raindance Writers' Lab Write + Sell the Hot Screen Play*. London : Focal Press, Butterworth-Heinemann, 2001.

Guerin, L. Wilfred, *et al*. *A Handbook of Critical Approaches to Literature*. New York : Oxford University Press, 1999.

Gulzar. "Music : In Tune with the Times". *Encyclopaedia of Hindi Cinema*. Eds. Gulzar, Govind Nihalani and Saibal Chatterjee. New Delhi : Encyclopaedia Britannica and Mumbai : Popular Prakashan, 2003. 271-278.

Gulzar, Govind Nihalani and Saibal Chatterjee, eds. *Encyclopaedia of Hindi Cinema*. New Delhi : Encyclopaedia Britannica (India) Pvt. Ltd. and Mumbai : Popular Prakashan Pvt. Ltd., 2003.

Gupta, A.R. *Women in Hindu Society*. Delhi : Jyoti Prakashan, 1982.

Gupta, Chandra, Bhan. *The Indian Theatre*. New Delhi : Munshi Ram Manohar Publications, 1954.

Hammett, Jennifer. "The Ideological Impediment : Epistemology, Feminism, and Film Theory." *Film Theory and Philosophy*. Eds. Richard Allen and Murray Smith. New York : Oxford University Press, 2000. 244-260.

Handy, J. William and Max Westbrook, eds. *Twentieth Century Criticism The Major Statements*. New York : The Free Press A Division of Macmillan, 1974.

Hartstock, Nancy. "The Feminist Standpoint : Developing the Ground for a Specifically Feminist Historical Materialism." *Feminisms*. Eds. Sandra Kemp and Judith Squire. New York : Oxford University Press, 1997. 152-160.

Harvey, David. *The Conditions of Post Modernity : An Enquiry into the Origins of Cultural Change*. Blackwell : Oxford University Press, 1984.

Hayward, Susan. *Cinema Studies The Key Concepts*. New York : Routledge, 2000.

Hodson, H.V. *The Great Divide Britain- India- Pakistan*. U.K. : Oxford University Press, 1969.

Hooks, Bell. "Feminism:A Movement to End Sexist Oppression." *Feminisms*. Eds. Sandra Kemp and Judith Squires. New York : Oxford University Press, 1997. 22-27.

Huyssen, A. "Mass Culture as Modernisms 'Other'." *Studies in Entertainment: Critical Approaches to Mass Culture*. Ed. Tania Modleski. Bloomington : Indiana University Press, 1986.

Irigaray, Luce. *This Sex Which Is Not One*. Trans. Catherine Porter with
    Carolyn Burke. New York : Ithaca, 1985.

————, "When our lips speak together." *The Feminist Theory and the Body*.
    Eds. Janet Price and Margaret Shildi. Edinburgh : Edinburgh University
    Press, 1999. 82-90.

Iyengar, Srinivasa, K.R. "Rabindranath Tagore." *Indian Writing in English*.
    New Delhi : Sterling Publishers, 1962. 99-144.

Iyer, Pico. "The End of Happy Ending." *The Hindustan Times* February 15,
    2004 : 6.

Jackson, Stevi. "Theorising Gender and Sexuality." *Contemporary Feminist
    Theories*. Eds. Stevi Jackson and Jackie Jones. Edinburgh : Edinburgh
    Press University, 1998. 131-146.

Jain, Jasbir and Sudha Rai, eds. *Films and Feminism Essays in Indian Cinema*.
    Jaipur and New Delhi : Rawat Publications, 2002.

Jain, Jasbir. "Gender and Narrative : An Introduction." *Gender and Narrative*.
    Eds. Jasbir Jain and Supriya Agarwal. Jaipur and New Delhi : Rawat
    Publications, 2002. ix-xxiv.

Jain, Devaki. *Indian Women*. New Delhi : Publications Division, Ministry of
    Information and Broadcasting. Govt. of India, 1975.

Jain, Rikhab, Dass. *The Economic Aspects of Film Industry in India*. New Delhi
    : Atma Ram, 1960.

Jameson, Fredric. "Pleasure : A Political Issue". *In Formation of Pleasure*.
    London : Routledge and Kegan Paul, 1983. 1-15.

Jayanti, Mahendra. "Some Mystic Currents in Bengali Literature." *The Indian
    Culture*. Calcutta : Bharat Sanskriti Parisat. Nalanda Press, 1951. 275-
    316.

Jeffrey, Particia. *Frogs in a Well : Indian Women in Purdah*. New Delhi : Vikas,
    1979.

Jha, Akhileshwar. *Sexual Designs in Indian Culture*. New Delhi : Vikas, 1979.

Johar, Karan. "Home Thoughts Abroad." *The Times of India* 9 Dec. 2004: 12.

Johnston, Claire. "Women's Cinema as Counter Cinema." *Feminist Film
    Theory:A Reader*. Ed. Sue Thornham. Edinburgh : Edinburgh University
    Press, 1999. pp.31-40.

Johnstone, Barbara. *Stories Community and Place*. Bloomington:Ind. Indiana
    University Press, 1990.

Jung, C.G. *Development of Personality : The Collected Works*. Vol.17. London :
    Routledge, 1991.

————, "Archetypes of Collective Unconscious." *Twentieth Century Criticism
    The Major Statement*. Eds. William J. Handy and Max Westbrook. New
    York : The Free Press A Division Macmillan, 1974. 205-232.

Kak, Siddhartha. "Commercial Cinema : Breezes of Change?" *Cinema Vision
    Indian*. (1.3 July), 1980 : 25-7.

Kakar, Sudhir. *The Inner World*. Delhi : Oxford University Press, 1978.

————, "Feminine Identity in India". *Women in Indian Society a Reader*. Ed.
    Rehana Ghadially. New Delhi : Sage Publications, 1988. 44-68.

Kanga, Fareeda. "So You Want To Write? The Projection Room." *The Sunday Times of India*. 19 September 2004 : 3.

Kaplan, E. Ann. *Women and Film : Both Sides of the Camera*. New York : Metheun, 1983.

———, *Looking for the Other : Feminism, Film, and the Imperial Gaze*. New York : Routledge, 1997.

Kapur, Anuradha. "The Representation of Gods and Heroes : Parsi Mythological Drama of the Early Twentieth Century." *Journal of Arts and Ideas* 23/24 (January, 1993) : 85-107.

Kapur, Geeta. "Mythic Material in Indian Cinema." *Journal of Arts and Ideas* 14/15 (1987) : 79-108.

Kaul, Gautam. *Social Reforms Movement in Indian Cinema*. New Delhi : Sterling Publishers, 1995.

Kaviraj, Sudipta. "The Imaginary Institution of India." *Subaltern Studies VII: Writings on South Asian History and Society*. Eds. Partha Chatterjee and Gian Dev Pandey. New Delhi : Oxford University Press, 1992.

Kazmi, Fareed. *The Politics of India's Conventional Cinema Imaging a Universe, Subverting a Multiverse*. New Delhi : Sage Publications, 1999.

Kazmi, Nikhat. *The Dream Merchants of Bollywood*. New Delhi : UBS Publishers, 1998.

———, *The Sunday Times of India* New Delhi : 20 Jan., 2002 : 4.

Kemp, Sandra and Judith Squires. *Feminisms*. New York : Oxford University Press, 1997.

Khan, Ullah, Amir and Saibal Chatterjee. "Stereotypes and Cliches." *Encyclopaedia of Hindi Cinema*. Eds. Gulzar, Govind Nihalani and Saibal Chatterjee. New Delhi : Encyclopaedia Britannica (India) Pvt. Ltd. and Mumbai : Popular Prakashan Pvt. Ltd., 2003. 403-404.

Kishwar, Madhu. "The Daughters of Aryavarta." *Indian Economic and Social History Review*, 32/2 1986.

———, *In Search of Answers Indian Voice from Manushi*. Eds. Madhu Kishwar and Luth Vanita. New Delhi : Horizon India Books, 1991.

Kohli, Suresh. "Memories Too Painful to Recall." *Spectrum The Tribune* 22 Dec. 2000.

Krishnaraj, Maithreyi. "Preamble Boundaries Ideal Images and Real Lives". *Women in Literature and History*. Eds. Alice Thorner and Maithreyi Krishnaraj. Mumbai : Orient Longman Limited, 2000. 1-34.

Krishnaswamy, Shanta. *Glimpses of Women in India*. New Delhi : Ashish Publishing House, 1983.

Kuhn, Annette. *Women's Pictures: Feminism and Cinema*. London: Routledge and Kegan Paul, 1982.

Laing, Stuart. "The fiction is already there : Writing and Film in Blair's Britain." *Writing and Cinema*. Ed. Jonathan Bignell. New York : Pearson Education Limited, 1999.134-149.

Lakshmi, C.S. "Feminism and the Cinema of Realism." *Women in Indian Society A Reader*. Ed. Rehana Ghadially. New Delhi : Sage Publications, 1988. 217-24.

Landry, Donna and Gerald Maclean. *The Spivak Reader Selected Works of Gayatri Chakravorty Spivak*. New York and London : Routledge, 1996.

Langer, Susanne. *Feeling and Form A Theory of Art*. New York: Charles Scribner's Sons, 1953.

Lerner, Gerda. *The Majority Find its Past: Placing Women in History*. New York : Oxford University Press, 1999.

Llewellyn, J.E. *The Legacy of Women's Uplift in India*. New Delhi : Sage Publications, 1998.

Loomba, Ania. *Colonialism/Post Colonialism*. London : Routledge, 1999.

MacCabe, Colin. *Theoretical Essays : Film, Linguistics, Literature*. U.K : Manchester University Press, 1985.

Malhotra, Kamini. *The Sunday Magazine Indian Express* 10 Nov., 2002 : 3.

Malik, Farhad. "Fact and Fiction." *Cinema in India* August 1981: 5-8.

Manekar, Purnima. *Screening Culture Viewing Politics, Television, Womenhood and Nation in Modern India*. New Delhi : Oxford University Press, 1999.

Mani, Lata. "Contentious Traditions: The Debate of Sati in Colonial India." *Recasting Women. Essays in Colonial History*. Eds. Kumkum Sangari and Sudesh Vaid. New Delhi : Kali for Women, 1989. 88-126.

Martin, Emily. "The Egg and the Sperm: How Science has Constructed a Romance based on Stereo Typical Male-Female Roles." *Feminist Theory and The Body*. Eds. Janet Price and Margrit Shildi. Edinburgh : Edinburgh University Press, 1999. 179-189.

Mast, Gerald, *et al.* (eds.). *Film Theory and Criticism*. New York : Oxford University Press, 1992.

Masud, Iqbal. *Dream Merchants Politicians and Partitions*. New Delhi : Harper Collins, 1997.

———, "Gharey Bhairey." *Satyajit Ray An intimate Master*. Ed. Santi Das. New Delhi : Allied Publishers, 1998. 148-152.

Mayne, Judith. *Cinema and Spectatorship*. London : Routledge, 1993.

Mendilow, A.A. *Time and the Novel*. London : Oxford University Press, 1952.

Metz, Christian. *Film Language : A Semiotic of Cinema*. Trans. Michael Taylor. New York: Oxford University Press, 1974.

Michie, Helena. "Not One of the Family:The Repression of the Other Woman in Feminist Theory." *Feminisms*. Eds. Sandra Kemp and Judith. Squires. New York : Oxford University Press, 1997. 55-58.

Mill, James. *The History of British India, 2 Vols*. New York : Chelsea House, 1968.

Miller, Nancy. "Feminist Confessions. The Last Degrees are the Hardest." *Feminisms*. Ed. Sandra Kemp and Judith Squires. New York : Oxford University Press, 1997. 101-104.

Minzer, Wilson. "Hollywood Cinema." *The Sunday Express Times* 12 July 2003 : 3.

Mirza, Saeed. "How Far Can a Film Maker Go?" *Cinema Vision India* 1.3 (July 1980) : 72.

Modi, Girish, Chintan. "A Novel Adaptation! From books to the big screen." G Ed. Julius D'Souza. 3 Jan. 2005 : 35-38.

Mohanty, Chandra. "Under Western Eyes: Feminist Scholarship and Colonial Discourses". *Feminisms*. Eds. Sandra Kemp and Judith Squires New York : Oxford University Press, 1997. 91-96.

Moi, Toril. *Sexual Texual Politics Feminist Literary Theory*. New York : Routledge, 2002.

Monaco, James. *How to Read a Film : Movies, Media, Multimedia*. New York : Oxford University Press, 2000.

Mukherjee, Prasad, Bimal. "History, Studies in Bengal Renaissance." *India Awakening and Bengal*. Calcutta : Nana Nivandha, 1954. 1-35.

Mulvey, Laura. "Visual Pleasure and Narrative Cinema." *Feminist Film Theory A Reader*. Ed. Sue Thornham. Edinburgh : Edinburgh University Press, 1999. 58-69. Original article in Screen 16 : 3, 1975, 6-18.

Nabar, Vrinda. *Caste as Woman*. New Delhi: Penguin Books Limited, 1995.

Naikar, Basavraj, Dr. "The Conflict between Bondage and Liberation in the Home and the World." *Studies in Indian English Fiction*. Ed. Amar Nath Prasad. New Delhi : Sarup and Sons, 2001. 39-53.

Nair, P.K. "Partition in Cinema". *Partition Films. South Asian Cinema*. Ed. Lalit Mohan Joshi. London : South Asian Cinema Foundation, 2004. 8-14.

Nandi, S. K. *Studies in Modern Indian Aesthetics*. Simla : National Institute of Advanced Study, 1975.

Nandy, Ashis. "Woman Versus Womanliness in India." *Women in Indian Society*. Ed. Rehana Ghadially. New Delhi : Sage Publications, 1988. 69-80.

———, *The Secret Politics of our Desires Innocence Culpability and Indian Popular Cinema*. Delhi : Oxford University Press, Cinema, 1998.

———, "Indian Popular Cinema as a Slum's Eye View of Politics." *The Secret Politics of our Desires Innocence Culpability and Indian Popular Cinema*. Delhi : Oxford University Press, Cinema, 1998. 1-17.

Narayan, Shovana. *Indian Theatre and Dance Traditions*. New Delhi : Harman Publishing House, 2004.

Nihalaini, Govind. *Talking Films*. Eds. Rajiv Rao and Rafique Baghdadi. New Delhi : Harper Collins Publishers, 1995 (xi-xiv).

———, "Bollywood". *Encyclopaedia of Hindi Cinema*. Eds. Gulzar, Govind Nihalani and Saibal Chatterjee. New Delhi: Encyclopaedia Britania (India) Pvt. Limited and Mumbai : Popular Prakashan Pvt. Ltd., 2003. 24.

Niranjana, Tejaswini. *Interrogating Modernity : Culture and Colonialism in India*. Eds. Tejaswini Niranjana, P. Sudhir and Vivek Dhareshwar. Calcutta : Seagull Books, 1993.

———, "Integrating Whose Nation ? Tourists and Terrorists in Roja." *Economic and Political Weekly* 15 January 1994 : 79-82.

Noble, G. Allen. *India : Cultural Patterns*. U.S.A. : Westview Press, 1982.

O Flaherty, Wendy, Doniger. *Hindu Myths*. Harmondsworth : Penguin, 1978.

Oakley, Ann. *Sex, Gender and Society*. New York : Harper and Row, 1972.

Oldenburg, Veena. *The Making of Colonial Lucknow, 1856-1877.* Princeton: Princeton University Press, 1984.

Pandey, Rekha. *Women from Subjection to Liberation.* Delhi : Mittal, 1989.

Pandit, Sneh. *An Approach to the Indian Theory of Art and Aesthetics.* New Delhi : Sterling Publishers, 1989.

Panja, Shormishtha. *Many Indians, Many Literatures New Critical Essays.* New Delhi : Worldview Publications, 1999.

Panofsky, Erwin. *Studies in Iconology.* Oxford : Oxford University Press, 1939.

Paul, Sukriti. "Cementing the Fissure Urdu Literature from Across the Border." *Crossing Boundaries.* Ed. Geeti Sen. New Delhi : Orient Longman Limited, 1997. 80-91.

Pfleiderer, Beatrix and Lothar Lutze. *The Hindi Film: Agent and Re-agent of Cultural Change.* New Delhi : Manohar, 1985.

Phalke, D.G. "Swadeshi Moving Pictures." Research and Trans. Narmada S. Shahane. *Continuum* 2.1 (1988/89), 51-73.

Pole, David. "Appendices." *Aesthetics of Form and Emotion.* Ed. George Roberts. London : Gerald Duckworth Co. and Ltd., 1983. 200-260.

Prasad, Madhava, M. *Ideology of the Hindi Film A Historical Constructions.* Delhi: Oxford University Press, 1988.

Premchand. *Gaban.* Trans. Christopher R. King. New Delhi : Oxford University Press, 2000.

Prempati, D. "Train to Pakistan : Some Reflections." *Three Contemporary Novelists Khushwant Singh, Chaman Nahal and Salman Rushdie.* Ed. R.K. Dhawan. New Delhi : Classical Publishing Company, 1985. 109-114.

Probyn, Elspeth. "Materialising Locations : Images and Selves." *Feminisms.* Eds. Sandra Kemp and Judith Squires. New York : Oxford University Press, 1997. 125-35.

Proferes, T. Nicholas. *Film Directing Fundamentals from Script to Screen.* USA : Focal Press, Hienemann, 2001.

Rajadhyaksha, Ashish. "Neo-Traditionalism Film as Popular Art in India." *Framework* 32/33, 1986 : 20-67.

Rajadhayaksha, Ashish and Paul Willemen, eds. *Encyclopaedia of Indian Cinema.* New Delhi : Oxford University Press, 1994.

Rajadhyaksha, Ashis. "Indian Cinema." *World Cinema : Critical Approaches.* Eds. John Hills, Pamela C. Gibson *et al.* London : Oxford University Press, 2000. 151-56.

Rajan, Anuradha. "Metrosexual Myth Gender Inequality a part of Modern India." *The Times of India* 25 Dec. 2004 : 2.

Ramchandani, Indu. "Editing : From the Editor's Table." *Encyclopaedia of Hindi Cinema.* Eds. Gulzar, Govind Nihalani and Saibal Chatterjee. New Delhi : Encyclopaedia Britannica Ltd. Popular Prakashan, Mumbai, 2003. 163-168.

Rangacharya, Adya. *The Natyashastra English with Critical Notes.* New Delhi: Munshiram Publications, 1986.

Rangoonwala, Feroze. "The Age of Violence." *Illustrated Weekly of India* 4-10 Sept. 1993.

Rao, Maithili. "To be a Woman." *Frames of Mind Reflection of Indian Cinema*. Ed. Aruna Vasudev. New Delhi : UBS Publishers, 1995. 240-260.

———, "Rebels Without a Cause." *Encyclopaedia of Hindi Cinema*. Eds. Gulzar, Govind Nihalani and Saibal Chatterjee. New Delhi: Encyclopaedia Britania (India) Pvt. Limited and Mumbai : Popular Prakashan Pvt. Ltd., 2003. 241-256.

Rao, Rajiv and Rafique Baghdadi. *Talking Films*. New Delhi : Harper Collins Publishers, 1995.

Rao, Vidya. "Seeing Radha/Being Radha." *Researching Indian Women*. Ed. Vijaya Ramaswamy. New Delhi : Manohar Publishers, 2003. 360-390.

Ray, K. Rajat. "Man, Woman and the Novel." *The Rise of a New Consciousness in Bengal (1858–1947)*. IESHR : 16 No. 1 March, 1979. 1-9.

Ray, Pratibha. *Yajnaseni:The Story of Draupadi*. Trans. Pradip Bhattacharya. Calcutta : Rupa and Company, 1995.

Ray, Satyajit. *Our Films, Their Films*. Hyderabad : Orient Longmann Ltd., 1976.

Renu, Phaniswernath. "Teesri Kasam, Mare, Gaye Gulfam." *Meri Priya Kahaniyan*. (Hindi). New Delhi : Rajpal and Sons, 1982. 23-57.

Rich, Adrienne. "Compulsory Heterosexuality and Lesbian Existence." *Feminisms*. Eds. Sandra Kemp and Judith Squires. New York : Oxford University Press, 1997. 322-325.

Roberge, Gaston. *The Subject of Cinema*. Calcutta : Seagull Books, 1990.

Roberts, Graham and Heather Wallis. *Introducing Film*. London and New York : Oxford University Press, 2001.

Robinson, Andrew. *Satyajit Ray The Inner Eye*. London:Andre Deutsch Limited, 1989.

Robinson, Andrew and Krishna Datta. eds. *Rabindranath Tagore. The Myraid Minded Man*. New York : St. Martin's Press, 1996.

Rockwell, John. *Fact in Fiction*. London : Rouledge Kegan Paul Ltd., 1974.

Ronald, deSouza, Peter, ed. *Contemporary India-Transitions*. New Delhi: Sage Publications, 2000.

Rotham, William. "Alfreds Guzzetti's Family Portrait Settings." *The "I" of the Camera. Essays in Film Criticism, History and Aesthetics*. USA : Cambridge University Press, 1999. 188-205.

Russo, Mary. *The Female Grotesque Risk Excess and Modernity*. New York and London : Routledge, 1986.

Ruswa, Hadi, Mirza. *The Courtesan of Lucknow Umrao Jaan Ada*. Trans. Khushwant Singh and M.A. Husaini. New Delhi : Hind Pocket Books Ltd., 1970.

Sangari, Kumkum and Suresh Vaid, eds. *Recasting Women: Essays in Colonial History*. New Delhi : Kali for Women, 1989.

Sangari, Kumkum and Uma Chakravarti, eds. "Disparate Women : Transitory Contexts, Persistent Structures". *From Myths to Markets Essays on Gender*. New Delhi : Manohar Publishers, 1999. x-xxix.

Saraswati, Pandita, Ramabai. *The High Caste Hindu Woman (1888)*. New Delhi : Inter-India Publications, 1984.

Sardar, Ziauddin. "Dilip Kumar Made Me Do It." *The Secret Politics of our Desires Innocence, Culpability and Indian Popular Cinema*. Ed. Ashis Nandy. New Delhi : Oxford University Press, 1998. 19-89.

Sarkar, Sumit. *A Critique of Colonial India*. Calcutta : Papyras, 1985.

Sarkar, Tanika. 'Strisiksha and its Terrors : Re-reading Nineteenth Century. Debates on Reform". *Gender and Literature*. Eds. Supriya Chaudhuri and Sajni Mukherji. New Delhi : Orient Longmann, 2002. 153-184.

Sartre, Paul, Jean. *What is Literature?* Trans. Bernard Frenchtman. New York, 1949.

Sastri, P.S. *Indian Theory of Aesthetic*. Delhi : Bharitya Vidya Prakashan, 1984.

Saxena, S.K. *Aesthetical Essays Studies in Aesthetics, Hindustani Music and Kathak Dance*. New Delhi : Chanakya Publications, 1981.

Schneir, Miriam. *The Vintage Book of Feminism The Essential Writings of Contemporary Womens Movement*. London : Vintage, 1995.

Scorese, Martin. "The Refracted Ray. What the World said after hit by the Ray of Sensitivity." *50 years of Ray Outlook* August 30, 2004 : 59-65.

Scott, F. James. *Film, the Medium and the Maker*. New York : Holt Rinehart and Winston. Inc., 1995.

Sen, Aparna. Interview on *Star News* at 6.30 p.m., 30.11.2002.

Sen, Geeti, ed. *Crossing Boundaries*. New Delhi : Orient Longman Limited, 1997.

Sen, Mrinal. *Views on Cinema*. Calcutta : Ishan, 1977.

Sethi, Vijay Mohan, and Satnam Kaur. "The White and the Brown Colonial Encounter in the Short Stories of Khushwant Singh." *Colonial Consciousness Black. American African and Indian Fiction in English*. Ed. Ramesh K. Srivastava. Jalandhar : ABS Publications, 1991. 199-212.

Shah, Panna. *The Indian Film*. Westport Cann : Greenwood Press, 1950. Rpt. 1981.

Shahane, A. Vasant. " 'The Novel as Realistic Epic' : 'Train to Pakistan'." *Three Contemporary Novelists*. Ed. R.K. Dhawan. New Delhi : Classical Publishing House, 1985. 51-96.

Shildrick, Margrit and Janet Price, eds. *Feminist Theory and the Body A Reader*. Edinburgh : Edinburgh University Press, 1999.

Shukla Anuradha. "An Interview with Dr. Manjula Sachdev." *The Hindustan Times* 7 Sep., 2004. 6.

Sidonie, Smith. *A Poetics of Women's Autobiography : Marginality and the Fiction of Self-Representation*. Bloomington:Ind : Indiana University Press, 1987.

Silverman, Kaja. "The Acoustic Mirror." *Feminisms*. Eds. Sandra Kemp and Judith Squires. New York : Oxford University Press, 1997. 388-390.

Singal, R.L. *Two Aspects of Hindu Culture, The Spiritual and The Material*. Chandigarh : Arun Publishing House, 2000.

Singh, B.P. *India's Culture the State and the Arts Beyond*. New Delhi : Oxford University Press, 1998.

Singh, Dyal. *Premchand An Interpretation*. Lahore : Minerva Book Shop, 1946.

Singh, Khushwant. *Train to Pakistan*. New York : Grove Press, 1956. Rpt. New Delhi : Ravi Dayal Publishers, 1988.

———, *Truth, Love and a Little Malice : An Autobiography*. New Delhi : Penguin Books in Association with Ravi Dayal Publishers, 2002.

Singh, Nonika. Shabana Azmi quoted in an Interview. "Indian Heroine no Longer a Glamour Doll." *The Hindustan Times* 25 Dec. 2004 : 7.

Singh, K. Pankaj and Jaidev. "Decentring a Patriarchal Myth : Bhisham Sahni's Madhavi". *From Myths to Markets Essay on Gender*. Eds. Kum Kum Sangari and Uma Chakravarti. New Delhi : Manohar Publications, 1997. 3-17.

Singh, Prakash, Indu. *Indian Women : The Captured Beings*. New Delhi : UBSD Publishers, 1995.

Skeggs, Beverly. *Feminist Cultural Theory, Process and Production*. Manchester : Manchester University Press, 1995.

Smith, D. Anthony. *Nationalism and Modernism*. New York : Routledge, 1998.

Smith, Sharon. "The Image of Women in Film, Some Suggestions for Future Research". *Feminist Film Theory*. Ed. Sue Thornham. Edinburgh : Edinburgh University Press, 1999. 9-19.

Sobti, Krishna. "Memory and History In Conversation with Alok Bhalla". *Crossing Boundaries*. Ed. Geeti Sen. New Delhi : Orient Longman Limited, 1997. 55-78.

Somaya, Bhawna. *Cinema, Images and Issues*. New Delhi : Rupa and Co., 2004.

———, "Sex Symbol or Woman of Substance." *Encyclopaedia of Hindi Cinema*. Eds. Gulzar, Govind Nihalani and Saibal Chatterje. New Delhi : Encyclopaedia Britannica (India) and Mumbai : Popular Prakashan Pvt. Ltd. 2003. 391-402.

Sonali, Kanwar and Jolly Wadhwa, eds. "Myth or Reality." *A Cross-Cultural Perspective*. New Delhi : Gyan Publishing House, 2000. 37-45.

Spiegel, A. *Fiction and The Camera Eye : Visual Consciousness in the Film and The Modern Novel*. USA : Charlottesville University Press of California, 1976.

Spivak, C. Gayatri. "Can the Subaltern Speak ? Speculations on Widow-Sacrifice." *Wedge* 7/8 (Winter/Spring 1985) : 120-130.

———, "Can the Subaltern Speak ?" *Marxism and the Interpretation of Culture*. Eds. Cary Nelson and Larry Grossberg. Urbana : University of Illionis Press, 1988. 271-313.

———, "How to read a 'culturally different' book." *Colonial Discourse/Post Colonial Theory*. Eds. Francis Barker Peter Hylme and Margaret Iverson. New York : Manchester University, 1994. 126-150.

———, *Imaginary Maps Three Stories by Mahasweta Devi*. Trans. Spivak. Calcutta : Routledge, 1995.

Srivastava, K. Ramesh. *Colonial Consciousness in Black African and Indian Fiction in English*. Jalandhar : ABS Publications, 1999.

Stam, Robert. *Film Theory An Introduction*. U.K: Blackwell Publishing Limited, 2003.

Subramanyam, Lakshmi. *Cultural Behaviour and Personality.* New Delhi : Mittal Publication, 2001.

Sullivan, O' and J. Hartley, eds. *Television and Popular Culture in India.* New Delhi : Anand Mitra Publishing House, 1998.

Suraiya, Jug. "The Practice of Reality." *The Sunday Times* 20th Jan. 2002 : 8.

Swarup, Harihar. "Bhupen:His Songs Touch Our Heart." *The Sunday Tribune* 7 March, 2004 : 17.

Tagore, Rabindernath. *The Home and The World.* New Delhi : Penguin Books, 1919, Rpt. 1999.

Tendulkar, Vijay. "Scripts : Writing Screenplays for Indian Cinema." *Encyclopaedia of Hindi Cinema.* Eds. Gulzar, Govind Nihalani and Saibal Chatterjee. New Delhi : Encyclopaedia Britannica and Mumbai : Popular Prakashan, 2003. 319-324.

Thapar, Romila. *India Another Millennium.* New Delhi : Penguin Books Ltd., 2000.

————, "Sakuntala Histories of a Narrative." *Narratives and the Making of History Two Lectures.* New Delhi : Oxford University Press, 2000. 1-23.

————, *History and Beyond.* New Delhi : Oxford University Press, 2000.

Tharu, Susie and K. Lalita, eds. *Women Writing in India 600 BC to the Present Vol. II.* New Delhi : Oxford University Press, 1993.

Tharu, Susie. "Looking at Film Hoardings." *Gender Culture Politics Conditions of Visibility.* Calcutta : Published by STREE, 2000. 59-76.

Thomas, Lyn. *Fans, Feminism and Quality Media.* New York : Routledge, 2002.

Thomas, Rosie. "Indian Cinema: Pleasures and Popularity." *Screen* 26/3-4 August, 1985 : 116-31.

Thorne, Gay. *Designing Stage, Costumes.* Marlborough, Wiltshire : The Crossword Press, 2001.

Thornham, Sue. "Feminist Media and Film Theory." *Contemporary Feminist Theories.* Eds. Stevi Jackson and Jackie Jones. Edinburgh : Edinburgh University Press, 1998. 213-231.

————, *Feminist Film Theory : A Reader.* Edinburgh: Edinburgh University Press, 1999.

Thorval, Yves. *The Cinemas of India (1896-2000).* New Delhi : Macmillan India Limited, 2000.

Uberoi, Patricia, Dipankar Gupta, and Veena Das, eds. *Tradition, Pluralism and Identity.* New Delhi : Sage Publications, 1999.

Uberoi, Patricia. "Feminine Identity and National Ethos." *Ideals Images and Real Lives.* Eds. Alice Thorner and Maitreyi Krishnaraj. Hyderabad : Orient Longman Ltd., 2000. 322-346.

Ukadike, N. Frank. "African Cinema." *The Oxford Guide to Film Studies.* Eds. John Hill and Pamela Church Gibson. New York : Oxford University Press, 1998. 569-577.

Valicha, Kishore. *The Moving Image A Study of Indian Cinema.* Bombay : Orient Longman Ltd., 1988.

Vasudev, Aruna. *The New Indian Cinema.* New Delhi: MacMillan, 1986.

————, *Frames of Mind Reflections on Indian Cinema.* New Delhi : UBS Publishers, 1995.

Vasudevan, Ravi. "The Melodramatic Mode and the Commercial Hindi Cinema : Notes on Film History, Narrative and Performance in the 1950's." *Screen* 30.3 (Summer 1989) 29-50.

———, "Shifting Ports, Dissolving Identities. Hindi Social Film of the 1950s as Popular Culture." *Journal of Arts and Idea* New Delhi : 1993 : 23-24.

———, "The Politics of Cultural Address in a 'Transitional' Cinema : A Case Study of Indian Popular Cinema." *Reinventing Film Studies*. Eds. Christine Gledhill and Linda William. London : Oxford University Press, 2000. 130-165.

———, *Making Meaning in Indian Cinema*. New Delhi : Oxford University Press, 2000.

Vatsyana, Kapila. *Traditional Indian Theatre*. New Delhi : National Book Trust, 1980.

Visvanathan, Shiv. "From the Front Stalls." *The Hindustan Times* 13 July, 2004 : 6.

Wadley, Susan."Women and the Hindu Tradition." *Women in Indian Society* A Reader. Ed. Rehana Ghadially. New Delhi: Sage Publications, 1998. 23-43.

Walby, Sylvia. "Woman and Nation." *Ethnicity and Nationalism : International Studies in Sociology and Social Anthropology*. Vol. IX. Ed. A.D. Smith Leiden. London : Verso, 1992. 81-100.

Walia, Nona. "Muzaffar Ali, The Poet as Filmmaker." *The Sunday Review* November 2001 : 2.

———, "Meet the Contrasexuals." *The Sunday Times of India* 19 Dec. 2004: 4.

Walimbe, Y.S. *Abhinvagupta on Indian Aesthetics*. New Delhi:Ajanti Publications, 1980.

Walter, Natasha. *The New Feminism*. London : Virago Press, 1999.

Weedon, Chris. *Feminist Practice and Post Structuralist Theory*. Oxford: Blackwell, 1987.

———, *Feminism, Theory and the Politics of Difference*. Oxford : Blackwell Publishers Limited, 1999.

Whelehan, Imelda. *Adaptations Text to Screen, Screen to Text*. Eds. Deborah Cartmell and Imelda Whelehan. London and New York : Routledge, 1999.

Willemen, Paul. *Looks and Frictions : Essays in Cultural Studies and Film Theory*. Bloomington : Indiana University Press, 1994.

Williams, Raymond. *Culture and Society : 1780-1950*. London : Chatto. 1958.

Wollen, Peter. *Signs and Meaning in the Cinema*. Bloomington : Indiana University Press, 1972.

Wollstonecraft, Mary. *Vindication of the Rights of Women*. Dent : Everyman, 1977.

Wood, H. John. "Satyajit Ray." *The Essential Mystery Major Filmmakers of Indian Art Cinema*. New Delhi : Orient Longman Limited, 2000. 53-102.

Wood, Robin. "Ideology, readers, pleasure:post-structuralism, deconstruction, psychoanalysis". *Reading Popular Narrative A Source Book*. Ed. Bob Ashley. London : Leicester University Press, 1997 : 189-192.